Single Men Are Like Waffles Single Women Are Like Spaghetti

Bill and Pam Farrel

HARVEST HOUSE™ PUBLISHERS

Published in association with the literary agency of Alive Communications, Inc., 7680 Goddard Street, Ste #200, Colorado Springs, CO 80920

Cover illustration © Krieg Barrie

Cover by Left Coast Design, Portland, Oregon

SINGLE MEN ARE LIKE WAFFLES—SINGLE WOMEN ARE LIKE SPAGHETTI
Copyright 2002 by Bill and Pam Farrel
Published by Harvest House Publishers
Eugene, Oregon 97402
www.harvesthousepublishers.com

ISBN-13: 978-0-7369-2249-4

The Library of Congress has cataloged the edition as follows:
Farrel, Bill, 1959-
    Single men are like waffles, single women are like spaghetti / Bill and Pam Farrel.
        p. cm.
    Includes bibliographical references.
    ISBN-13: 978-0-7369-0280-9

    1. Single people—Religious life. 2. Man-woman relationships—Religious aspects—Christianity. I. Farrel, Pam, 1959- II. Title.
    BV4596.S5 F365 2002
    248.8'4—dc21   2002003621

To Jeff and Micky

The singles at NorthCoast Church are fortunate to have you as shepherds over their hearts, and we are fortunate to have you as friends.

To all the singles who gave their valuable insights and opinions, may God bless your lives as you have been a blessing to so many.

Contents

So God created man in his own image,
in the image of God he created him;
male and female he created them.

—Genesis 1:27

Accept one another, then,
just as Christ accepted you,
in order to bring praise to God.

—Romans 15:7

Nobody realizes that some people expend tremendous energy merely to be normal.

—ALBERT CAMUS

Male and Female He Created Them

At the very beginning of history God said, "'Let us make man in our image, in our likeness'...So God created man in his own image, in the image of God he created him; male and female he created them" (Genesis 1:26-27).

It was in God's plan from the moment He imagined us to make us different from each other. Our differences can be a starting point for building fulfilling relationships. Unfortunately, what was intended to be an advantage often turns out to be a universal source of frustration. Because we are all experientially familiar with the turmoil of relationships, we easily laugh at stories like this one:

> Mel's son rushed in the door. "Dad! Dad!" he announced. "I got a part in the school play!"
>
> "That's terrific," Mel said proudly. "What part is it?"
>
> "I play the part of the dad."
>
> Mel thought this over. "Go back tomorrow," he instructed, "and tell them you want a speaking role."[1]

Despite the frustration, the vast majority of us have an undeniable desire to have great relationships with the opposite sex. We want both male and female friends; we want successful business relationships with both men and women; and we want to meet just the right person, fall in love, and live "happily ever after."

But many singles have become frustrated trying to bridge the gender gap. We asked some singles to suggest titles for this book. Here are a few of the responses:

Why Aren't You Married Yet?

Why Should I Make the First Move?

Danger! Caution! Ouch!

It's Not That Bad if You Know What You're Getting Into!

Good Luck! You'll Need It!

It's Not Me—It's You!

It's Going to Take a Lot More Than a Book to Help Me!

Is This as Good as It Gets?

Hold Your Nose and Jump In

It Doesn't Have to be Terrible

Face It—There's No One for You!

You're Not Alone!

It's a Whole New World!

I Stink at Dating!

Shouldn't I Be Married by Now?

But All My Friends Are Married

Stick a Fork in My Eye (And 100 Other Fun Things to Do on a Friday Night)

How to Scare a Great Person Away After Just One Date

Seems the emotions are running high in this whole guy-girl thing. One suggested title sums up the ultimate question rather succinctly: *Can Male/Female Relationships Really Work in the New Millennium?*

The answer, of course, is *yes.*

How is a bit more difficult.

Knowing that men and women are so different, *how* can you have healthy, happy relationships with the opposite sex that actually work? And *how* can you create an atmosphere in your life that helps you relate to someone of the opposite sex— someone who might turn into the love of your life?

Although it's possible to make too much out of the differences between men and women, it's also possible to *not* make enough out of the differences. If you want to have relationships that add to your life rather than make you exhausted, the best place to start is with an understanding of the basic uniqueness each gender brings to relationships.

Dive into the Differences

So how are you to understand the differences between men and women? Put simply: *Men are like waffles, women are like spaghetti.* At first, this may seem silly, but stay with us. It's an analogy that works, and men "get it" (because it involves food).

Men Are like Waffles

By this statement we don't mean that men "waffle" on decisions and are generally unstable. What we mean is that men process life in boxes. If you look at a waffle, you see a collection of boxes separated by walls. The boxes are all separate from each other and make convenient holding places. These boxes resemble how a man typically processes life. His thinking is divided up into boxes that have room for one issue and one issue only. The first issue of life goes in the first box, the second goes in the second box, and so on. The typical man then spends time in one box at a time and one box only. When a man is at work, he's at work. When he's in the garage tinkering around, he's in the garage tinkering. When he's watching TV, he's simply watching TV. That's why he can look like he's in a trance and ignore everything else going on around him. Social scientists call this "compartmentalizing"—putting life and responsibilities into different compartments.

As a result of experiencing life in boxes, men are by nature problem solvers. They enter a box, size up the "problem" that exists, and formulate a solution. In their careers, they consider what it will take to be successful, and they focus on it. In communication, they look for the bottom line and get there as quickly as possible. In decision-making, they look for an approach they can "buy into" and apply as often as possible.

A man will strategically organize his life in boxes and then spend most of his time in the boxes *he can succeed in*. This is such a strong motivation that he will seek out the boxes that "work" and ignore the boxes that confuse him or make him feel like a failure. For instance, a man whose career holds the possibility of success will spend more and more time at work at the expense of other priorities. On the other hand, a man who always falls short at work or feels he never meets the expectations of those around him may find out that he's pretty good at being lazy. He will then develop a commitment to being lazy because he knows he can do that today with the same proficiency as yesterday.

A man also takes a "success" approach to communication. If he believes he can successfully talk with the opposite sex and reach a desirable outcome, he will be highly motivated to converse. If, on the other hand, conversation seems pointless or women seem impossible to understand, he loses his motivation to talk and clams up. "Hanging out with the guys" can become a pattern for men—sometimes they truly enjoy the male bonding, but other times they're avoiding the consistent conversation women often enjoy.

That's why men say such profound things as, "Is there any point to this conversation? Is this conversation leading anywhere? Can you just get to the point?" These are statements a man makes out of frustration because he doesn't know how to make conversation with the women in his life work.

The "success" drive is also why men find it so easy to develop hobbies that consume their time. If a man finds something he does well, it makes him feel good about himself and about his life. Because men tend to be good with mechanical and spatial activities, they get emotionally attached to building, fixing, and chasing things. Yard projects become expressions of a man's personality. The car becomes his signature. Fishing becomes an all-consuming pursuit of the right equipment, the right fishing spot, and the right friends. The computer, once simply a tool of work, transforms into an educational, entertaining, even intimate friend. It makes predictable moves and gives predictable feedback. Because a man knows what he will get back from his computer, he spends more and more time facing the monitor and less and less time face-to-face with people.

The bottom line with men is this: *they feel best about themselves when they're solving problems.* Therefore they spend most of their time doing what they're best at, while they attempt to ignore the things in which they feel deficient.

Women Are like Spaghetti

In contrast to men's waffle-like approach, women process life more like a plate of spaghetti. If you look at a plate of spaghetti, you notice that there are individual noodles that all touch one another. If you attempted to follow one noodle around the plate, you would intersect a lot of other noodles and you might even switch to another noodle seamlessly. That's how women process life. Every thought and issue is connected to every other thought and issue in some way. Life is much more of a process for women than it is for men.

This is why women are typically better at multitasking than men. A woman can talk on the phone, prepare a meal, do the laundry, make a shopping list, work on the planning for tomorrow's business meeting, watch her favorite talk show, and not skip a beat. Because all her thoughts, emotions, and convictions are connected, she's able to process different strands of information and keep track of different activities all at once.

As a result, most women try to connect life together. They solve problems from a much different perspective than men do. For most women, it's an act of denial to quickly solve a problem that involves a lot of disconnected issues. Women consistently sense the need to talk things through. In conversation, a woman can link the logical, emotional, relational, and spiritual aspects of the topic. These links come to her so naturally that the conversation is effortless for her. If she's able to connect all the issues together, the answer to the question at hand bubbles to the surface and is readily accepted.

This often creates significant stress when a man and a woman talk because while she's making all the connections, he's frantically jumping boxes, trying to keep up with the conversation. The man's eyes are rolling back in his head while the tidal wave of information is swallowing him up. When the woman is finished, she feels better and he's overwhelmed. The conversation might look something like this:

Joan calls John and says, "Hey, I drove by your favorite truck store today—the one where you got that cool cup holder. You remember…that day when we went to my mother's for my cousin's birthday. It was the day I wore that peach dress you said you liked. I think you like it because it's my color. You know, I went to that color seminar at work and they said I was a "Spring" so that's probably why I look good in peach. Hey, this spring, I think I want to go to *Memphis in May*—maybe a whole group of us can go. It's so pretty then and they have great jazz there. It shouldn't be too hot then. It has been so hot here lately…makes me want to go to the beach. What do you think? Should we?"

At this point, John isn't sure what the question is. "Should we go to Memphis? The beach? Shopping for peach dresses? And he has no idea what any of it has to do with his truck! He admires her ability to connect seemingly unrelated thoughts, but he just can't seem to understand how she does it.

Out of Words

Waffles and spaghetti are very different from each other, but there's more—most men have boxes in their waffle that have no words. There are thoughts in these boxes about the past, their work, and pleasant experiences, but the thoughts do not turn into words. A man is able to be quite happy in these boxes because the memories he carries in these wordless boxes have significant meaning to him. The problem is that he cannot communicate these experiences to others, and so the women in his life may feel left out.

What's more, not all of the wordless boxes have thoughts! There are actually boxes in the average man's waffle that contain no words and no thoughts. These boxes are just as blank as a white sheet of paper. They're empty! To help relieve stress in his life, a man will "park" in these boxes to relax. Amazingly, if there is any woman in eyeshot (sister, mother, girlfriend, coworker) it's as if she has radar for these moments when he's in park. She notices his blank look and relaxed posture. She assumes this is a good time to talk, and so she invariably asks, "What are you thinking?"

He immediately panics because he knows if he tells the truth, she will think he's lying. She cannot imagine a moment without words in her mind. If he says, "Nothing," she thinks he's hiding something and is afraid to talk about it. She becomes instantly curious and mildly suspicious. Not wanting to disappoint, his eyes start darting back and forth as he hopes to find some box in close proximity that has words in it. If he finds a box of words quickly, he will engage in conversation and both will feel good about the relationship. If he's slow in finding words, her suspicion fails to be extinguished and he feels a sense of failure. He desperately wants to explain that he sometimes just goes blank. Nothing is wrong, he's not in denial about anything, and nothing is being hidden. This is just the way he has been his whole life, but she cannot imagine it.

These blank boxes can get in the way of meaningful conversation. In the middle of conversation, as a man moves from one box to another, he may pass through one of these blank boxes. Right in the middle of conversation, he goes blank. He knows he should have something to say, but he's blank. He knows it's awkward to go blank in the middle of a thought, but no amount of effort can prevent it. It's an awkwardness he must live with, and he hopes there are kind women who might learn to accept it.

Consider the following interaction. MaryBeth came to Tim's apartment after a particularly stressful day at work. She began unpacking her emotions by lamenting, "Tim, it was so awful today. It's like I couldn't do anything right. And everyone wanted something from me. 'Do this MaryBeth. Do that MaryBeth!' I feel like everyone is so self-absorbed. No one takes thirty seconds to care about what I might want or need. It's like no one talks anymore. Now that you got your new job we don't even talk much. I don't even know how you feel. How *do* you feel, Tim?"

Well, Tim has also had a stressful day—so busy that he missed lunch. "I feel hungry!" he answers.

"Tim!!"

"What? You asked me how I feel. I feel *hungry*. I want a cookie."

At this point, someone has to jump over the gender wall. MaryBeth could say, "I want a cookie too—or an entire carton of Ben and Jerry's ice cream!"

Or Tim can say as he wraps his arms around her, "I care how you feel. Let's go get some dinner and talk." Tim knows he will really just listen and eat, but MaryBeth will be happier—and he will too, after he eats. He might even care about MaryBeth's day!

These gender differences aren't limited to conversation. God made men and women different in *many* ways. They think differently, they process emotions differently, they make decisions differently, and they learn differently. And yet men and women complement one another so beautifully that healthy relationships will enhance *both* genders. Consider the following ways that modern research has highlighted our uniqueness.

Viva la Difference!

According to Leah Ariniello of the Society for Neuroscience,[2] "Now research is confirming that the brains of men and women are subtly different." The differences start in the physical structure of the brain. "For example, studies show that human male brains are, on average, approximately 10 percent larger than female brains. Certain brain areas in women, however, contain more nerve cells."

The differences extend to the operation of the brain. "One study shows that men and women perform equally well in a test that asks subjects to read a list of nonsense words and determine if they rhyme. Yet imaging results found that women use areas on the right and left sides of the brain, while men only use areas on the left side to complete the test." We find it amusing that even when it comes to the use of the brain, women connect both sides of the brain while men keep it as simple as possible by using only one side.

It then follows that men and women excel at different tasks. "Tests show that women generally can recall lists of words or paragraphs of text better than men. On the other hand, men usually perform better on tests that require the ability to mentally rotate an image in order to solve a problem." As a result, men use different strategies and different parts of their brains to navigate, and they really are better than women at finding their way when they're lost.

"Researchers scanned the brains of 12 men and 12 women as they tried to escape a three-dimensional virtual reality maze.

The volunteers pushed buttons to move their virtual selves left, right, or ahead. In the real world, that might be like trying to find a specific place in an unfamiliar city," said neurologist Dr. Matthias Riepe of the University of Ulm in Germany.[3] "The men got out of the maze in an average of two minutes and 22 seconds, versus an average of three minutes and 16 seconds for the women." In regard to finding their way, men use geometry to figure it out, such as following a map, while women depend on their memory advantage and landmarks, such as "turn right at the drugstore." And it appears this difference is associated with the different parts of the brains that are used.

Another interesting development in our understanding of male and female brains is that "on average, women synthesize the chemical serotonin at a lower level than men. Currently serotonin is a popular drug target because it has been implicated in a number of diseases, including depression."[4]

We find these differences fascinating. Sometimes it's difficult to adjust to someone else's ways, but it can also be humorous and enjoyable. Here are a few of the ways that men and women approach life differently.

- Men are more aggressive than women when they drive sports cars and light trucks; women are more aggressive than men when they drive SUVs and luxury cars.[5]

- Most people believe men are safer drivers than women.[6]

- Women are less likely to be caught and convicted of speeding than men.[7]

- A research project was done on the quiz show "Jeopardy." It was discovered that "men were more likely than women to appear as contestants, made most of the selections in the game, and won more money....Wagering strategies differed late in the game, as men bet a higher percent of their earnings than did women, but only when wagering on masculine topics.[8]

- When men perform as well as they expected at a particular task, they tend to attribute their success to their own skill or intelligence. If they perform below their expectations they tend to blame it on bad luck or some other factor that is out of their control.[9]

- When women meet their low expectations, they tend to attribute it to their lack of ability or intelligence. When women exceed their low prediction for achievement they tend to attribute it to good luck or some other factor beyond their control.[10]

- Men, on average, are willing to take greater financial risks than women. "For example, in the 1989 Survey of Consumer Finances sponsored by the Federal Reserve System....Roughly 60 percent of the female respondents said they were not willing to accept any risk, while only 40 percent of the men said they were unwilling to take risks.[11]

- Women make safer choices than men when it comes to smoking, seat belt use, preventative dental care, and having regular blood pressure checks.[12]

- Little girls in groups learn to blend in, be sensitive to one another's feelings, avoid boasting, and believe they're punished by exclusion when they're bossy.

- Little boys are primarily concerned with dominance and are rewarded for being the boss, whether in Little League or on the corner selling lemonade. Boys in groups know who is on the top and who is on the bottom.

• Girls in groups tend to include everyone and be nice. "Men are the people of the ladder, women are the people of the circle."

• 75 to 93 percent of interruptions in conversation are made by men.[13]

• Studies show that parents believe math is more difficult for their daughters, and they're likely to interpret their daughters' success as a consequence of hard work. Parents attribute their sons' success to high ability.[14]

• A recent study asked students to imagine they woke up the next morning as the opposite sex. Here are some of the responses:

Boys:
Boys wanted to look at and touch their new breasts.

For most boys, becoming the opposite sex was difficult to imagine.

Most boys also felt that becoming a girl would be constricting.

They did not want to study as much as girls.

They did not relish the loss of their physical freedom.

Girls:
They talked about the increased freedom they would have.

They couldn't wait to be able to stand while they urinated.

They would now be able to joke around in class, do homework only rarely, and still make good grades.

They would be able to sit in any position they wished.

They could greet each other in the hall with a punch.[15]

- American men overwhelmingly believe that it's harder to be a guy today than it was 20 years ago.[16]

- Men are split on their opinion whether it's harder to be a woman than it was 20 years ago.[17]

- Within relationships, women resolve the day-to-day issues and men settle the life-changing disputes.[18]

- Men grow less satisfied with their current relationship when they're exposed to physically attractive women whereas women are relatively unaffected by exposure to physically attractive men.

- Women grow less satisfied with their current relationship when they're exposed to socially dominant men whereas men are relatively unaffected by exposure to socially dominant women.[19]

- Women take criticism of their abilities quite seriously. Men discount criticisms and tend not to incorporate the criticism into their evaluation of themselves.[20]

- Women underestimate their own intelligence, and men overestimate theirs.[21]

- Audiences listen to men more than to women.[22]

• When asked to give a description of a painting, women ask more questions; men give more answers and talk longer.[23]

What We Love, What We Hate

During the writing of this book, we interviewed and surveyed singles and found some interesting results (and some interesting comments!).

The biggest frustrations single women had with single men were...

1. They won't talk.

2. They won't listen.

3. They won't commit.

Men may have at least one reason they don't commit. The relationship advice they say they have received more than anything else is, "Don't be in a hurry. Take your time!"

Single women said the traits they appreciated most in men were their ability to be objective even under pressure, their strength and protectiveness, and vulnerability—nothing was as attractive to a woman as a man who was vulnerable enough to share his feelings.

Single men said their biggest frustrations with single women were...

1. They give mixed signals.

   • "They have different expectations at different times."

   • "I never know what she's thinking!"

   • "They never say what they mean. They want us to know them, but the clues don't make sense!"

2. They're oversensitive.

One man said, "They read something into everything! If I don't talk as much, or if my phone conversation is shorter, she thinks I don't love her as much and the relationship is in trouble—but I didn't talk as long because I had a boring day so there just wasn't much to say!"

3. They have too many long, detailed conversations!

What do single men appreciate most about single women?

1. Caring

2. Beauty (Nearly every man added an apology for this. For example, "I like their appearance. I know, I'm shallow—so sue me!" and "Beauty— sorry to admit it—but it's true!")

3. Good listeners

As you read this book, you will be exposed to the most important differences between the genders. You will come across funny stories and jokes. We hope you will laugh with us because developing a good sense of humor is one of the best ways to break the tension that exists between sexes. Mostly, we hope you gain insight into the way you have been designed and develop skills that will make you glad men are like waffles and women are like spaghetti.

Things Women Want

In the *Chicago Tribune*, Cheryl Lavin lists the things women want:

1. Don't ever lie to us; we always find out.

2. If you're in a bad mood, we're going to assume it's our fault. So, tell us what's bothering you.

3. Quit complaining about your boss. Find another job.

4. Sunday is usually the only day we can relax. Be flexible about the all-day sports rule.

5. Buy yourself some decent clothes.

6. Pay attention. We like to give clues. "Susie and Bob tried a great new restaurant" means "Why don't you ever take us anywhere nice?"

7. Yes, it's true. Sometimes we like to call up and talk about nothing. Get used to it.

8. We are self-conscious by nature; we can't help it.

9. The kissing must never stop.

10. If you ask us what's wrong and we say nothing, ask us again. And this time, look sincere.

11. When we say something, it's necessary for you to respond. At the very minimum, nod your head.

12. Real men run dishwashers and dust furniture.

13. If you only knew how much a tender word, a thoughtful act, or an unexpected gift means to us, you would do it, and your life would improve exponentially.

14. When no one's home, stand in front of a mirror and practice this until you can say it in public: "I was wrong."

15. After you've mastered that, work on "I'm sorry."[24]

Men's Rules for Women

Cheryl Lavin also writes about the rules guys wish girls followed. Here is a sampling of 17:

1. If you ask a question you don't really want an answer to, expect an answer you didn't want to hear.

2. Sometimes, we're not thinking about you. Live with it.

3. Don't ask us what we're thinking about unless you are prepared to discuss topics such as navel lint, the shotgun formation, and monster trucks.

4. When we have to go somewhere, absolutely anything you wear is fine. Really.

5. Crying is blackmail.

6. Ask for what you want. Let's be clear on this one: Subtle hints don't work. Strong hints don't work. Really obvious hints don't work. Just say it!

7. No, we don't know what day it is. We never will. Mark anniversaries on a calendar you know we check.

8. We're not mind readers and we never will be. Our lack of mind-reading ability is not proof of how little we care about you.

9. Yes and no are perfectly acceptable answers to almost every question.

10. Come to us with a problem only if you want help solving it. That's what we do. Sympathy is what your girlfriends are for.

11. It's neither in your best interest nor ours to take any quiz together.

12. Anything we said six months ago is inadmissible in an argument. All comments become null and void after seven days.

13. If something we said can be interpreted two ways, and one of the ways makes you sad or angry, we meant the other one.

14. You can either ask us to do something or tell us how you want it done, not both.

15. Whenever possible, please say whatever you have to say during commercials.

16. Our relationship is never going to be like it was the first two months we were going out.

17. If we ask what's wrong and you say "nothing," we will act like nothing's wrong. We know you're lying, but it's just not worth the hassle.[25]

2

Don't Overcook Communication

Men and women have very different approaches to communication. When a man starts a conversation, it's generally to fix a problem. If there is no problem, there is no need to talk. The man is comfortable in his box, and so everything must be all right. In fact, he enjoys his box so he assumes the person he's talking with enjoys it too. Computers, sports, his favorite hobby, or his personal philosophy of life—if he finds someone who wants to be in the box with him, he can talk at length. Consider this conversation I (Bill) recently had with another man.

I started the conversation with a question, "I read recently in the book *Wild at Heart* that men like to be dangerous in a safe way. What do you think about that?"

Frank responded, "That's a cool way to put it. I have always loved fast things. I have a motorcycle and a Corvette, and I love to drive them."

"A Corvette, really! So, why did you choose a Corvette? I would have bought a Porsche if I had the opportunity."

"I have always loved Corvettes. The first time I saw one, I was 13 and I knew I would have one some day. The way the fenders are curved is exciting, and I love the feel of that big engine in front of me. It's such a rush!"

"I rode in a Corvette once. A friend of mine in Bakersfield owned one and he gave me a ride. We were getting on the freeway when he put the pedal to the metal. I had never been pushed back into the seat like that. Wow!"

"Yeah, there's nothing like speed!"

I believe we could have gone on forever with that one subject if we had not been interrupted. But a female friend of ours, Kendyl, walked up and asked us what we were talking about.

"Frank's Corvette," I said with great enthusiasm in my voice.

"Again? Doesn't Art have a Corvette also?" she asked, feigning interest in cars.

"No, Art has a Camaro. It's still a Chevrolet, but it's a different model," Frank quickly added.

"Oh," said Kendyl with a rise in her voice that revealed her lack of interest in this topic, "So how is Art? I haven't seen him in months."

At this point, both Frank and I temporarily stalled. We were both wondering, *How is Art? The real question is, "How is Art's Camaro?" We were talking about cars. How did this change to personal questions? I guess we should care, but I didn't think to ask last time we were together. Hmm, how should we answer that question?*

Kendyl had succeeded in changing subjects and it froze Frank and me.

This happens often in male-female interactions because all of life is connected for most women. It's natural for her to connect all subjects to each other and to the important people in her life. She will regularly have seamless conversations with her girlfriends about multiple subjects. She will assume her male friends and coworkers will appreciate this also because it's so natural for her. It's hard for her to imagine that anyone would not approach life this same way.

Houston, We Have a Problem

If two girlfriends had a similar conversation, it might sound like this.

"Did you see Frank's car? He sure looks good in it. It looks kind of like Peter's car."

"What have you heard about Peter? Is he still dating Sherri? I always wondered if they would stay together."

"I don't think they're going together anymore. But you know who would know—Shawna. She's a good friend of Sherri's. They work together in accounting and see each other a lot."

"How is it going for you at work? I know you wanted to get in the accounting office, too. How did it work out?"

"Oh, I thought I wanted to follow that path, but I was offered a position in personnel and I find I like that much better. I get to meet so many interesting people. I just met Anthony who moved back from Korea. It's so fascinating to hear him talk about a foreign country."

"I had the opportunity to work in Africa for a couple of years and I loved it. If you ever get the chance to travel, take it!"

When a woman begins a conversation, a man naturally assumes she's bringing up a problem that needs to be resolved. But generally, she's starting the conversation because it seems natural to talk about whatever is on her mind. While she's in conversational mode, her male listener turns on the "fix it" mechanism and the conflict begins. She gets her feelings hurt because he's trying to figure her out rather than just visit with her. He gets impatient because there seems to be no point to the exchange. What started out as a hopeful point of contact becomes another disappointment.

How do men and women make communication work for them? We believe the most important skill anyone can develop to promote effective communication between the genders is learning to take turns.

Whose Turn Is It?

Whoever begins a conversation should be able to set the pace for the conversation. Let me (Bill) talk with the men first. When an important woman in your life begins a conversation with you, assume that she needs to connect the issues of her life together. She doesn't need you to work your male logic into her thinking process. She simply needs you to help her make the connections. You will do well if you view the conversation as a journey she's going to lead you on. *Pack your bags, go on the journey, and encourage her to take the conversation wherever she wants.* Many men refuse to do this because they're afraid that if they ever give a woman permission to talk until she's finished, the end will never come. This just isn't true. Most men don't know this, however, because they have never helped a woman finish a conversation.

Women are driven to connect. Because they're aware of all the issues of their lives and because it's impossible to fix every issue all at once, they approach things differently than men do. Before they look for solutions, they interact with each part of their lives and experience the appropriate emotion of each issue. The things that should be upsetting get them upset. The things that are sentimental bring soft words and flowing tears. The things that are exciting bring giggles and enthusiasm. The things that are intense bring focused concentration. Each issue gets its own emotional reaction. That's why women can experience such a range of emotions in one conversation. Just because you, as a man, cannot keep up with them doesn't mean your way is better. If you're willing to encourage this need of hers, you will develop much healthier friendships with women. You may not really understand what she's going through, but it will definitely make her life better.

A common complaint among men is that women ramble on...and on...and on...and on—seemingly with no point. Since men can't figure out where the conversation is leading, they feel powerless to do anything about it. The sense of failure sets in, and the man concludes women are unreasonable and unable to think through important issues.

A New Goal!

A new perspective is needed, men. To help you understand your female friends' need to finish conversations, imagine everything in your life ending early. What if you were never able to finish a meal because it was taken away from you when you were halfway through? What if every sporting event you watched on TV was turned off five minutes before the end of the game? What if every project you started had to be abandoned before you were able to finish it? How would you feel? Frustrated? Irritated? If life were actually like this, your anger would always be close to the surface, and your motivation to keep pursuing these activities would be drained.

This is the way a woman feels when she's unable to finish conversations with you. She's frustrated and irritated, and she isn't very motivated to keep talking with you.

I shared this concept at a conference, and one of the men left more than a little frustrated. He accepted that women have this need to connect everything in their lives, but he couldn't figure out how to help meet that need. As he continued to ponder the issue, it occurred to him that he could develop a listening box in his waffle, so to speak. In this box, he defined the problem and invented a solution. He set a goal for himself to learn to listen to others for up to 30 minutes at a sitting. If he succeeds, he rejoices because he conquered the challenge.

Stay in the Box

Ladies, when it's the men's turn to talk, you need to practice staying in the box they want to open. You see, when a man brings up an issue for discussion, he actually intends to talk about that issue. So when he says to you, "Do you like your job?" he most likely wants to have a conversation about work. If he says he wants to talk about your upcoming vacation, he probably wants to talk about your vacation, and so on. He's hoping this time will be different. He wants to have what he considers to be a reasonable conversation with you. He wants it to stay on track. He wants to identify the problem, evaluate the options, commit to a solution, and see it work out.

But tension develops because you immediately recognize all the issues that are related to the one he brought up. It's as if you can see every box touching the box he has opened. You want to open all those boxes because they're relevant to the discussion. If you don't open them, the loose ends will never be addressed. You know that it has backfired in the past, but you haven't ever really understood why, so you try again.

The problem is we women are very impatient listeners. We often think that because men don't process life like we do they're unfeeling or uncaring, but nothing could be further from the truth. We just don't let them stay in one box long enough to discover their feelings. Sometimes we even think men don't have feelings. One cartoon I saw explains how we usually view men and their feelings.

A niece came into the room where her uncle was sitting in his recliner. He had done some favors for her, and she wanted to express her thanks. The young woman rambled, "Thank you so much—you always come through for me. What would I do without you?" On and on she prattled...

The uncle took a business card out of his pocket, gave it to his niece and said, "If you take this down to the petroleum store they'll give you ten percent off your petroleum."

His wife witnessed the interaction and said, "What were you doing? She was pouring her heart out to you, and you gave her a business card? Have you no feelings?"

"I have feelings. I was *afraid* she was going to hug me. I was *scared* it was going to go on and on, and I was *happy* when it was over! I have feelings!"

But if we stay focused on one topic and resist the urge to open up all the surrounding boxes, we buy our men the time they need to work through their box. They may even trust us enough to share with us their well of emotions that are deep in the box. It's a lot like drilling for oil. When you drill deep enough, you can reach a valuable gusher! However, we ladies must remember that we are drilling for valuable treasure; we're not interrogating a prisoner. Patient listening will sometimes bring to the surface the emotions that we love to see.

The Emergency Shutoff Valve

Have you ever wondered why many men reach a point in a conversation when they either shut down or get frustrated with you? When a man starts a conversation, there is one problem on the table to be solved. When you open a second box, there are two problems. When you open a third box, there are three, and so on. Every man has his own limit of how many problems he can deal with at once. He started the conversation in problem-solving mode, and every box you open feels like a separate problem to him. At some point, there are too many issues for him to handle, and he gets overwhelmed.

A man's reactions to being overwhelmed can be varied, but they seem to fall into two categories. He either shuts down or gets angry. If your male friend's tendency is to shut down, he may walk away from the conversation or give you the silent treatment. He feels there's no way he can succeed in the conversation, so he loses motivation. He doesn't know how to keep up with you and thinks he's going to lose the conversation. The only way he thinks he can get on level playing ground with you is to bail out.

If his tendency is to get angry, he might throw accusations at you, storm around and disappear for a while, or aggressively call off the conversation by telling you to stop talking. The whole time he's telling himself he shouldn't be this angry, but he feels lost and doesn't know how to recover his composure. Rather than exposing his lack of control, he protects himself from any further feelings of inadequacy by getting angry. Either approach ends with a failed conversation.

Don't Make Me You

Instead of taking turns listening to each other, most people spend their time trying to change one another. As women are breaking down the walls that allow men to separate the issues in life, men are trying to cut up women's spaghetti into squares. They're sincerely trying to make sense of each other, but they only end up confusing each other more. It's as if she's always putting marinara sauce on his waffles and he's always putting syrup on her spaghetti.

Taking turns is hard work, but *not* taking turns is agonizing. For those of you who want to find a way to make the differences work in communication, you *must* become good listeners. The amazing thing is that the same listening techniques work for both sides. The man who wants to be able to travel in conversation with women must be a focused listener. The woman who wants to be able to camp in the boxes men find themselves in must also be a focused listener.

First, let's take a look at what listening is not.

Listening Is Not an Attempt to Understand the Opposite Sex. We try hard to sound insightful when we say to one another, "I understand." It comes in various forms—

"I understand how you feel."

"I understand what you're thinking."

"I understand how upset you must be right now."

"I understand your hurt."

"I understand how happy you are right now."

These sound like compassionate, caring, even insightful statements, but in reality they're escape clauses. We get tired of listening and want to start sharing our own thoughts, so we interrupt with the statement, "I understand."

The intention is definitely sincere, but the problem is we can never truly understand each other. We women know that men will understand us the day they have a menstrual period. And we men tell women that they will understand us the day they experience an aggressive rush of testosterone. These two experiences are so common and so intertwined with our self-image that to say we can understand each other without sharing these experiences is naïve. But don't lose hope—even though you can never fully understand each other, you can discover enough about each other to enrich your lives.

Listening Is Not an Attempt to Become Each Other's Counselor. Good listening does not always start with you leaning toward your friends, looking deeply into their eyes, and with a compassionately whiney voice, asking, "How are you feeling today?" There is a time and place for counseling, but it's not usually in the midst of your everyday conversations. When something is wrong in your life or some transition of life is getting the better of you, it's wise to schedule time with a counselor. But you also need to be able to communicate effectively whether you are on the run or relaxing. You need to stay connected without neglecting the housework, the yard work, or the homework. Listening should be slow and relaxed, but it should also be energetic and active.

Listening Is Not an Attempt to Fix Your Friends. Avoid asking, "Why do you feel this way?" This question comes in a myriad of forms—

"Why are you thinking that?"

"Why do you think you had that reaction?"

"Why are you so upset?"

"Why can't you just accept that this is the way it is?"

We want to ask why because we don't understand what's going on. We keep hoping we're going to get a reasonable answer. But the answer never comes. The question we are actually asking is, "Why do you have emotions?" We all have emotions, and even though they're not logical, they often motivate us to love what we love and do what we do. So the answer to the "why" question is, "I am emotional."

This is why emotional intimacy is so important to a healthy relationship but is difficult to achieve. We process emotions differently, and yet we expect others to feel the way we do. Our emotions don't have the ability to think. We feel what we feel because of our personalities, past influences, and developmental progress. Emotions are not rational in their makeup; they don't think before they express themselves. The goal in conversation with your friends is not to analyze emotions and come up with some kind of solution that will make them never feel this way again. The goal is to get better acquainted.

A friend may say, "I am often intimidated by my boss." Try not to respond with, "There's no reason to be intimidated. You are bright, intelligent, and talented. Your boss is just threatened by how good you are. Be brave. It will be all right!" In doing so, you shut him down. He's probably trying to get a conversation started with you that is bigger than work. It may have to do with his lack of confidence or lack of understanding of how competition works in an adult world. Or he may be contemplating a job change and he's checking to see how wise this decision is. Or he may be intimidated by you and trying to lead into the conversation by blaming his boss first! Whatever the case may be, you will never know if you attempt to fix him rather than let him work through the process with your listening help.

Listening Is Not a Personality Trait. You do not have to, or want to, become someone else in order to listen to others. Listening is a skill, just like driving or typing or playing music. You must practice and develop your own style over time. The basic elements of listening such as empathy, attentiveness, and asking compassionate questions are shared by all good listeners, but no two people listen exactly the same. Two guitar players sound a little different even though they're playing the same song. Two drivers have different styles of driving even though they arrive at the same destination. You too will develop your own style of listening that will fit well in your lifestyle. But you will never develop your own style until you learn the basic skills. And you will never develop the skills unless you practice.

Listening Is Not Easy for Anyone. Nobody is born a good listener. Just like no one is born a good driver or a great athlete, listeners must develop the little bit of natural talent that each of us has to become better listeners. Your ability to listen strategically is determined by how much value you place on it and how hard you are willing to work at it.

Levels of Communication

Now let's define what listening is. To develop a strategic approach to listening, we must first understand that communication takes place on four levels.

The first level is for small talk. This is where you deal with the straightforward stuff of life. How is the weather? Are you going to the Super Bowl party? What time are we getting together? It's important that small talk remain relatively uncomplicated. If you begin asking questions such as "How do you feel when you go to the store to get milk?" or "Does it freak you out that it might rain today?" communication will wear you out. Issues like the weather and groceries need to be handled as simply and nonemotionally as possible.

The second level is for thoughts and opinions. These areas require a little more than the obvious, but they're not inherently emotional. Questions such as "Where would you like to go to dinner tonight?" "What is your favorite color?" and "Which outfit do you like better?" are questions that should not throw a conversation into a tailspin. We should let each other have our own opinions on these issues without loading them up with emotional freight. This, however, seems to be the level where complications begin. We argue over what cars are best, and we criticize others when they make choices different from ours. We point out differences in the way other people dress. We make a big deal out of the eyeglasses others choose to wear or the style of their hair or the music they prefer. When areas of life do not involve moral choices, we need to enjoy the variety of the human race. Too often we create divisions over preferences in life and miss out on some great friendships.

The third level is where people share their opinions and convictions. This is where spiritual and moral convictions are revealed to one another. This is the level at which compatibility is discovered and friendships are made. But even among friends, it's impossible to establish compatibility in all areas of life. Your gender differences, personality differences, family backgrounds, and personal preferences guarantee that some parts of every relationship will be incompatible, but you don't need to see eye-to-eye in every area. You will, however, discover that your closest friends share your convictions on the core issues of life. If you differ on your preference for hobbies or your favorite colors or how organized you are, you will most likely continue to get along and find workable compromises. If, however, you differ on the role of God in your life, your moral values, or the level of respect you hold for people in general, this friendship will be too much work and one or both of you will lose interest. If you are in a romantic relationship, it will keep progressing if you discover you are compatible in these basic values. However, if you are not compatible, creating a quick end to the relationship will save you both from the hurt you will later experience as these values clash.

The fourth level is the area of emotional intimacy. This level is reserved for your very closest friends and those with whom you are romantically involved. This is the level where you give one another insight into what makes you the unique individual that you are! It's where you share your dreams, your fantasies, your fears, the ridiculous ways you think and feel, and the things in your life you are most proud of. This is the risky road where few people travel.

Most people misunderstand what emotional intimacy is, and they avoid it because of their misconceptions. We falsely assume we have to become a soft-spoken counselor to communicate at this level. Because that is unattractive to most people, the pursuit's abandoned or sabotaged. Emotional intimacy is a much more aggressive pursuit than just quietly talking. Emotional intimacy happens when you reveal to another person the things that motivate you at an emotional level.

We are all a mixture of thoughts and emotions. Our thoughts are logical and relatively easy to describe to other people. They're safe because they can be justified and supported with evidence. When others disagree with our thoughts, we generally do not get hurt, and we are all pretty good at holding our ground.

Mixed in with these thoughts are our emotions. At the core of who we are, there are emotional drives that make life the fascinating adventure it is. These emotions add joy and pain to our lives. They get us excited and make us cry. They draw us to the activities that make us feel alive, and they drive us away from the activities that steal the joy from life. They're God's gift to us to make life more than just a responsibility. Unfortunately, these emotional drives don't make sense. They cannot be logically evaluated, and they cannot be fully explained. They're the illogical part of us that makes us interesting to others. Without them we would simply be chemical machines carrying out the tasks of life.

Let me (Bill) give you a couple examples from my life. I get great joy in life from winning. It amazes me that it doesn't matter what it is. It can be an important transaction at work, or it can be a trivial game. I just love to win. Some of you know exactly what I mean. We are hard pressed to explain to others why winning is so exciting to us, but we cannot deny it. At the same time, I hate for anyone else to lose! This can cause a significant amount of confusion if I am guided by my emotions. I can live in limbo between victory and defeat if I do not deliberately guide my life with my thinking.

Another example from my life was evident even as a young child: I want to be a hero! When I was a child, I would only watch superhero cartoons. If the star of the show didn't fly or swim at super speeds or defeat the armies of evil, I wasn't interested. I didn't just watch these heroes in action, I *was* these heroes. As I have matured, I have come to realize there is only one hero in life, and His name is Jesus Christ. It's our job to point as many people as possible to Him so they can meet their Hero. At the same time, I cannot dismiss this hidden desire to be a hero in the lives of other people. It could easily get out of hand, but I have found it to be a great source of motivation for being involved in other people's lives.

In addition to these positive emotional ties to life, there are a number of negative emotional drives in my life also. I grew up around a controlling mom who struggled with a mental illness. She was afraid of most of the things in life I loved. She worked hard to hide from these fearful things and to isolate our family from anything in life she couldn't control. As a result, I react intensely to any female who attempts to control me. At the same time, Pam grew up with an alcoholic father who could not be counted on. When he was sober, he was one of the greatest dads on earth. When he was drinking, he was unpredictable and unreliable. Being the eldest daughter, she learned to take control of situations and to make something positive come of them. These reactions are as much a part of who we are as anything else, and they profoundly affect every aspect of our lives. To really know us you have to know this about us.

Risky Rewards

Life will require you to communicate on the first three levels previously mentioned. You only reach level four if you choose to go there, and you will only choose to go there with a few very close friends in your lifetime. The goal is to reveal to the important people in your life the emotions that drive you. When others discover your motivations, they're drawn to you. If all they see is your reactions, they may be repelled.

It's common for people to fear this kind of openness. We are afraid that people won't like us if they really know who we are. We are sure that the following could be the story of our lives.

> A pious church member, who thought himself to be a
> great Christian, visited the Junior Department of the

Sunday school. The Superintendent asked him to say a few words to the boys and girls. He stood pompously before them, and asked, "Why do you think people call me a Christian?"

There was an embarrassing silence, then a small voice from the back of the room said, "Because they don't know you."[1]

It's certainly risky to be known by others, but the reward is that you learn more about yourself in these vulnerable conversations than in all the other levels combined.

Blake and Jeannie had been talking after a Bible study for about 20 minutes and she sensed he was losing interest and drifting to other thoughts.

"You haven't heard a word I have been saying!" Jeannie said with obvious disappointment in her voice.

"What are you talking about?" returned Blake with obvious frustration. "We've been talking for almost half an hour, and you think I haven't been listening? I just think you are being too emotional!"

"How would you know if I am emotional? You haven't ever heard one single beat of my heart," Jeannie blurted out, knowing her words would inflame the conversation. "I thought you were special, but you really are just like any other man. How can I ever trust you if you won't listen to me?"

"Whoa! You are really hurt about this, aren't you?" responded Blake desperately looking for some way to turn this conversation around. "I thought I was trying hard to talk to you more."

"You have been talking to me more. You just haven't been listening!"

Listen to Key Words and Phrases

Blake and Jeannie are stuck at a point where many people find themselves. They're spending quite a bit of time talking to each other, but they seem to be getting nowhere in their relationship. They want to connect with each other, but in all their talking they don't know how to listen in a way that creates intimacy. The reason for this is that we are all slow communicators. We throw out hints rather than boldly telling our friends how we are doing. As we learn to respond to these "hints," we encourage others to reveal more of what is really going on in their hearts.

Disclosure happens gradually. People reveal themselves slowly and in stages. They start out with "safe" statements and progressively share more risky and vulnerable truths if the atmosphere of the conversation is conducive.

The key is encouraging your friends to share more by being a "safe" person. If they can share without being judged or prematurely "fixed," new information will emerge. You'll get to know the emotions that motivate their actions and decisions. These skills encourage open disclosure:

1. Repeat key words or phrases with the voice inflection that says, "I have heard what you said, and I am ready to listen to more."

2. After your friend has been talking for a few minutes with your encouragement, summarize his or her thoughts and then ask, "Is that what you have been saying?"

3. After a significant amount of sharing, when you think you have a good idea of what is motivating your friend, describe a time in your life when you felt the same way. When you are finished describing this event, ask, "Is that what it's like for you?"

You won't complete all three of these steps very often. Most of the time when you share your experience and ask your friend if it's similar to hers, she'll say, "Not really." That may sound like bad news, but don't worry—just a little success can give you a great relationship! If a professional batter hits the ball only one-third of the time, we call him a great baseball player. If a basketball player misses six out of every ten three-point shots, we call him a great shooter. In the same way, people who connect at this level about 10 percent of the time will be great friends!

"Let's try again," Blake said in a way that indicated, *you're safe with me.* "You mentioned that I don't listen, tell me what you mean by that."

"I tell you how I feel and you just tell me how I should act," Jeannie cautiously said.

"So I just tell you how you should act?" Blake responded with a reassuring curiosity in his voice.

"Blake, when you tell me what to do as if it's a simple thing, you make me feel stupid." Jeannie was hesitatingly becoming more vulnerable.

"I make you feel stupid?" Blake asked with genuine surprise in his voice. He had always thought Jeannie was one of the brightest people he had ever met. Her statement made him feel pity and anger all at the same time, both of which he swallowed for her sake.

She sensed his genuine concern and was amazed at herself when she blurted out, "It makes me feel the same way my parents used to when they told me I was an accident and they wished I'd never been born."

"They told you that?" Blake's astonishment was obvious to Jeannie.

"I was 16. I couldn't believe it when my dad said it first. We were having this really big fight. I was being pretty difficult, I admit, but I don't think I deserved that. I looked at my mom and asked if it was true that I was an accident—that I was unwanted. When she just looked down at the ground in silence, I felt my heart fall through my feet. I've tried hard to cover up my pain all these years, but it keeps coming back to haunt me. Whenever you treat me like I don't know what I am doing I feel that same pain again."

"I am sorry, Jeannie. I didn't know."

"I know, Blake. I try to tell myself that others don't mean to make me feel this way, but sometimes it just overwhelms me. I didn't know whether to tell you or just be angry with you to protect myself."

Even though neither of them knew what to do about these thoughts of inadequacy, they marveled at the new sense of warmth and trust in their relationship. Blake decided that night he would be wise if he learned how to listen more.

Get Him to Open Up

Men like to feel successful. If you have a quiet man in your life and you'd like to get him to open up, give him a topic ahead of time—he might get out of the blank box and into one with thoughts and opinions. You'll be even more successful if you talk in an environment he feels successful in. He's more likely to be vulnerable if he's feeling successful already.

A female friend of Pam's came to her and said, "I really love my fiancé, but I'm afraid to marry him because he's…he seems, well…shallow."

"Tell me about him." I was looking for a box he felt successful in.

"He's a race car driver."

"Maybe he will be more open with you if he's in a comfortable environment, like driving in a car or being in the garage. Just go into his favorite box, the garage, and listen. Just keep him talking by repeating key phrases."

So she went into the garage one day and just kept listening to him as he talked on and on about the parts of cars. She was feeling a little frustrated and very bored, but she dutifully kept repeating key phrases. Suddenly her fiancé, who was under the car, slid out, stood up and said, "No one has ever cared about my world like this. No one has ever loved me so unconditionally before. I can't wait to marry you. I want to build us a new house and put a white picket fence around it. We can get that puppy you've always wanted, and someday we can let our kids play safely in the backyard. I'll build a big front porch so we can sit in a swing and watch the sunset. We'll just hold each other all evening, and we'll still be in love when we are old and gray! Honey, I feel like the luckiest guy on earth!"

She told me later, "I never wanted to leave the garage!"

Look for the Positive

Communication is a challenge. As you get older you may be tempted to just give up or accept less than the best. Consider these two men.

Two old fellows were walking along the shoreline of a lake when a frog came hopping up to them. Creaking with age, one of the old-timers slowly bent down and scooped up the frog in his hands. As he stood there gazing at the frog, fascinated by its ugliness, the frog croaked, "Hey, mister! I'm not really a frog. If you kiss me, I'll turn into a beautiful princess who will do anything your heart desires."

Startled, the old man slipped the frog into his pocket and headed on down the shoreline. For the longest time he and his friend trudged along in silence.

"Well?" his buddy finally blurted out. "You gonna kiss it?"

"Naw, I guess not," the first codger replied. "At my age, I think I'll have more fun with a talking frog."[2]

WAFFLES
SPAGHETTI

The His-and-Hers Guide to Drive-Through Automated Teller Machines

HIS:

1. Pull up to drive-through Automated Teller Machine

2. Insert card

3. Enter PIN number

4. Take cash, card, and receipt

HER:

1. Pull up to drive-through Automated Teller Machine

2. Check makeup in rearview mirror

3. Shut off engine

4. Put keys in handbag

5. Get out of car because you're too far from machine

6. Hunt for card in handbag

7. Insert card

8. Hunt in handbag for tampon wrapper with PIN number written on it

9. Enter PIN number

10. Study instructions for at least two minutes

11. Hit "cancel"

12. Reenter correct PIN number

13. Check balance

14. Look for deposit envelope

15. Look in handbag for pen

16. Make out deposit slip

17. Sign cheques

18. Make deposit

19. Study instructions

20. Make cash withdrawal

21. Get in car

22. Check makeup

23. Look for keys

24. Start car

25. Check makeup

26. Start pulling away

27. STOP

28. Back up to machine

29. Get out of car

30. Take card and receipt

31. Get back in car

32. Put card in wallet

33. Put receipt in chequebook

34. Enter deposits and withdrawals in chequebook

35. Clear area in handbag for wallet and chequebook

36. Check makeup

37. Put car in reverse gear

38. Put car in drive

39. Drive away from machine

40. Travel three miles

41. Release handbrake

Now, the most important thing is, we have to work as a team, which means you do everything I tell you.

—FROM THE MOVIE *CHICKEN RUN*

3

Waffles and Spaghetti at Work

Men and women love to achieve. We have both been created with an incredible capacity for intelligence, ambition, and achievement. Both men and women feel better about themselves when they've mastered a new concept or found an effective avenue for reaching goals. This is one of the great areas of life that men and women share in common. The result, of course, is that in pursuing their similar goals, men and women often find themselves sharing the workplace. And the same gender differences that can prove hazardous in relationships with those we *choose* to be with in our social life can be even more awkward in our jobs, where we work alongside those whom we *did not choose* as companions.

We are all competitive, ambitious, and stubborn to some degree. It's not fair to say that men love to produce while women love to nurture—both genders love to produce and we all should see ourselves as intelligent, creative, nurturing people.

In addition, being an adult brings certain responsibilities that require many of us to work outside the home. Living costs money. There are bills to pay, groceries to buy, cars to maintain—and a whole host of other "living expenses." As a result, many men and women must work at jobs that aren't their first choice. In fact, some people must work at jobs they dislike simply to make ends meet. And so we work, and we work hard.

Different from the Get-Go

The assumption that is made too often, however, is that men and women work the same. But in reality men and women approach achievement from much different perspectives. The difference begins to emerge during childhood and appears to last for a lifetime. Several years ago, makers of children's computer games came to the startling conclusion that boys and girls like different types of games—a fact most parents have known for years. "Finally, the computer industry has awakened to the fact that girls have lots of money to spend, but they don't want the same games that boys have," said Chris Byrne, editor of *Market Focus: Toys*, a New York-based trade publication.[1]

Software makers have been hesitant to accept this conclusion, not because of the facts, but because they were "nervous about demand and fearful of stirring gender issues."[2] Nobody wants to go so far as to say that girls never like the games boys like, or vice versa, but the fact is that boys and girls find satisfaction in different ways. And what is this difference? "Girls like cooperative play instead of competitive play," Byrne said. "They want to involve their creativity into playtime, and some games geared for boys don't offer that."[3]

Nancy Deyo and Brenda Laurel, founders of Purple Moon, spent five years studying girls' interests before concluding that girls "don't care about winning and losing. They want a good story plot, and they want to actually love a character, who they want to be as real to them as their best friend."[4]

"What girls and boys value as entertainment is different," said Laura Groppe, president and chief executive of Girl Games, based in Austin, Texas. "Boys get into one subject matter, while girls spread their interests across many fronts."[5]

There it is again—men are like waffles, women are like spaghetti.

This is not just a kid issue, however. Boys and girls take these same traits into adulthood—and into the workplace. The work and career preferences for most men are significantly different than those of women. A practical understanding of these differences can be a big help in choosing a career that's likely to bring success. In addition, your gender differences have vital implications of how you can best encourage one another as you pursue your dreams. Let's look first at the differences in how men and women approach work.

Men like to take more risks than women. Generally, men are more willing to take risks and gain a greater level of satisfaction from any resulting success than their female counterparts. This is not to say that women are afraid of or are unwilling to take risks in their career pursuits. It's just that men enjoy risk more. In video games, boys are incessantly looking for someone or something to defeat. In the workplace, men are looking for challenges they can conquer. "The study, called *The Testosterone Rush: A Study of Senior Marketing Executives,* found that men 'shot more from the hip,' while women carefully considered the alternatives before choosing a course of action. When it comes to decision-making, men were perceived to be faster on the draw…and were more apt to take risks….Men also 'pay too much attention to the competition,' and are more short-term oriented."[6]

Women like consensus more than men. If you consider that life for the average female is a web of interconnected relationships and issues, it makes sense that women at work would interconnect their relationships and decisions. This does not mean that she has to get along with everybody in the office. It simply means that she will consider the broad impact of her decisions, and she will want the decision to benefit as many of the important people in her life as possible. "Women…build more consensus during decision-making…and acted more thoughtfully when choosing their course of action."[7] It's interesting to note that "men work longer hours" than women, but they "perceive significantly lower coworker support compared to women…" and "…women are substantially more likely than men to report that they can talk to their coworkers and are close to and appreciated by their coworkers."[8]

Men and women lead differently. As much as we like to think that we all face challenges the same and that we all follow the same leadership styles, research does not support this conclusion. Men and women tend to lead differently. Men typically emphasize the achievement of organizational goals as the highest priority of the work environment while women typically emphasize people and relationships. I think the reason many people are uncomfortable with statements such as these is that too often these general principles are carried to the extreme. We think that emphasizing one part of leadership must mean that we exclude the rest. Balanced research, however, reveals that "women leaders emphasize both interpersonal relations and task accomplishment more than do men" and that "women tended to adopt a more democratic style than men."[9] In other words, women tend to take a more connected view of the work environment while men tend to focus on single issues.

Modern research reveals some evidence for a very interesting trend among men and women. Since men are problem solvers by nature, they will tend to want to divide labor so it's fair. A typical man will want an "equitable" arrangement (however he defines "equitable").

Women, on the other hand, because they're driven to connect all of life together, will want help with the mundane tasks they're responsible for. The typical woman feels valued and more productive when others get involved with chores she's responsible for. You would think that she would also include the responsibilities of others in the discussion and that she would want to get involved in the things that others must get done. But this does not seem to be the case.[10] It appears that it's easy for men to seek out equity in the division of labor and that they must learn to jump in and help when sharing responsibility is vital. It also appears that women are adept at seeing how others can help keep their lives connected by sharing responsibilities and that they must learn to keep responsibilities divided when it's in the best interests of the group.

Sally Helgesen, in *The Female Advantage,* kept a diary that followed the lives of successful female executives and entrepreneurs. She found that women managers had many of the same characteristics as their male counterparts, but they also had a few unique character traits.[11] She found that women managers...

- worked at a steady pace. Men did too, but women guarded short "downtimes" to catch their breath and clear their mind throughout the day.

- made a deliberate attempt to be accessible. One study showed that women managers were twice as accessible as their male counterparts.[12]

- integrated family and work. Men tended to compartmentalize their lives while women blended them. (Hmm, there it is again—*Men are like Waffles, Women are like Spaghetti!*) It may be natural for a woman manager to make out her grocery list or talk to her children on the phone in the five minutes between meetings. However, both men *and* women who were torn between family and work responsibilities wanted company policies that were more family friendly such as job sharing, flextime, and childcare.[13]

- preferred live personal contacts. Just like the male managers, females prefer conversations and delegation to be as personal as possible: face-to-face or on the phone as opposed to using a memo or fax.

- maintained a complex network of relationships outside her organization. Male managers also spent equivalent time in outside contacts, but the women's networks were broader, often including volunteer organizations, ministry, and personal interests that didn't seem as connected to the job.

• focused on the ecology of leadership. They kept the long term in focus when some male counterparts often felt buried in "today."

• see their own identities as complex. A woman is not her career. Her career is just one element of who she saw herself to be.

• scheduled time to share information. Women in leadership held relationships in high value. Women tended to see interruptions by people as an opportunity to share and build the relationship, not an interruption of a task.

However, these differences are very slight, and they're narrowing. Women are slightly better at verbal skills, reading nonverbal clues, and maintaining high energy and their own inner work standard. Men are slightly better at spatial tasks, attentiveness to power structures, and task-oriented behaviors.

Most importantly, men had a better ability to see themselves as leaders. It was almost a self-assigned role.[14] However, women only truly identified themselves as leaders after they had interacted with a group and members of the group had defined them as leaders.[15]

Men and women learn differently. One of the reasons men and women approach the workplace differently is that they learn differently. Although we think in remarkably similar ways and are able to learn the same information, we *process* it differently. "Men, for example, tend to think more in terms of principles, while women think more in terms of relationships. Men generally learn on a less personal level, while women tie thoughts to emotions." This is why "on achievement tests, men score higher on math and spatial concepts, while women outscore men in areas of language."[16]

As a pastor, I see this all the time. Men consistently talk about the principles of the Bible and how to apply them to their lives. Women are more concerned about the well-being of the members of their families and the spiritual motivation of the ones they love. It's also interesting to notice that women have no trouble meeting new women and getting them involved in Bible studies. Men, on the other hand, feel awkward meeting new men and asking them to get involved in anything. The men would rather just make an announcement and expect interested people to come.

The fact that women tend to tie knowledge to their emotions may help explain why women often have better memories than men. Women attach the events of their lives to their emotions, which makes the memories stronger. Memories are more intense for women than for men. Men go through life one activity at a time and usually do not attach activities to vivid emotions. As a result, the memory of the activity is rather bland. In my relationship with Pam, this is a pretty consistent frustration. She often says to me, "Don't you remember?" The problem is, I *don't*. She has such vivid memories of times we have spent together that at times I wonder if I was really there.

Men and women cope with work stress differently. When men are faced with stress at work, they tend to either focus on the task and get it done or divert attention to an easier activity. In school, male students will distract themselves by watching more television than their female counterparts. It's almost comical to walk through the student union of any university and watch the young men sitting watching TV while the young women are in huddles talking. Conversely, women seek out conversation with others to cope with the pressures of work. They find that when they can talk through their expectations, they can face the stress. Women may talk with parents, friends, trusted co-workers, or mentors, but the stress remains until they can talk it out.[17]

Women feel they have to work harder than men. In high school, women begin believing they have to work harder than men to achieve the same level of success. In high school "women spent more hours in studying and less hours in watching TV. This may be due to the fact that women…tend to attribute their achievement outcomes to effort while men attribute theirs to ability."[18]

Once a woman enters the work force, she quickly realizes she has entered a male-dominated domain. As a result, women who hope to maximize their career find they often have to adapt their work style.[19] Researchers Eagly and Johnson discovered in 1990 that women feel the pressure "to adopt more typically male styles in order not to lose authority and position."[20]

The struggle doesn't stop here, however. Because men get so attached to their work, they defend it by making women feel they're not as capable. It has previously been shown that women already tend to underestimate their abilities, so they're susceptible to believing this report. Also, since it's not natural for women to act like men, they're criticized when they try. As a result, women are often placed in "a 'double bind situation.' If they adopt stereotypically masculine styles of leadership that may be required for that particular job, they're considered to be abrasive or maladjusted. However, if women utilize stereotypically feminine styles, they're considered less capable and their performance may not be attributed to competence."[21]

Women are affected more by their home life than men are. This is one of the most obvious differences between men and women. Because men see their lives in individual boxes, they approach work as an end in itself. It's not attached to family life, not attached to friendships, and not attached to the emotional climate of their relationships. When a man goes to work, he goes to work. It has often been said that people need to leave their personal lives at home in order to succeed in their careers—an observation no doubt made by a man.

Because women connect everything in life, work is an integrated pursuit. Her day at work affects her personal relationships and her relationships affect her work. She would like to separate the two but finds that it's more work to keep them separate than it is to relate them to one another. As a result, she enjoys her work more when her personal life is going well and she enjoys her personal life more when her work is going well.

Women are more easily satisfied with their work than men. Modern research has brought this important distinction to the surface. "Although women work for less pay and in jobs that are less intrinsically rewarding, they do not appear to be any less satisfied with their jobs than men, a finding that has come to be known as the 'paradox of the contented female worker.'"[22] This is quite a compliment to women. It appears that men need to have a job that is satisfying to them in its own right, or they become restless. Women, on the other hand, can feel good about a job that's less satisfying if it fits into the overall plan of their life.

Maximum Effectiveness

So what is the best way to go about dividing up the responsibilities of life? What tasks are most effectively overseen by men? By women? What responsibilities should be handled together? Each generation wrestles with these questions in its own culture.

The challenge of the twenty-first century has been expanded because of the balance between men and women in the work force. "Since the 1950s, there has been an exponential increase of women in paid jobs and careers so that currently approximately 75 percent of U.S. women now work in paid jobs."[23]

Historically, women's work has centered around the home. It has been assumed that women are more domestic and have a natural desire to develop a nurturing environment in their homes. Men, on the other hand, have gravitated to the areas of yard work, analytical pursuits, and the maintenance of the family machinery.

Yet we all know men who are good at housework and women who prefer working with mechanical equipment. But we should not assume men and women will approach their responsibilities in the same manner. Because women have the ability to connect everything in life, the average woman can manage several tasks at a time better than the average man. The tasks she considers vital must be addressed with a workable plan, or everything in her life may feel out of place. It doesn't necessarily matter to her if she attends to these tasks herself or if others get them done as long as they're accomplished. It doesn't appear that the individual tasks are as important as the balance between them.

Because men tend to process life in individual boxes, the average man prefers tasks that can be done one at a time. He wants to do the first task until it's done and then move on to the next one. If it's a creative task, he even wants to stay in the box and admire the work for just a little while. The particular task is not as important as the opportunity to focus on one task at a time.

A Job Well-Done

Bill was working on a project in our unfinished home. The younger boys needed closet doors hung in their room. Bill worked painstakingly all day to finish the job before out-of-town company arrived. Finally, he announced the doors were hung. I ran upstairs and looked, gave him a hug, said thanks, and off I went. After about a half an hour of getting things ready for our guests, I began looking for Bill. I knew he was done with the closets, but I couldn't find him. I checked the shower. (A logical place to go after a dirty job and ten minutes before guests arrive.) I looked in the garage, the office, outside in the yard...then I finally charged up the stairs. Bill was still standing in the exact place I'd left him thirty minutes before. He was gazing at his closet door creation! "You're still here? Bill, they look terrific. What's wrong?" I asked.

"Nothing. It just feels so good to be done with something!" Bill exclaimed. "All day long every day, I work with people. People are never done—at least, not this side of heaven. Those doors are done! They're *done!*"

Now I understood why Bill took so long to do each project. He wanted the project to be done well—and stay done! The list of chores that I consider a cumbersome drag, Bill sees as a gold mine. Those chores bring balance to his life.

We have seen in the last three decades an attempt to minimize gender differences. Women are sometimes considered the underprivileged class who have been oppressed by men. The script is being rewritten so that men and women have equal opportunity and equal choice in their pursuits.

Men and women should have equal opportunity because they're equally talented. But men and women will approach these opportunities in different ways. The best way to allow both men and women to be as effective as possible is to allow them to tackle challenges in their own way. Men will want to organize their work in individual tasks. They will be at their best when they focus on one thing until they have gone as far with it as they can. Women will be most effective when they can organize their work in relation to all that is currently on their minds.

Maximum Motivation

Our relationships are profoundly affected not only by our gender differences but also by our personalities. Many helpful studies have been done in the past century focusing on two primary personality traits. The first trait is extroversion versus introversion. The other trait is task-orientation versus people-orientation.

The introverted-versus-extroverted discussion has often been misunderstood. It has been assumed that all extroverts are loud and boisterous. It has likewise been assumed that all introverts are quiet and shy. However, the real distinction is that extroverts process life from the outside in, while introverts process life from the inside out.

When an extrovert evaluates a relationship with God, he or she will ask questions such as, "Am I spending enough time reading the Bible, attending church, and praying?" Extroverts evaluate careers with questions such as "Is this job meeting my goals in life? Will this position help get me where I want to be in life? Does this job hold the potential for advancement that I desire?"

When an extrovert is thinking about an important relationship, he or she will ask, "Are we spending enough time together? Are we doing the things that will keep this relationship moving forward? Is there enough fun in this relationship to keep it fresh?" And when an extrovert approaches a decision, he or she will want to talk it out or diagram it. By stating the problem and the possible solutions, the issue is moved outside the person and made clearer. When an extrovert holds his or her thoughts within, the issue remains cloudy and confusing.

Introverts evaluate a relationship with God with questions such as "When I read the Bible, attend church, or pray, do I connect with God?" The evaluation of a career for an introvert involves questions such as, "Is this job a good fit for me? Will this position bring personal satisfaction to my life?" When an introvert is thinking about an important relationship, he or she will ask, "Do we connect with each other when we spend time together? Are we gaining any insight into one another's heart? Is there a desire to understand what is important to one another?" And when an extrovert approaches a decision, he or she will want to think it through before expressing it to other people. Introverts place high value on every thought and idea. They're slow to share these ideas because every idea is too important. As a result, they get their feelings hurt easier than extroverts when their ideas are evaluated or criticized.

When you put these traits together, you get four personality profiles. Looking at these profiles is helpful because it gives you insight into the natural motivation that is inherent in each personality. Each of us must mature and learn to operate in each personality style, especially in the arena of work. Life flows best, however, when the majority of our time, and the time of those we work with, is spent in those pursuits that are connected with our natural motivation style.

Look over the personality profiles below. See if you can pick yourself out. Also see if you can discern which type of personality your friends have. Then see if you can identify the profiles of the people you work with most often. The more you can tap into their natural motivation, the more satisfying your workplace will be for everybody.

Personality Type 1: Knight in Shining Armor, Queen of Hearts

People who have this personality: Lancelot, James Bond, Robin Hood, Crocodile Dundee, Joan of Ark, Lois Lane, the apostle Paul

Personality type in profile surveys: Choleric, Dominant, Lion[24]

Characteristics of this personality type: They're task-oriented, extroverted, dominant, and focused. They love new experiences, co-operative environments, and being active. They prefer to be the leader who is focused, in control. They're skilled in making decisions and want to get on with it once the decision has been made. These people are great natural leaders.

Preferences in romance: They like adventurous activity (if they're in charge), Club Med, hiking, anything they decide is a good idea, making lists, and checking off the goals. Never take them on guided, directed tours because they will want to take it over.

Motivated by: Control of the decisions that affect his or her life. If this person is not in charge, he or she needs to always have options to choose from.

Personality Type 2: The Hopeless Romantic

People who have this personality: Anne of Avonlea, Cupid, the apostle Peter

Personality type in profile surveys: Sanguine, Inspirational, Otter

Characteristics of this personality type: They're people-oriented and extroverted. They love to be the center of attention. They like to meet lots of people, and they prefer new experiences that are fun, unique, exotic, daring, active, and adventurous. They're fascinated with personal, once-in-a-lifetime experiences. The more public their life is, the better they like it. They make great sales people and help others enjoy life more.

Preferences in romance: They like anything new, entertainment that is personal and touches the heart, human drama (plays, musicals, concerts, sporting events), adventurous outings, exotic getaways, and any time they get surprised with their own idea.

Motivated by: Attention (the more public, the better)

Personality Type 3: Wind Beneath My Wings

People who have this personality: Superman, Robert and Elizabeth Browning, Barnabas

Personality type in profile surveys: Phelgmatic, Steady, Retriever

Characteristics of this personality type: They're people-oriented and introverted. They're naturally relaxed, easygoing and stress free. They take life as it comes. They do not like aggressive problem solving, busy schedules, or high expectations. They mostly prefer time with people to talk.

Preferences in romance: A light schedule, simple activities, time to relax, escape from reality, flexible options, and entertainment when there is plenty of time to enjoy it. For them, the most valuable thing is an atmosphere of acceptance because the best event is good company!

Motivated by: Acceptance for who they are rather than for what they do. Respect.

Personality Type 4: True Blue Lover

People who have this personality: Jane Eyre, Romeo and Juliet, the apostle Thomas

Personality type in profile surveys: Melancholy, Cautious, Beaver

Characteristics of this personality type: They're task-oriented and introverted. They like what is predictable, scheduled, significant, and controlled. They love to learn and handle details very well. The key to working with them is to do what we said we would do.

Preferences in romance: Do what you said you would do. Events that are discussed ahead of time, guided tours, meaningful entertainment, educational outings, museums, historical tours, constant encouragement with flowers, notes, and sincere feedback, honest and complete discussions, and exploration of the emotional complexity of life. The key is to remember significant dates and details—anniversary, birthday, first kiss, favorite color, etc.

Motivated by: Structure and order

Set Up Successful Communication

When communicating at work, give one another an occasional "heads up." When men want to communicate with women, they need to choose which style they want to follow. Are they going to ask the women to stay in one box as they discuss the problem at hand, or are they going to travel through many subjects at once? When women communicate with men, they must likewise choose.

In my office, we identify ahead of time the type of conversation we are going to have. I will say to our staff, "You all need to get in the same box with me." Or I will say, "I want us all to noodle on the issues for a while." This sets the context for the conversation and gives everyone an opportunity to adjust, making the conversation much more successful. When the context is not set ahead of time, somebody inevitably winds up frustrated. Either men get overwhelmed by the conversation and bail out, or women get frustrated because they sense too much was left out of the conversation and the issues were left unresolved. Both genders would be further ahead if they checked their own misconceptions and biases about the opposite gender and looked at the idea or innovation for its own value rather than considering the gender of the person who spoke the idea. Make "win-win" your goal at the workplace. Motivational speaker Zig Zigler explained this concept at a seminar we attended: "You will get what you want out of life if you help enough people get what they want out of life."

Focus Your Pursuits

No matter your gender, to be an effective contributor to the work force you need to be a growing, productive individual. To work this out in your life, you have to figure out what is important to you as a person and what your personal goals are.

Let's start with the questions, What are the important areas of your life? What makes you feel like your life is worthwhile and complete? Take the quiz below. Rank each item with a 1, 2, or 3. A 1 means it's very important to you. You would keep your 1 activities even if you never could do a 2 or a 3. A 2 means it's important; not a main focus, but you don't feel like it can go undone. A 3 means if it gets done, fine, but if it doesn't, no sweat. The 3s are those things that can be dropped when life gets hectic, or the quality can suffer a bit without making you crazy.

Life Responsibilities

____Being in good physical shape

____Having a neat, clean home

___Having your finances in order

___ Maintaining correspondence

___Having quality intimacy/romance

___Having fun

___Succeeding in your career

___Having a personal ministry/involvement in church

___Extra-curricular activities (community involvement, career enhancement, philanthropic activities)

___Having a nice car

___Furthering your education

___Achieving more financial success

___Time alone

___Time with God

___Time for a hobby

___Other_____

Use this list to gain insight into yourself. When the most-satisfying areas of your life are getting attention through either your career or your personal life, you will look forward to each day and enjoy the adventure of life. On the other hand, if your life is consumed with your least-satisfying obligations, you will feel a consistent sense of loss or emptiness. The goal is to fill your life as much as possible with the things you consider important. Another area of personal conflict you will need to watch out for are those areas you marked as 3s but in reality are 1s in daily life. Whether we like it or not, bills have to be paid!

Ask others how important your 1s are to them. These are the key emotional priorities in your life, and your best friends will share these desires. If you are dating someone, ask him/her to mark the list also. Compare your lists. Which things are ranked the same? Mark those with an asterisk. You're probably less likely to argue over those areas. Circle the areas that have the greatest differences—such as yours is a 1 and his is a 3. These are hot spots. If too many areas are hot spots, you will probably find this relationship to be tense. If, on the other hand, most of the areas are compatible, you will probably find it easy to spend time together.

In order to make sure the important areas are being addressed you need goals to keep you focused. So what types of goals will help you maximize achievement? In order to maintain a balanced life, it's helpful to write goals in four major areas. Write goals that will help you take another STEP forward:

- Your **S**piritual Life

- Your **T**eam

- Your **E**nergy

- Your **P**roductivity

Your Spiritual Life: This area includes goals that build a closer walk with God, including a daily personal devotional time with God, Bible studies, church attendance, verses you'd like to memorize, and growth activities such as retreats, conferences, Christian radio, and books you'd like to read. When you are connected to God, your perspective is renewed, and your decision-making skills sharpen because you will be thinking more like God.

Your Team: Included in this section are goals that affect your significant relationships such as mentors, family, and close personal friends. One author recommends that we prioritize our lives by who will cry at our funeral.[25] When you maintain healthy relationships, you will have more emotional stability to tackle life. Your motivation for life will increase as your relationships are strengthened.

Your Energy: To maintain a high level of energy you must manage the areas of life that are of importance to you as an individual. These will include your personal finances, emotional well-being, health, and social life. It will also include those activities such as hobbies, sports, reading, leisure activities, and areas of study or crafts.

Your Productivity: This area includes goals in your career, education, and ministry (both public and personal). What type of work do you want to pursue? What position do you want to attain to in that field? What type of education do you need to fulfill these pursuits? Who are the people you would like to personally influence for Christ? How would you like to use your gifts in your local church ministry?

How to Write a Goal

To know whether you are making any headway on a dream, you need to write a set of goals that explain how to get to the dream.

A goal must be specific. How will you know you've fulfilled a dream unless you can articulate what that dream looks like? A nonspecific goal would be, "I'd like to be happy." Well, what makes you happy? What are you like when you are happy? Is happy something that God even wants you to set as a goal?

A better example might be, "I'd like to have an income that would adequately supply my housing, food, and basic lifestyle desires and also allow me to help others." You could then list those desires and estimated costs to come up with a target income need.

After that you could brainstorm on how to meet that income need and decide if meeting the need is worth the required lifestyle. If meeting the income is too great a strain, you might adapt the list, look for another geographic location, or look at other options for income.

Goals must be realistic. I cannot write a goal that I cannot control. For example, I can't say, "I wish I were Afro-American or Hispanic." That is out of my control. I also can't say, "I wish my friends were more considerate." You can't control your friends. You can, however, be more considerate yourself.

Goals need to be achievable with God's help. We want goals that are just out of our power to achieve because these kinds of goals stretch us and make our faith grow. Each speaking engagement that comes in for Bill and me is a faith builder. We can only let people know we are available and what topics and seminars we have in our portfolio. We really believe God fills our speaking slate. We can't make anyone invite us to speak.

In business, all you can do is persist at working your plan, and then trust that God will work behind the scenes to make the connections you can't.

But I Hate Goals!

Some people feel overwhelmed by the goal-setting process. Goal setting may feel as intimidating as painting the Empire State building with a toothbrush. It doesn't have to be that overwhelming. Think of goal setting as climbing stairs. You want to get to the top, and each stair (goal) helps you get there.

Other people feel like they can't obey God and set goals at the same time. Somehow they feel they're usurping His control or direction. That is impossible! We are not in complete control of our futures. There are always variables we cannot control. But we are stewards of our futures, and we are commanded to "be very careful, then, how you live—not as unwise but as wise, making the most of every opportunity, because the days are evil" (Ephesians 5:15-16).

The key is flexibility—that is, ranking our will lower than God's will. We set goals with the attitude that "this is our educated guess at life. God, if you want it changed, we know you'll make it very clear!" The commands of God found in the Bible are an expression of His goals for us. Often He leaves the application of the goals up to us.

15 Rules for Women to Live By

1. Don't imagine you can change a man—unless he's in diapers.

2. What do you do if your boyfriend walks out? You shut the door.

3. If they put a man on the moon, they should be able to put them all up there.

4. Never let your man's mind wander—it's too little to be out alone.

5. Go for younger men. You might as well—they never mature anyway.

6. Men are all the same—they just have different faces so that you can tell them apart.

7. Bachelor: a man who has missed the opportunity to make some woman miserable.

8. Women don't make fools of men. Most men are the do-it-yourself types.

9. The best way to get a man to do something is to suggest he's too old for it.

10. Love is blind, but marriage is a real eye-opener.

11. If you want a committed man, look in a mental hospital.

12. The children of Israel wandered around the desert for 40 years. Even in biblical times, men wouldn't ask for directions.

13. If he asks what sort of books you're interested in, tell him checkbooks.

14. Remember, a sense of humor does not mean that you tell him jokes. It means that you laugh at his.

15. Sadly, all men are created equal.

Why It's Great to Be Male

1. We know stuff about tanks.

2. A five-day trip requires only one suitcase.

3. We open all our own jars.

4. We go to the bathroom without a support group.

5. We leave a motel bed unmade.

6. We kill our own food.

7. We get extra credit for the slightest act of thoughtfulness.

8. If someone forgets to invite us to something, he can still be our friend.

9. Everything on our faces stays the original color.

10. Three pair of shoes are more than enough...maybe too many.

11. Car mechanics tell us the truth.

12. We can sit quietly and watch a game with a friend for hours without thinking, "He must be mad at me."

13. Same work, more pay.

14. Gray hair and wrinkles only add character.

15. We can drop by and see a friend without having to bring a little gift.

16. If another guy shows up at a party in the same outfit, you just might become lifelong friends.

17. Your pals will never trap you with, "So, notice anything different?"

18. We are not expected to know the names of more than five colors.

19. We are totally unable to see wrinkles in our clothes.

20. The same hairstyle lasts for years—even decades.

21. We don't have to shave below the neck.

22. A few belches are expected and tolerated.

23. Our belly usually hides our big hips.

24. We can do our nails with a pocketknife.

25. Christmas shopping can be accomplished for 25 people on the day before Christmas and in 45 minutes.

*Let's put the Fun back in
Dysfunction!*

—T- SHIRT SLOGAN

Relationship Ready

How do you know if you are really ready to date? How do you know your heart is ready—or repaired—from the last go-round with love? How do you know if you have what it takes to navigate the adventurous seas of heterosexual relationships? How do you develop the discernment to effectively tell the difference between healthy and unhealthy people? Modern history is painfully decorated with individuals who set out to have fulfilling relationships, only to find themselves trapped in heavy responsibility and surrounded by ongoing disappointment.

Teresa thought she was the most fortunate woman in the world when she married her husband. She became vaguely aware of some growing tension with the birth of each of their three children but concluded this was normal. She was truly shocked the day he announced he was leaving her for another woman. Now she is raising three boys whose dad only spends time with his sons when it's convenient.

Randall, too, thought he had found the love of his life. She was so attentive when they were dating that he ignored her constant need for attention. She eventually became overwhelmed with the responsibilities of motherhood and left him with their two toddler-age sons.

Chris found herself pregnant when she was 15 and has never married. Often people think her 12-year-old daughter is her little sister.

Carmen is a beautiful mom of five children. Her husband, a successful lawyer, hit midlife and simply checked out of their marriage and left his family behind with only the monthly check his secretary sends.

Renee wishes she had a monthly support check. Her husband abandoned the family with no means of support and hasn't been seen since. Long ago she ran out of resources to try to find him. The family went from living in an upscale suburban neighborhood to a two-bedroom apartment in a marginally safe area of town.

None of these people set out to have a difficult life. No one ever does! But the reality is that many people end up getting into relationships that appear to be awesome at first but turn out to be disastrous. Why do some people seem to be a magnet for losers while others seem to regularly attract healthy people? We have found in our experience in working with people that there are some subtle characteristics that make up the "loser magnet." People with these characteristics are usually living productive lives. They are generally disciplined, hard-working people with steady careers and good friends. These characteristics lie dormant until a romantic attraction begins. Then the emotional attraction overshadows the problems until it's too late. If an individual can identify which of these characteristics are active and gain reasonable victory over them, he or she can enjoy a successful dating life. If, on the other hand, an individual ignores these characteristics and assumes they are a "normal" part of life, he or she will find unhealthy people attractive.

Pull the Trigger

Whenever you experience a traumatic event in your life, you respond with an intense emotional reaction. You may be frightened, angry, or intensely focused. You may feel like hiding in a corner, or you may feel like running away. You may feel like standing and fighting, or you may feel that you have to control your environment. You may feel totally defeated or you may feel you have to take on the whole world. These are all part of the "fight or flight" response built into each one of us as a part of our survival instinct. These feelings may be useful in sharpening our senses in times of danger, but they can also betray us.

It's common for these responses to create emotional triggers in our lives. If you have a trigger in your heart, it will go off when it is stimulated. You encounter a situation today that feels like a dangerous situation from your past, and the same "fight or flight" response kicks in. The situation doesn't feel safe so you intensely react. You know your reaction is overstated, but you can't turn it off. The reaction takes on a life of its own, and for a brief time you are out of control. You hate the fact that you do this, but you feel powerless to do anything about it.

Tom grew up in a home with a very controlling mother. She demanded strict adherence to everything she said. She regularly used guilt to make Tom feel bad about thinking for himself. If he disagreed with her, she would hit him across the face then scream at him for 20 to 30 minutes. His mother picked out his clothes for him until his fifteenth birthday. Outwardly he would silently comply, but inwardly he was seething. He couldn't wait for the day when he could leave the house and get out from under her smothering influence. As soon as he graduated from high school, he got a job and moved out with two friends. He has been on his own for eight years, and he thoroughly enjoys his freedom. He finds women attractive, but strangely, every one of them turns out to be controlling. At some point in the relationship, she makes some demand of him. He immediately feels guilty and erupts. He is vaguely aware that his reaction is too strong, but the thought of allowing another woman to control his life is unbearable.

Joanne is a bright, talented young lady who grew up with an alcoholic father. When he wasn't drinking, he was responsible and fun to be around. When he was drinking, though, he became belligerent and unpredictable. Joanne loved her dad and longed for his attention. The contrast between the drinking and nondrinking dad was so extreme that she would freeze when he became belligerent. She would quietly move to a corner and hope he wouldn't hurt her. She felt that the safest thing she could do was hide. Now, as an adult, Joanne keeps running into guys who are pushy and manipulative. They all seem to be nice guys at first, and she finds them very attractive. Just when she thinks she has gotten to know one of them, he does something. One guy reached up the back of her shirt at a park and started to undo her bra—she froze. Another guy started driving recklessly on the way to a restaurant for dinner. Instead of asking to go home, Joanne froze. A third guy started screaming at her before they even left on their second date. Instead of canceling the date, she froze.

You would think people would avoid these situations that set off their triggers but it's just the opposite. We are so emotionally tied to these triggers that we find situations that give them a stage.

The Dramatic Flashback

Flashbacks are not as specific as the triggers, but they are just as powerful. A flashback presents itself as a general sense of doom that descends upon the landscape of your life like a thick fog. The catalyst for the fog is a situation that is similar to a past experience. These are common with people who were abused in some way during their childhood. When a child of yours, a niece or nephew, or the child of a close friend approaches the age you were when the abuse happened, a sense of doom sets in. You may not be plagued with specific memories, and you may even be confused as to why you feel so bad. You only know that you are off balance and not functioning well. These flashbacks can also arise if a significant setback happened at a key time in your life or if your parents handled some developmental transition poorly. Transitions such as your first period, your first date, the physical and emotional changes of puberty, and early challenges you faced in life are all critical moments that profoundly shape your future. If these didn't go well, watching others approach these stages can be unduly stressful.

Jane was 11 when her 30-year-old dad went into a deep depression and took his life. She found out later that the men in his family have a hereditary predisposition toward depression, but this still hasn't erased the thought that there must have been something she and her mom could have done. Since then, every time someone she knows gets close to his or her thirtieth birthday, Jane's mood changes, and she fights despair. She has never paid much attention to it because it always passes. She isn't even aware that she is afraid to get close to anyone—she doesn't want to see them die like she did her dad.

Getting It Perfect

The third characteristic that helps create the "loser magnet" is perfectionism. Most people think perfectionists try to get things perfect. That is true, but it's not the whole truth. Perfectionism causes someone to bounce back and forth between two extremes. The first extreme says, "If I am going to do something, I have to do it right." Since it's impossible to do things perfectly, exhaustion sets in and gives rise to the second extreme, which says, "Since I can't do it perfectly, I am going to do nothing." The perfectionist shifts back and forth from hyperactivity to inactivity. The perfectionist never feels good about himself or herself because the hyperactivity never yields the expected results, and the inactivity yields guilt. The most tyrannical aspect is that perfectionism eliminates priorities. Everything looks just as important as everything else so that there is really only one priority left—everything!

Dave has a hard time making friends. He is constantly evaluating his friendships because they never seem good enough. He gets his feelings hurt easily because he feels like others are always letting him down. He is also upset with himself most of the time because he always thinks he's coming up short in his part of the friendship. He finds it easier to just focus on work most of the time—but then he gets lonely. He ventures out to make friends and enjoys it at first. But then he starts to analyze the friendships again until he gets exhausted. At that point he refocuses on the relative safety of work and hides again in his career.

The Power of Decisions

People hold on to the elements of the "loser magnet" because they are emotionally attached to them. These responses to life have become a vital part of who they are. These responses make them feel safe because they're familiar. And most people don't know how to change their emotional reactions to life. They can't reason with their emotions because emotions are not rational. The emotional reactions seem to be involuntary so there appears to be no alternative.

The key to changing your emotional reactions to life is the willingness to make decisions. Every time you make a deliberate decision, your emotions move. When you take a courageous step in your career, your confidence level builds. When you confront a person who is intimidating to you, your courage grows. When you choose the reaction you *want* to have rather than the one you would *normally* have, your sense of self-control is strengthened.

That's right! You can choose the reaction you want to have. It may be slow at first because you have to take the long route, but it is very doable. When you have one of these overstated emotional reactions, step one is to stop the reaction. Step two is to decide the reaction you would rather have. Step three is to move your reaction from the one you have to the one you want. Like any other skill in life, it will be awkward at first. It may seem hard to do—even impossible—but in reality it's very possible. The second time you try to reassign your emotional reactions will also be awkward. If you refuse to get discouraged and you keep trying, you *will* see progress. Through diligence, you will learn that you really can choose the emotional reactions of your life rather than be a victim to them.

In my own life (Bill), I have an ongoing challenge with my mom. She has a very strong personality. If she was healthy, she would be a natural leader and would exercise significant influence over others. But mom grew afraid of life somewhere in her adult years. As a result, she has made up her own way of thinking that does not always line up with reality. I currently work in an office on Navajo Street. If she knew this she would tell me I should not work there because only Native Americans should work on Navajo Street, and I am not a Native American. This is the kind of logic I grew up with.

As a result, whenever I encounter a female who is not making sense to me, I begin to react. At first I get frustrated and then I get angry, but then I feel a desperate need to retreat. I never succeeded in "winning" any discussion with my mom. Her illogical energy was more than I could combat so I would just shut down around her. But although I am conditioned by my past to shut down around anything that appears illogical, I don't let it rest there anymore. I have *chosen* to move my emotional reaction to gratitude for what God has done in my life. When I feel like shutting down, I start an inward conversation with myself that sounds something like this: *Wow! That is some weird logic. It reminds me of the stuff I heard growing up. Now, Bill, you know you normally shut down at this point, but God is bigger than that in your life today. Aren't you glad you don't think like this? Give thanks right now that God rescued you from this. Say it out loud if you have to. Choose to rejoice in the changes in your life. This is not your mother, and you are not living under her influence anymore.*

When I do this, I am amazed at what God has done in my life. He actually feels bigger and stronger than my mom. In the same way, if I don't choose my emotional reaction my mom feels bigger and stronger than God and my past just takes over my heart. *We cannot erase the past, but we can rewrite our response to the past.* You always have a choice, but you must deliberately choose.

First Things First

Priorities also disarm the "loser magnet." Intense emotions about the past can make whatever is in front of you appear to be the most important priority of your life. The present is always demanding your attention. Confusion sets in as the tyranny of the urgent runs your life. The confusion is heightened if multiple issues in your life all claim to be the most important. Changing a light bulb can feel just as important as a deadline at work. Bringing in the newspaper may seem just as urgent as visiting a friend in the hospital. Answering a casual e-mail may appear to be just as important as taking time to pray, and so on.

The only way out of the tyranny is to live by priorities. Because you can't *feel* what your priorities should be, you must deliberately *choose* what you want them to be. Having made the list, put them in the order of importance they hold to you. Now comes the hard part: Ruthlessly decide to give more time and attention to the higher priorities on your list. The higher the priority, the more of your focus it should receive. The lower the priority, the less of your attention it should dominate. If you struggle with perfectionism, this will be a challenge because you must decide that the lower priorities do not need to be done as well as the higher priorities and that will "feel" wrong. Finally, stop apologizing for not giving more of yourself to the lower priorities. This may sound harsh to some, but it will maximize your effectiveness in life.

Forgive Everything!

There is much confusion about what forgiveness is and what it isn't. If we are going to exercise forgiveness in our lives, we must understand what we're dealing with. In order to be effective at forgiving others, each of us needs to avoid some common misconceptions.

Forgiving Is Not Forgetting. It's common to think that an individual who has forgiven another will forget the offense. Somehow we are expected to take emotionally significant events in life and put them out of our memories. We are not supposed to do this with good memories because they help shape who we are and how we view life. But the negative events in life can also add to our development and mold our convictions. If you have had money stolen from you, you will most likely have strong convictions about robbery and financial integrity. If you have been abused, you probably have intense opinions about the need for children to be protected and treated with fragile concern. If you have been raised in the home of an alcoholic, you will certainly not be neutral on the issue of the proper role of alcohol in life. If you have experienced the horror of rape, you probably hold strong values regarding the safety and protection of women.

The reason you have such strong opinions about these areas is that you *do* remember. You care because you understand what others will experience. If you are trying to forget what happened, you run the risk of dulling your senses and establishing blind spots in your life. The key is to remember the event in a way that builds character and conviction in your life. You do not, however, want to remember the events in a way that causes you to reexperience the emotions associated with the event. If you go through the emotional trauma every time you remember the past, the past will be your master. You want to use the past to solidify your convictions, but you don't want the past to build fear that causes you to freeze in the face of challenges.

Forgiveness Is Not Saying, "It's Okay." In our relativistic world, it seems that the highest goal in life is happiness. We're told that if we attain a satisfying level of happiness, we have reached the top. We have become a society that has replaced the idea that there are rights and wrongs with a frantic pursuit of personal peace. Something is considered right if it makes you happy and wrong if it doesn't. As a result, many people mistakenly think forgiveness is simply a process of accepting other people's decisions. It's assumed that each of us is seeking our own happiness and that we have the right to do so.

But such a philosophy is doomed to failure. It's not possible for everyone to be happy in a world that is broken. Everybody has shortcomings, and all of us make mistakes. Our inconsistencies in human behavior hurt other people. We cannot say that another's actions are okay, when their behavior is wrong. If somebody beats you, it is wrong. If someone steals from you, it is wrong. If another disregards your opinions and treats you with disrespect, it is wrong. We often sabotage our own healing because we won't face the moral reality of life. With no standard by which to evaluate life, forgiveness cannot be applied. Because forgiveness is the only recourse for many of the events of life, the offended individual is left in a powerless state where freedom from bitterness is impossible to realize. In order to empower forgiveness, there must be a desire to discover God's best in life.

Forgiveness Is Not Denial. Forgiveness drives us to look ahead. It challenges us to overcome the past and move triumphantly into the future. In a relationship with Christ we are transformed from a life of foolishness to a life of productive service. In describing this process the apostle Paul says, "And that is what some of you were. But you were washed, you were sanctified, you were justified in the name of the Lord Jesus Christ and by the Spirit of our God" (1 Corinthians 6:11). In a similar way, our relationships can continuously improve. Many people avoid forgiveness because they haven't chosen to grow beyond the intense feelings associated with their pain. Replacing the hurt with a positive outlook and renewed hope in their relationship seems too hard.

Ignoring the irritations of life, rather than growing beyond them, will only prolong the suffering. The reality is that life is a mixture of pleasure and pain. Some great moments in life create lifelong memories and sweeten our experience as human beings. But some agonizing moments threaten to drive us into a shell where we no longer risk the thrill of intimacy or the challenge of new opportunities. None of us can run away from life by denying that bad things happen.

Forgiveness and Reconciliation

Although forgiveness and reconciliation are related to one another, they are not twins. We often see people stall in their growth because they define forgiveness as reconciliation. Reconciliation may be frightening or repulsive because the offender has shown no remorse and has made no significant change. The offended one isn't convinced that a new relationship would be any better than the previous one. Because he doesn't know how to forgive without reconciling, he falls into limbo and lives in the misery of thinking he is required to restore a relationship that has caused great pain.

There is a very distinct difference between forgiveness and reconciliation. Forgiveness is a process that takes place within the heart of an individual. Reconciliation is a process that takes place between two parties. Forgiveness is an internal decision to release the heart from continued pain and manipulation. Reconciliation is a decision to restore a relationship back to unity.

The greatest distinction between forgiveness and reconciliation is the extent to which we apply them. *Forgiveness must be applied to every situation in our lives if we want to grow.* Bitterness is a process that will destroy the one who holds onto it. It will not coexist with an individual and maintain respect for that person. Pastor Ron McManus says, "Bitterness is like drinking poison and waiting for the other person to die." *Reconciliation, on the other hand, is only to be applied to those who repent.* If the person who has caused you pain has not repented, apologized, and committed to making changes in life, reconnecting to that individual may cause further pain and seriously affect your confidence.

In our ministry, we have tried to pattern forgiveness after Christ and His ultimate act of forgiveness on the cross. To give forgiveness handles that you can grasp in a practical way, we have come up with six statements that provide a working definition.

1. I forgive _____ for _____ .
               (name the person)   *(name the offense)*

It is important to specifically name the offense. Vagueness in dealing with forgiveness only leads to doubts about whether forgiveness has truly been achieved.

The greatest example of forgiveness in the world is the forgiveness Jesus Christ has offered us. He has granted each of us who would trust Him freedom from guilt. This is indeed good news! But the good news starts with a very tough reality. "All have sinned and fall short of the glory of God" (Romans 3:23).

Too often this step is skipped. Maybe you think your hurt feelings are your problem. Maybe you are upset by what others have done, but you think they had the right to do whatever made them happy. Maybe you are afraid to bring up pains from the past. Or maybe you just didn't know how. If you are looking for a clear path of freedom, *get specific.*

2. I admit that what happened was wrong.

Paul increases the seriousness of forgiveness in Romans 6:23 when he writes, "The wages of sin is death..." Paul understands forgiveness to be a life-and-death issue that begins with the honest confession of something done wrong. In our politically correct world, we often feel uncomfortable saying something was wrong. We may feel like we are being critical or judgmental. But if nothing wrong was done, there is nothing to forgive. And if the goal is forgiveness with the hope of restored freedom, we aren't being a critic or a judge—we are taking courageous steps of growth.

3. I do not expect _____ to make up for what he or she has done. *(name the person)*

This is a courageous statement of reality. Those who have hurt you cannot make up for the mistakes that have been committed. Their actions will continue to hurt you, and the memory of the irritation will linger. Nothing can ever undo what was done. Once an offense is committed it cannot be *un*committed, so you need to take them off the hook. Even if they apologize for what they did, it doesn't make up for it. Even if they make some sort of restitution for what they did, it doesn't make up for it. If you have been hurt, what you *can* do is forgive and give the opportunity for repentance. You can't make up for mistakes, but you can start over.

The real tragedy in not forgiving shows up here. If you persist in waiting until others make up for their mistakes, the pain of those actions will control your life. Every time you are reminded of the event, the pain will shoot through your heart. Every time you try to trust, the pain will trip you up.

4. I will not use the offense to define who this person is.

When you define others by the negative impact they have had on your life, you make them bigger than life. You certainly make them bigger than you because you give them control of your emotions.

When it comes to forgiving yourself for the things you have done, this step is vital. When you define yourself by the things you have done wrong, you encourage a process of decay. It has been well established that we live out what we think about ourselves. If you think you deserve an unhealthy life, you will live out an unhealthy life. If you think you deserve to be punished, you will live out a self-destructive life. If you think you are a failure, you will avoid the path of success. If, on the other hand, you define yourself as the object of God's grace and an adopted child who is in line for God's favor, you will pursue healthy avenues of growth and development.

5. I will not manipulate this person with this offense.

Manipulation is an attempt to emotionally blackmail another person. It's an attempt to protect yourself from the other person. There is something in the human spirit that believes we can control others through manipulation. The tragedy is that every act of manipulation confirms that the one who hurt you is still very much in control. Your very approach to life shows that you're still afraid of what this person might do to you, so you try to get to them before they get to you. You run in an endless circle of self-protection, never enjoying the freedom of truly living.

Jesus does not manipulate us by bringing up our past sins to force us to do His will. Rather, He calls us to walk with Him as new creatures who have been set free from the past and our mistakes. We are encouraged to live as saints rather than recovering sinners. This does not mean God ignores the influence of our past. He has committed Himself to helping us grow through our past and reach up to a whole new life. We too would be wise to look forward to the life ahead of us rather than overcome the past that is behind us.

6. I will not allow what has happened to stop my personal growth.

This is probably the most important statement. Too often we allow the sinful offenses of others to dictate the course of our lives. It is as if we think we are punishing the ones who hurt us by refusing to pull our lives together. Or we are emotionally committed to keeping things the way they have historically been in our families. If our ancestors were bitter, we are bitter. If our ancestors were prone to depression, we are prone to depression. This applies to everything from alcoholism to anger to lack of confidence.

Forgiveness is not easy, but it will set us free. It will not happen all at once. Forgiveness peels away layers of offense, just like a cook peels away layers of an onion. We must exercise forgiveness regularly to weaken the "loser magnet."

A Special Note for Single Parents

Single parents have all kinds of stories, all kinds of pressures, and all kinds of issues. How do you know if and when you are ready to date when you have kids to raise and the memory of a broken relationship to live with? It's common for people to compound the hurt in their lives by getting into new relationships before settling the issues of old ones. Here are some questions that are vital to ask yourself if you're trying to balance parenthood and a personal social life.

1. Are you completely finished with *all* court hearings of any kind? In other words, is your divorce really *final?*

2. Have you completed divorce recovery counseling or been in a divorce recovery group?

3. Have you and the children settled into a new routine?

4. Do you have at least one group of single friends, or are you a part of at least one organization where single parents can socialize as a group?

5. Have you forgiven your former spouse?

6. Are you attending a church that has programs for single parents, divorce recovery, and counseling that help single parents heal so they can integrate into the general congregation?

7. Do you have a childcare system in place so that your children are encouraged and ministered to when you socialize?

8. Have you talked with the children about their feelings of you dating again?

9. Have you determined what you might have done to contribute to the end of the last relationship?

10. Have you created a list of qualities you are looking for in the next person you marry?

If you can't answer yes to *all ten,* then you are not ready to date yet. Let's take a look at each.

Are you completely finished with** all court hearings of any kind? In other words, is your divorce* really *final?

The biggest mistake we see individuals make is getting involved in another relationship too soon. (In many cases, getting involved with another person is what ended the first marriage—that's definitely too soon!) Divorce is traumatic—to yourself and to your children. Give God time to heal you and your children. Too often, the wounded parties think they are okay because the immediate shock and turbulence is over—untrue. After both the Vietnam War and the Gulf War, veterans who came home soon discovered many harmful side effects from what they'd been exposed to in the war. Divorce carries its own "agent orange" and you are probably shell-shocked, so give yourself some time to recover. As a basic *minimum* rule of thumb, for every year you were married, you should take a month off from dating. This formula goes into effect only *after* the divorce is *final*—not just after the papers are filed. It's not fair to another person, nor to your children, to expose them to the whole divorce process and a new relationship at the same time. Bob Burns and Tom Whiteman, in *The Divorce Recovery Handbook,* say this:

> Go slow. That will be frustrating, but be patient. Research shows that it takes three to five years to learn to trust again, to fully reenter society. That's how long you can expect to be recovering from the grief of divorce, attaining a level of acceptance. But it's usually another year or more before you can really turn your attention outward again, restoring

relationships and overcoming vulnerability. It's a long slow road.[1]

Have you completed divorce recovery counseling or been in a divorce recovery group?

If the divorce was a mutual decision, then you have some sorting out to do. Why didn't the first relationship work? Are there new skills to learn? If you left your mate, why? Was it their unhealthy choices—or yours? If your mate left you, you are going through grief just as real as if you lost someone to death—or maybe worse because in divorce, the person *chose* to leave you. Rejection often feels worse than bereavement.

Any new relationship will have plenty of issues of its own. And there will be issues you can't help but carry forward such as custody and parenting with your ex. Why compound the problem by carrying *unnecessary* baggage forward? Many issues can be effectively dealt with in a counseling office or small group setting. An added benefit of counseling and small groups is that your life will be very stressful as you navigate the divorce and the recovery. You will want to talk out these issues (women really want to talk them out), and your friends may get tired of hearing them. Counseling and small group settings are a safe haven for your feelings. *The worst thing you can do is put your child in the place of a counselor!* Commit early on that you won't vent your emotions when you're with your children. As much as possible, try to help your child have a normal, happy childhood. They are grieving too, so they really don't need adult-level problems added to their already hurting hearts and minds.

Have you and the children settled into a new routine?

Give your kids some time and space to get used to a new routine. Your economic status may have changed. Your living quarters may have been rearranged. Your kids may be getting used to having two rooms, one at mom's and one at dad's. Or they might have a room while with one parent and then feel like a camper or overnight guest while with the other.

In addition, divorce takes a lot of time. Whether you sought the divorce or it was thrust upon you, divorce is time consuming and steals time away from your children. Invest in some extra time with them. Get their lives stabilized before you add another relationship to it.

Do you have at least one group of single friends, or are you a part of at least one organization where single parents can socialize as a group?

The longer you were married, the more important this step is. Single dating is stressful. Get used to the dating dynamic by group dating first. Investigate what organizations or groups might be available in your community. Many single parents discover new friendships by joining *Parents Without Partners* or church single-parent groups. To find some healthy singles, look through the yellow pages for single parenting groups, call your local Christian newspaper or bookstore, or call a local social services organization for referrals.

Have you forgiven your former spouse?

This issue was dealt with in length earlier in the chapter; this is just a reminder that to go forward you have to let go of the hurts of the past.

In addition, your children may have to forgive your ex, especially if there were any issues of abuse, an affair, or abandonment.

Are you attending a church that has programs for single parents, divorce recovery, and counseling that help single parents heal so they can integrate into the general congregation?

Some of the best help for handling dating and single parenting can be the modeling you receive from other healthy Christian single parents and from other parents in general. A local church is a great place to meet others who are at least desiring to live a more emotionally, spiritually, and morally healthy lifestyle. A local church is often a great resource for low- or no-cost counseling, recovery groups, and small groups that deal with specific issues. In addition, when you do begin dating, churches often have many safe social events. If a relationship progresses and you begin dating seriously, that same church can offer pre-engagement counseling. Your pastor, whom you now have a relationship with, can perform your wedding, and there will be follow-up help if the next relationship hits any stressful bumps in the new emotional road you're traveling.

Do you have a childcare system in place so that your children are encouraged and ministered to when you socialize?

No one likes feeling left out or abandoned, especially children who might already feel like a parent has left them emotionally. This is common in single-parent homes. Make a plan for your dating life. Date on the weekends the children are with the other parent. Create a single-parent baby-sitting co-op where single parents take turns creating a partylike atmosphere for the children. You'll need to take your turn hosting a fun night for the kids. Or arrange to hire a consistent childcare provider who really cares for your children. Even a teen who is like an older brother or sister will help a child feel like they are in a family again. Older couples can act as surrogate grandparents (or the children's actual grandparents can be a nice option as well). The important issues to consider are:

- Does the child look forward to this childcare option?

- Is it safe—emotionally, physically, and spiritually?

- Does it buy you *more* time (not less) with your child?

Have you talked with the children about their feelings regarding you dating again?

After the children have settled into a new routine, the divorce is final, and you feel you have personally recovered and set a healthy plan for your dating life, then approach the children about your dating. If you have younger children, they might have already brought up the topic—often with some uncomfortable questions such as "Why don't I have a dad?" and "Why don't you get married again and get me a mommy?" Teens might make comments like "Mom, you need to get out once in a while." However, don't let your children's concerns and questions be the determining factor on dating. Date when *you* and *your children* are *both* ready.

What do you do when you think you are ready, but your children aren't? Perhaps they are holding out for a miraculous reconciliation between you and your ex. Or maybe they don't want to give up being "the man of the house" or "the woman of the house." What if you find resistance?

First try talking it through. Often, if you set aside time to *listen* to your child, you may discover an underlying fear or frustration which you can address. Also, it helps if they hear from you the kind but honest reality of a situation. For example, "I know you want mommy and daddy to live together again, but honey, that is something that just isn't going to happen." Then explain why in a simple one- or two-sentence explanation. "Daddy is dating another person." "It just isn't safe to live with Daddy anymore." Try to be honest without degrading the other person. It often helps to explain that you want to go do things with your friends. This sounds less threatening than "Mom's dating" or "Dad has a girlfriend."

Also, keep your child(ren)'s best interest in mind. When my own parents divorced (Pam), my mother went for years without dating much. She had a few men in her life as friends, but she quickly saw that she wasn't ready for a relationship and neither were any of us kids. We were all between the ages of 15 and 20, but we'd been hurt by our father and hurt from all the disruption the divorce caused. Soon my mother realized that it was healthier for her relationship with all of us if she waited to date until my youngest brother was away at college. She put her social life on hold for the greater good of our family. I respect her so much for this decision. Instead of dating, she put her time into personal growth for her. She spent time assessing the hurt we'd been through and found ways to help us recover. And she spent a huge amount of quality time developing deeper relationships with each of us. She also created ways for my brother to gain healthy male role models in his life.

My mother worked hard after the divorce at a new career, so she could have easily felt she "deserved" to date and have a little fun. Instead, she looked at what her children deserved and put us first. After my brother went away to school, mom did invest more into group social activities and met a wonderful man who shared her same values. They eventually married and were quite happy until his untimely death from a heart attack. We wondered if mom felt her time with her new husband was robbed because she delayed dating, but she reassured us that she'd do it all again—only she would have decided even sooner not to date until my brother was away at college. My mother made a short sacrifice that has paid long-term benefits.

Have you determined what you might have done to contribute to the end of the last relationship?

Before you go out to begin new relationships, it is imperative that you look yourself in the mirror and ask, "Did I contribute anything to the dissolution of the marriage?"

We see individuals all the time who blame all the problems in a marriage on the other spouse. They run away, often to another relationship, only to find similar problems cropping up in the new relationship. We can't run away from ourselves!

When you begin dating, be ready to be honest with your potential dates. One man, when asked by his first-time dates, "Why did your marriage go on the rocks?" would answer, "I know I contributed to the demise of the marriage. I was a different man then. After the marriage ended, I felt like a huge failure, so I took a long hard look at myself. I saw I was not good at managing stress. I was too short-tempered and impatient. I also hid my true emotions. I would just push down any negative emotions. When there was a seemingly minor infraction, I would overreact. I have worked on learning many new relationship skills, including some great new communication and listening skills. Also, the divorce caused a crisis of faith and I came to realize I was unable to control all of life. Now I know God is in control, so I don't have to be controlling. Even my children have seen a difference. Ask them!"

By being honest and open and giving permission for the date to "check him out" with others, this man opened the door for an honest relationship. A foundation for trust was laid on the first date.

Have you created a list of qualities you are looking for in the next person you marry?

On some side-view mirrors are the words, "Objects may appear larger than they really are." In the same way, loneliness, unmet emotional needs, and old patterns can make someone of the opposite sex appear to be much more attractive as a potential mate than they actually are. Know what you are aiming at. Take the advice of one of the people we surveyed for this book: "Be the kind of person you'd want to marry."

In addition to your list, ask your children what they want and don't want in the person you might marry. They might want someone with kids—or they might not. They might want a man who'll come watch them play sports or a woman who is a great cook. You won't know until you ask them.

Gradual Exposure

The best way to nurture your children and nurture your love life is to expose your children to the people in your social life gradually and naturally. Natural exposure is the best. By being involved in many group activities, your children will meet and spend time with those who are interested in you in a non-romantic setting. If your son and daughter see Mr. Jensen at church each Sunday, at the single parent picnic, at music concerts and the school football game, they won't feel so awkward relating to him when he shows up on their doorstep.

However, the time spent with someone of the opposite sex *and* your children should be planned out and incorporated gradually. Children attach very easily. It's much more difficult to break up with someone to whom your children are also attached. Cameron made that mistake. She met Jack on-line even before her marriage ended. She moved after the separation, and Jack was the only single male she knew in the city. He attached to Cameron immediately. He offered to baby-sit whenever she needed him to. He brought food over for meals nearly every night. He took her teen son jet skiing and bought clothes and games for her younger children when their own father was not providing in those ways.

Then he began to stay the night, first on the couch, falling asleep after a late-night movie with her and the kids. Then Cameron made the mistake of sleeping with him. He moved in, but he left his things at his mother's house. He was living with his mom because he was currently underemployed, working part-time and playing part-time. Before Cameron could realize she had fallen for a 35-year-old teenager, her children were best friends with the guy. She discovered his addiction to pornography. Then his immature relationship skills rose to the surface. He was demanding, controlling, and smothering—bordering on extreme possessiveness. She knew she needed to kick him out of her bed, out of her apartment, and out of her life, but the kids wouldn't hear of it. Months passed and the attachment the children felt only grew stronger—except for Chad, her teenage son. He began to show signs of anger and depression when he realized he was working harder than Jack. Chad watched the younger kids, fixed dinners, and worked part-time too. Jack had wedged his way into his mother's heart when she was vulnerable, and Chad hated Jack and his mother for it. Cameron watched her son spiral downward in his faith, his schoolwork, and his social life until she knew she had to make a change.

She packed up a box of Jack's things, drove them to his mother's, and left a note explaining the need to break it off.

Every time she tried to break up in person, she'd failed because of Jack's boyish charm and charisma. Then she called a couple friends and said, "Don't let me let him back in. Hold me accountable for this."

As Cameron looks back on this relationship she is amazed at herself. "I feel like I have wasted three years of my life—on what? A mama's boy who I thought was some great lover. He still doesn't work enough. How did I ever think he could be a dad to my kids? What was I thinking? The divorce was hard enough on the kids; then I went and brought this other guy into their life, and now it's like they are going through another divorce all over again. I know it's right to break up, but it's hard on the kids. The only thing harder is having such a bad role model stay with them!"

This book leads you through a series of decisions to define your sexual and social life. Maintaining these boundaries will safeguard your children as well. Model before them the kind of dating standards and boundaries you want them to maintain in their teen and college years. If you don't want your daughter to get pregnant as a teen, you'll probably tell her to date in public, date in a group, don't invite a boy into an empty apartment, and don't invite a boy into your bedroom. Model those same rules for your children.

In addition, protect their attachments. Introduce your children to your date in a casual way, as one of your friends. It helps if the introduction is done in a more public setting the first time—at church or a picnic—so the kids don't feel on the spot. They can stay and interact or they can run and play—whatever is most comfortable to them. Whether you have toddlers or teens, this same no-pressure introduction maintains your family unit's identity. Early on, have your family spend time with your date away from their home. This way if the relationship doesn't last, the memories of the person aren't so connected to your children's personal, private space.

Most importantly, *you* maintain the rules and discipline. Don't ask a date to be a parent. As the relationship progresses, communicate your expectations in this area clearly to your children and your dating partner. There may come a time when your dating partner is alone with your kids while you run an errand. Or you may decide to have them spend time together so your potential fiancé can learn to have a one-to-one relationship with your child. When doing so, communicate to each what the normal boundaries and expectations are.

Maintain your child's routine and privacy at all costs. For example, no matter how busy you are, don't ask your new boyfriend to bathe your toddler daughter. When you're in a pinch and can't get to the junior high to pick up your son from soccer practice, don't ask your girlfriend to pick him up. Instead, plan ahead and keep a list of phone numbers of your son's friends and coaches. You are doing this to protect not only your child but also the reputation of the person you are marrying. If your ex doesn't like the fact that you have a love life, he or she can twist simple boundary infractions and make them seem much worse in court. Or if a child is angry at you for not reconciling, he or she can scream false accusations of child abuse.

Earn the Right to Parent

Your date has a responsibility to earn the right to spend time with you and your children by giving you an ever-growing level of commitment. If you want to spend significant time together so your children can bond with someone you think will soon be your fiancé, do it wisely. For example, if you want to vacation together so you can get some uninterrupted quality time, don't go all in one tent. Instead, opt for a Christian single parent family camp and each maintain your own cabin. Meet at meal and recreation times.

When the relationship is approaching engagement, pre-engagement counseling is wise. If you have children, they need to be a major point of discussion. The pastor or counselor can facilitate a dialogue that helps you see the areas with your children that you and your dating partner might need to work on before the ring is purchased and date announced. Address those areas before you make it official so the children still feel they have input into the decision of adding more members to their family.

In one wedding my husband performed, the new husband gave each child a ring and wrote personal vows of promise to each child and read them as a part of the ceremony. Not only was that a moving moment and a lasting, positive memory for the children, it was also a public declaration. He was unlikely to just opt out of doing what he had promised after announcing it to those in attendance. Time has proven he meant every word. He not only has lived up to those promises, the oldest children see him as their "real" dad because their biological father dropped out of the picture entirely. Their new dad is stepping in and has become their hero.

How does all this apply if you are a parent who has never been married? It is nearly the same. You have also been hurt and have your own issues. No, they are not issues from a divorce, but since you didn't marry the mother or father of the baby, there are still issues of hurt that need healing. Your children might not feel the pull and tug of an abrupt change of lifestyle that divorce brings, but they have to grow up wondering why they don't have a mom or a dad or why their mom or dad doesn't live with them. They still need their boundaries protected. At least eight out of the ten questions (pp. 87-88) still apply. You might still be dealing with custody courts even though you've never married. And you probably have someone (or maybe just yourself) you need to forgive so you can go forward in life.

Loving After Loss

Loving after the death of a spouse is similar—and different—from loving after divorce. It's easier to move into a healthy relationship if you had a healthy marriage. You haven't experienced the rejection and abandonment that often comes with divorce. But you have to navigate through feelings of grief, loss, and loneliness. The person you date also has to handle your feelings of grief. He or she has to wrestle with where they fit in the family, living under the shadow of the dead (and often "perfect") spouse, and they also have the typical dating and relationship issues.

If you have children, use the questions on pages 87-88, but disregard issues of custody, and court. However, you will need to add the question, "Am I ready to move into a new relationship in a way that is fair to the person I date and to my children?"

To be fair to the people you might date, grief counselors recommend that no major decisions be made the first year after a loss. Starting to date *is* a major decision. This is further complicated if your children are ages 3 to 18 because they will have feelings about your dating. Each child is different. Some will feel you are being disloyal to the dead parent if you date. Others may want you to get on with your life so you find happiness again. Younger children may even ask, "When do I get a new mommy or new daddy?"

Most people just assume having a relationship is a right. It is not. It is a privilege—one which you can prepare your heart to receive. In our study guide for the married version of *Men Are Like Waffles, Women Are Like Spaghetti,* we give these keys to great marriages: To have a better marriage, become a better partner; to become a better partner, become a better person. Quality attracts quality and produces quality relationships. You deserve the best, so seek to be the best.

A Few Answers for the Question, Why Aren't You Married Yet?

- You haven't asked yet.

- I was hoping to do something meaningful with my life.

- What? And spoil my great life?

- Because I just love hearing this question.

- Just lucky, I guess.

- It gives my mother something to live for.

- My fiancé is awaiting parole.

- I'm still hoping for a shot at Miss America.

- I'm waiting until I get to be your age.

- It didn't seem worth a blood test.

A friend asked a gentleman how it is that he never married. Replied the gentleman, "Well, I guess I just never met the right woman. I guess that I have been looking for the perfect girl."

"Oh, come on now," said the friend, "Surely you have met at least one girl that you wanted to marry."

"Yes, there was a girl, once. I guess she was the one perfect girl—the only perfect girl I really ever met.

"Well, why didn't you marry her?" asked his friend.

The gent replied, "She was looking for the perfect man."

Sure Signs That You've Had a Bad First Date

- You find out her real name is Vinnie, and you used to play little league with her.

- She has a thicker moustache than you.

Single Women Are Like Spaghetti

- When you go to pick her up, her lawyer meets you at the door with a contract describing your duties and restrictions.

- You jokingly ask her if she wants to go down to Atlantic City and get married. She then informs you that leaving the state is a violation of her parole.

- You are the first guy she's gone out with who isn't her cousin.

- She keeps staring at you all through dinner, then finally asks if you want to meet Satan.

- She informs you that you can't go out again because her boyfriend doesn't like you.

*The smallest package we have
ever seen is a man wrapped up
in himself.*

—AUTHOR UNKNOWN

The Waffle Warrior

The Lord God formed the man from the dust of the ground and breathed into his nostrils the breath of life, and the man became a living being" (Genesis 2:7).

What exactly does it mean to be a man? To most men, it means to be adventurous and untamed, constantly looking for something in life to overcome. When life is too easy, a man becomes bored. When life is too challenging, he gets discouraged. A man is capable of remarkable feats of strength and courage. He's equally capable of astonishing feats of laziness and neglect.

Driven to Succeed

Men have a built-in drive to succeed. The waffle boxes in which a man is most likely to succeed are the boxes he will spend the most time in. When a man knows he can do something well—that's where he'll expend his energies. Other boxes—the ones in which he's less successful—are the ones where he'll spend the least time and energy.

A man who is highly productive at work will enjoy going to work and may even spend too much time there. A man who is adept at athletic competition wants all of it he can fit into his schedule. A man who reads well and thinks clearly is naturally motivated to extend his education. A man who is skilled at making things with his hands will always have a project going.

Unfortunately, this drive to succeed has a dark side. If a man figures out he's very good at unproductive things, he will be just as attracted to them as he is to his positive pursuits. A man who realizes he's good at being lazy will fill his schedule with idleness. A man who constantly hears from others that he's an underachiever will commit himself to underachieve for the rest of his life. If crudeness comes easily and is rewarded with laughter and attention, a man will become an expert at being crude. A man who's had his confidence shaken early in life through failure or disapproval will develop a remarkable ability to disappoint people throughout his life.

Untamed Sophistication

When God made man, He made him outside the garden, in the wilderness of life. John Eldredge, in his very insightful book *Wild at Heart*, captures the essence of what it means to be a man when he writes, "Adam, if you'll remember, was created outside the Garden, in the wilderness....Man was born in the outback, from the untamed part of creation....Adventure, with all its requisite danger and wildness, is a deeply spiritual longing written into the soul of man."[1] In the heart of every man is the love of adventure. He wants to conquer something, overcome something, discover something, kill something, or invent something. He's never interested in just keeping the status quo. God created him to subdue the earth and cultivate the ground. Man is designed to face the wild things of life and bring them under his submission. The last victory of his life is never enough to satisfy his soul. He needs a new horizon to discover each and every day of his life.

This is why men are more attracted to risk than their female counterparts are. When life is in order and a minimum of effort is required to maintain it, men get bored. This doesn't appear to be a learned skill but rather an inborn trait of males. "This leads us to one of the very few clear-cut differences in behavior between the two sexes: Whenever and wherever they're observed, boys engage in more rough-and-tumble play than girls."[2]

A California study of four-year-old children confirmed these differences in gender, even in play. The children were invited to play on a trampoline in groups of three, all of the same sex. "About a quarter of the boys engaged in fairly extreme types of horseplay, piling on top of each other on the trampoline or rushing into each other and collapsing in shrieks of laughter. None of the girls played really boisterously, although some of them took part in a more decorous type of high jinks. About a quarter of the girls went to the other extreme, organizing a rotation system in which they went on the trampoline one at a time, while the two other members of the group watched and waited their turn. None of the groups of boys organized such a system."[3]

When you put a ball in the mix with a group of guys it gets even more interesting. "In girls' games, the emphasis is usually on keeping the ball going back and forth. The groups of boys, on the other hand, tend to invent rules which ensure plenty of physical contact and an eventual individual winner. Interestingly, this difference between co-operative and competitive styles of playing is greatest between the ages of twelve and fourteen, when concern about gender role is at its peak."[4]

When you dial this competitive nature up to manhood, you get men who are willing to turn anything into a game with a winner. We like to win at work, and we like to win at play. We like to win at romance, and we like to win at decision making. When we are not the winner, we must recover. We have great respect for those who beat us in any competitive pursuit, but we're always looking ahead to the next time when *we* can end up in the winner's circle. Even when we're the spectator, we engage this competitive instinct. When a man who loves sports is watching *his* team win, his testosterone level rises by an average of 20 percentage points. Likewise, when *his* team loses, his testosterone level falls by an average of 20 percentage points.[5] The only conclusion you can reach is that a man feels more like a man when he wins!

Winning Words

Even when it comes to conversation we men have an aggressive approach. We like to know where the conversation is going at all times. It's not that we want to *control* the conversation as much as we want to *succeed* at the conversation. As soon as we recognize something we can talk intelligently about we want to jump in before the subject changes. We are easily intimidated by the women in our lives who can talk about anything at any time. We are amazed at men who can stay active in conversation. We are even highly critical of them because we don't want the pressure on us to have to be like them.

This is a trait that shows up early in life and is only extinguished by the grave. "Analysis of nursery school children's conversation shows that boys tend to interrupt other speakers nearly twice as often as girls. This establishes a pattern that continues throughout life: at primary school, the ratio of male to female interruptions of a teacher in lessons is very much higher, while in adulthood it has been calculated that men are responsible for no less than 98 percent of all the interruptions that occur in everyday conversation!"[6]

Men even put reading in boxes. A man's motivation to read is directly related to the level of interest he has in the subject. Seldom will a man read to simply read. He will read to learn something he thinks he needs to know. He will read to enhance his knowledge of something he's already interested in. He will analyze sports. He will investigate computers. He will lose himself in cars or trucks. But rare is the man who will read just to explore the nuances of life. "When they're interested in what they have to read, boys are found to perform much better, whereas girls seem to do equally well, irrespective of whether or not they find what they have to read interesting."[7] And why is this so? "Poor reading is associated with being impulsive, and there is evidence that boys are more impulsive, and girls more reflective, from a fairly early age."[8]

Meet Me On the Edge

A man's desire to be "dangerous in a safe way"[9] extends to the way we handle money. If there is no sense of risk in our investments, we're just not interested. If there's no reward for our expenses, we get bored with the whole process. When we shop, we want to hunt down our purchases, not graze in the mall. A recent study reveals that "single women exhibit relatively more risk aversion in financial decision making than single men.... Greater financial risk aversion may provide an explanation for women's lower levels of wealth compared with men's."[10]

Men approach every area of life with more risk than their female counterparts. Recent studies have "found that women appear to be less willing to risk being caught and convicted of speeding than men, and that on average women made safer choices than men when it came to making risky consumer decisions, such as smoking behavior, seat belt use, preventative dental care, and having regular blood pressure checks."[11]

Call Me the Navigator

Much to our joy, it has now been confirmed that we men are better at finding our way out of unfamiliar places than women. In the most recent research, a biological connection has been established for this ability. When men navigate their way in a new place, they not only use different parts of their brains but they only use one side of their brains. Women, on the other hand, have more connections between the two sides of their brains than men, and they use both sides when making navigational decisions. Even in the car, the waffle and spaghetti distinction holds true. Men approach navigation as a single task and isolate one part of their brain to carry out the task while women connect the two sides of their brain. It's interesting to note that men tend to remember directions such as left and right, while women give directions in relation to landmarks, such as "turn left at the grocery store."[12][13][14]

Men also have natural confidence in their ability to find their way. This frustrates those who have to ride with them, and this frustration probably gave rise to this bumper sticker I saw the other day:

> *Question: How many roads must a man travel down before he admits he's lost?*

> *Answer: No man is ever really lost. He just hasn't found his way out yet!*

To admit we are lost is to admit defeat. We will only admit defeat when the pain of admitting we are lost is less than the pain of continuing the search.

Guys Who Love Movies

When it comes time to choose a movie to watch, the battle between the sexes lights up. Men tend to like dangerous movies! It's safe to watch a movie filled with dangerous scenes and outrageous adventures. The man who wins the woman's heart while defeating the enemy with death-defying stunts is the ultimate man because there is no limit to his success or to his ability to overcome the major challenges of life. We love the hero. James Bond, Superman, Jack Ryan, and Indiana Jones encompass all that we find exciting. Their exploits make life worth pursuing. Many of us are locked into jobs that lack any sense of adventure. Our lives are filled with responsibilities that must be managed rather than pursued. We long to find an adventure that will capture our heart. We want to climb tall mountains, meet beautiful women that find us fascinating, conquer the evil masters of disaster, and figure out the impossible situation. Since there is so little of this in our everyday lives, we get lost in the movies that take us where we cannot go ourselves.

Most women wish we were more interested in stories of relationships and movies where real-life drama meets character development. We men ask, "Where is the danger? Where is the adventure? Where is the impossible situation that will be overcome by the hero of the day?" All of us men wonder, *Why would we want to be entertained by everyday life when it wasn't that exciting the first time?*

Consider Captain James T. Kirk. He makes a habit of boldly going where no man has gone before. If it's out there, he wants to discover it. If there are obstacles in his way, he will overcome them. If enemies are encountered, they will ultimately be done away with. If he confronts what seems impossible he will find a way to make it possible. He's the ultimate warrior.

In *Star Trek III: The Search for Spock*, Kirk is agonizing over his latest decision. The amazing thing about Captain Kirk is he has the ability to show his vulnerability while still being invincible. He engages his good friend Dr. McCoy in a conversation about the latest plight in his life.

Kirk asks, "My God, Bones, what have I done?"

Dr. McCoy fills our hearts with imagination when he reminds his friend, "What you had to do; what you always do: turn death into a fighting chance to live."

In *Star Trek: Generations*, Captain Kirk meets up with Captain Jean-Luc Picard. They will explore together, conquer together, and reaffirm themselves as winners against the forces of evil and mediocrity. In a classic interchange that stirs up everything it means to be a man, Captain Kirk says, "I take it the odds are against us and the situation is grim."

Captain Jean-Luc Picard responds, "You could say that."

To which Captain James T. Kirk says, "Sounds like fun!"

The Ordinary Adventurer

The next incarnation of James T. Kirk is Indiana Jones. Dr. Jones is so ordinary he could be any one of us. He has a responsible job and lives in an average neighborhood. At the same time, he cannot help but find adventures that take him away to exotic places on heroic adventures. That's what every man dreams his life could be. We are locked up in ordinary, responsible lives, but we long to find the adventure that will convince us we are stronger than life.

Willie Scott is just about overwhelmed in *Indiana Jones and the Temple of Doom* by Dr. Jones' ability to defeat death. In exasperation he says, "You're gonna get killed chasing after your fortune and glory!"

When Indiana Jones responds, "Maybe. But not today," my heart just about leaped out of my chest. In an instant, I knew I wanted to be Dr. Jones and not Willie Scott. Oh, how I long to think up things like this on the spot. In my mind, I know somebody labored over the script to make Indiana sound so spontaneous, but in my heart I want to spontaneously live just like this.

In *Indiana Jones and the Last Crusade*, we admire Sean Connery as Henry Jones, but we long to be Indiana. Henry is the devout, wise, intellectual discoverer. Indiana is the conquering, tenacious, dangerously exciting, fully alive treasure hunter. This difference is clearly displayed in this interaction between father and son.

> Henry: They're trying to kill us!
> Indiana Jones: I know, Dad!
> Henry: This is a new experience for me.
> Indiana Jones: It happens to me all the time.

In reality, none of us want to be shot at. We don't want people seeking to kill us. We don't want to live on the edge of disaster. But we do want to believe that we are resourceful enough to overcome just such challenges if the need arises.

The Fantasy Avenger

The other side of the story is just sheer fantasy. We love to entertain thoughts of the impossible. We love to laugh at men in movies who overstate their worth and value. We love to stand with men who overshadow the reality of life. We know it's not true, but there is something about it that transports us to a place in life that is better or more enjoyable than the stable reality of today. It's not that we want to live out the fantasy of the greatness of the unconquerable male. We just want to visit there often enough to relieve the stress of real life. Consider these bigger-than-life heroes and their bigger-than-life proclamations.

William Wallace in *Braveheart*: "They may take our lives, but they'll never take our freedom!"

Colonel Nathan Jessup in *A Few Good Men:*

> Son, we live in a world that has walls, and those walls have to be guarded by men with guns. Who's gonna do it? You? You, Lieutenant Weinberg? I have a greater responsibility than you can possibly fathom. You weep for Santiago and you curse the Marines. You have that luxury. You have the luxury of not knowing what I know: that Santiago's death, while tragic, probably saved lives. And my existence, while grotesque and incomprehensible to you, saves lives. You don't want the truth because, deep down in places you don't talk about at parties, you want me on that wall, you need me on that wall. We use words like honor, code, loyalty. We use these words as the backbone of a life spent defending something. You use them as a punchline. I have neither the time nor the inclination to explain myself to a man who rises and sleeps under the blanket of the very freedom that I provide and then questions the manner in which I provide it. I would rather you just said "thank you"

and went on your way. Otherwise I suggest you pick up a weapon and stand at post.

Lucilla in *Gladiator*, speaking about Maximus Decimus Meridius: "Today I saw a slave become more powerful than the Emperor of Rome."

At the climax of the story, Emperor Commodus and Maximus have a showdown that shows the superiority of the Gladiator.

> Commodus: "The general who became a slave. The slave who became a gladiator. The gladiator who defied an emperor. Striking story! But now, the people want to know how the story ends. Only a famous death will do. And what could be more glorious than to challenge the Emperor himself in the great arena?"
>
> Maximus Decimus Meridius: "You would fight me?"
>
> Commodus: "Why not? Do you think I am afraid?"
>
> Maximus Decimus Meridius: "I think you've been afraid all your life."

The President in *Independence Day:*

> Mankind. That word should have new meaning for all of us today. We can't be consumed by our petty differences anymore. We will be united in our common interest. Perhaps it's fate that today is the Fourth of July, and you will once again be fighting for our freedom. Not from tyranny, oppression, or persecution, but from annihilation. We're fighting for our right to live, to exist! And should we win the day, the Fourth of July will no longer be known as an American holiday, but as the day when the world declared in one voice, "We will not go quietly into the night! We will not vanish without a fight! We're going to live

on! We're going to survive! Today, we celebrate our Independence Day!"

Ian Malcolm in *Jurassic Park:* "God creates dinosaurs. God destroys dinosaurs. God creates man. Man destroys God. Man creates dinosaurs..."

Dr. Ellie Sattler: "Dinosaurs eat man. Woman inherits the earth..."

In *A League of Their Own,* Tom Hanks, as manager Jimmy Dugan, is feeling the exasperation of managing women in baseball. He loves the game and is committed to teaching it to his team, but there are certain aspects he just can't quite figure out. In frustration he blurts out, "Are you crying? Are you crying? There's no crying in baseball."

In *The Princess Bride,* Buttercup is afraid and attempts to point out to Westley that the adventure they're on is impossible. She blurts out, "We'll never survive!"

Sensing that she's about to spoil their perfectly dangerous adventure, he assures her in confident ridiculousness, "Nonsense! You're only saying that because no one ever has."

Simply Irresistible

A man's drive to find an adventure he can succeed at breeds in him an intense desire for simplicity. He longs to be able to focus on one box at a time in his life. He wants a manageable schedule and evenly paced expectations. It isn't because the other areas of life are less important to him. In fact, it's precisely because these areas are important to him that he must give them his attention. When he divides his attention, however, he begins to feel inadequate and the stress in his life grows.

As already mentioned, when it comes to projects, men like to work on them one at a time. He climbs in the box and gets immersed in the project. He forgets that anything else is going on in his life, and he loses himself in the work. When he can work this way, he finds life to be very satisfying. When the project is over, he will stand back and admire his handiwork. He will probably find the people who mean the most to him and ask them to join him in the admiration. Every comment about the beauty of the finished product increases the sense of accomplishment. Every criticism of the process deflates his pride and makes him wonder if it really was worth the effort.

The quickest way to steal motivation from a man is to make him change focus rapidly. This is often confusing to women because they tend to process life in short bursts. A woman travels the spaghetti noodles of her thought process and actively switches from one subject to another. This makes for a fascinating journey in life, and so she assumes that everyone is like she is. But men are very different. When a man has to switch subjects quickly, he gets exhausted and confused. He loses sight of what is most important and has a hard time figuring out what needs to be done next. When he can focus on one or two things he's very productive, but when he has to focus on many things he can easily become disoriented or frustrated. He will often get angry or just walk away from what looks like a mess to him.

Alec Baldwin gives all us ordinary men hope as Jack Ryan, the hero of *The Hunt for Red October*. He's the one man in the movie who is bigger than life and thereby indestructible. As the plot unfolds, it becomes apparent that Jack Ryan can overcome any obstacle and figure out any mystery. But he has a simple view of himself. When asked for his identity, his response is simply, "I'm not an agent; I just write books for the CIA." Every man knows that this simple view of his role empowers him to be great. To think about every exploit ahead of time would breed fear. Reviewing the detailed greatness of his accomplishments would overwhelm him. When he thinks of himself as a simple author caught in a moment of destiny, he overcomes all obstacles.

This drive for simplicity allows men to boil down the well-being of their lives to one issue. If this issue is good, life is good. If this issue is bad, life is bad.

Searching for Solutions

Men like to work on projects that have a solution. A man will lose himself in working on his car because there is a goal and an easily defined finish point. A man will bury himself in his computer because he can always tell when it's working correctly. If something is wrong, he will give himself over to pursuing the solution, and he will spend far too much time working on the problem because he anticipates the taste of victory. Having to divert attention from this one project to another disrupts his day. The women who know him don't get it because they think he should be flexible and take care of other simple responsibilities. They don't realize that even the smallest act can disrupt his momentum and throw him off schedule for hours, even days. A man's ability to focus on a single project is a beautiful and highly productive thing. It requires all his energy and consumes his life for the duration. Once the magic is broken, however, it's difficult to reconnect him to the task at hand. He feels ripped off and maybe even lost.

If this happens too often, he may even grow bitter or lazy. A man works best when he's able to concentrate on one goal. If he's repeatedly interrupted, he will develop a pattern of avoidance. He will despise his laziness, but he will find it less painful than pursuing tasks that always get interrupted. On the other hand, he may be driven to accomplish. He assumes that others know how important it is to him to be focused. When others interrupt him, it adds to the irritation. If specific people in his life are consistently demanding that he switch his focus, he will conclude they either don't know or don't care. If he takes time to explain this to his friend and the friend continues to downplay his need to stay focused, he will build up his resentment of this person. The resentment will linger until it turns into lingering bitterness. It lurks just under the surface and gets released with each interruption. It surprises him and it surprises those who get affected by it, but it's very real.

What's the Problem?

The boxes in a man's life contain questions to be answered or problems to be solved. A man finds no joy in pursuits that simply have opinions rather than an answer. He's more comfortable with the thought that there is a *best* way to do everything in life. Because there is a *best* way, there is no reason to talk about *possible* ways. He will often get stuck on this "best way" and refuse to see any other legitimate way through the situation. This is the cause of much of the stubbornness in men. We can't see any way but *our* way, and we resist efforts of others to help us see things differently. We continue in the same pattern of thinking and feeling despite the fact that things may be falling apart around us.

I was working with Pam's 70-year-old grandfather on the farm one day. The pump for the well was not working, and we were trying to figure out the problem. The pump house was only large enough for one of us at a time so I was standing at the doorway while grandpa went in with a wrench in each hand. The pump was wired to a 220-volt circuit and he was doing some "testing."

I became concerned so I asked, "Gramps, do you want me to turn off the power before you start feeling around with two metal wrenches?"

"Naw, I'll be alright," Grandpa shouted back. You see, Grandpa had decided that his way was best. He had decided there would be no problem. I thought about pushing the issue, but I knew it wouldn't make any difference, and I was concerned it might distract him.

As I was thinking this through, Grandpa bent over the pump in a 90-degree position and started in on the project. The next thing I knew, he was yelling something I can't repeat as 220 volts ripped through his body. From his bent-over position he jumped in the air so high that his feet went to my waist. Sparks were dancing in the air, and the accompanying electrical buzz broadcast itself through the airwaves. His feet crashed back to earth as he managed to let go of the wrenches.

He turned to me in stunned embarrassment and said, "I guess you can turn the power off now."

I feel bad telling you that I was laughing inside. I still think one of the funniest scenes I have ever seen is the feet of a 70-year-old man jumping three feet in the air because of his stubbornness. Fortunately, when we shared the story with the ladies later that day, he too was amused with himself. He had decided that his way was best and all it led to was one of the best laughs we have ever shared.

The Dark Side of Manhood

But sometimes, this stubbornness isn't funny at all. When a man hangs all his happiness on one issue, one box, he sets himself up to be angry. Anger is by far the most common emotion men experience. When it's focused on an injustice in the world, it can motivate him to heroic action that is admired by all. But more often, he thinks someone or something is standing in the way of his fulfillment, and he lashes out. History has proven that unhealthy anger is all too easy for men to discover in themselves.

Anger takes on many unwelcome faces in the life of a man. Anger can turn to abandonment as he flees the scene he has lost control of. Anger can turn into abuse—physical, mental or emotional—if he hasn't settled the issues of his manhood and allows himself to be threatened by those weaker than himself. Anger can produce tantrums, either of silence or childish behavior, when he feels powerless to get his way. Or anger can turn into addiction as he pursues outrageous behavior in an attempt to numb the pain of failure. Anger can even turn a man inward and make him passive. He takes his anger out on himself and falls into depression or physical ailment. He gets angry to try to get the things in life he desperately desires, only to find that anger drives them all away.

117

Men actually like the feeling of anger because it makes them feel powerful. Anger causes a man's heart rate and blood pressure to go up, and it sets off an increase in the levels of energy hormones, adrenaline, and noradrenaline. "Anger is a natural, adaptive response to threats; it inspires powerful, often aggressive, feelings and behaviors, which allow us to fight and to defend ourselves when we are attacked. A certain amount of anger, therefore, is necessary to our survival."[15]

But sadly, out-of-control anger is currently epidemic among men. Of the 140 million Americans who use illicit drugs, 77 percent are men. Half of all Americans report alcohol use, but one third *more* men than women are binge- and heavy drinkers.[16] Almost 14 million people in the United States have a drinking problem, and three times as many men are alcoholics as women. Forty percent of all rapes, 30 percent of all assaults, and one-half of all homicides and domestic violence cases are alcohol related. Forty-three percent of all Americans report that they have been exposed to alcoholism as a part of their family circle.[17]

John Gottman and Neil Jacobson, in the article "Anatomy of a Violent Relationship," explain that "batterers share a common profile: they're unpredictable, unable to be influenced by their wives, and impossible to prevent from battering once an argument has begun." This is vital information for singles when you consider that most battered women are live-in girlfriends, not wives. The authors further explain that "battering is physical aggression with a purpose: to control, intimidate, and subjugate another human being. It's always accompanied by emotional abuse, often involves injury, and virtually always causes fear in the battered woman."

Social scientists studying batterers still could not accurately predict when a man would cross over from emotional abuse to physical violence. The scientists further added, "We have discovered that once an episode starts, there is nothing that the woman can do to affect its course." However, they did see a common trait in batterers. They never heard the men say phrases like, "'That's a good point,' or 'I never thought of that'—comments that most married men (and women) say all the time during an argument. Instead, we observed that batterers became more aggressive when their wives asserted themselves."[18]

Normal couples have a withdrawal ritual when things get too intense, but abusive men never withdraw. It seems that once a man is "activated," even if a woman senses she's in danger and wants to leave, he won't let her. The only faint warning signs the sociologists spotted were belligerence and contempt during an argument combined with attempts to squelch, control, or dominate a wife's behavior. Eighty percent of batterers hold unrelenting contempt for women and yet are extremely dependent on them. Through abusive scrutiny (belittling, name calling, swearing) and constant demands, batterers establish control. Control is important to these men because they genuinely feel they will be abandoned if they do not maintain constant vigilance over their wives.

> One particularly sinister form of control they use is known as "gaslighting." This technique—which gets its name from the film *Gaslight*, in which Charles Boyer convinces Ingrid Bergman she's going insane—involves a systematic denial of the wife's experience of reality. For example, when one of our subjects slapped his wife in front of a neighbor, he denied that he had done it, telling her that this kind of behavior was inconsistent with his personality, and that her accusations of abuse came from her own disturbed mind. Although her face still hurt from the slap, she thought to herself that maybe she had made it all up. The neighbor, a friend of the husband's, went along and said he didn't see anything. This technique of denying the woman's reality can be so effective that when used in combination with methods to isolate the woman from other people, it causes battered

women to doubt their own sanity. This is the ultimate form of abuse: to gain control of the victim's mind.[19]

So how can a man learn to handle the anger? How can he avoid addictive behaviors? How can he gain the strength and courage to stay in a relationship rather than abandon it?

Seek God. God knows what it means to be a man. He understands your love of adventure. He loves the aggressive part of your soul, and He knows how to channel that aggression into productive and healthy pursuits.

Find the dream that resides in your heart. Men were made for adventure. We all look for excitement. If there is not a real challenge to face in life, we create one. When we can't fight a noble battle in life, we pick fights with people we love or we turn passive in an attempt to dull the pain of a boring life. A man without a dream to chase is much more susceptible to being angry than a man who is caught up in a great adventure.

Learn to look for options. Men get angry because they feel like failures. They have one solution to a problem, and that solution isn't working. Instead of looking for other ways to solve the problem, they get angry in an attempt to force their way to work.

Admit early when you are angry. Men feel weak when they admit anger. They feel they're giving up control and admitting they can't handle a situation. When a man learns to admit early in conversation that he's getting angry, those who care about him can help him find constructive ways to express his anger. The vulnerability raises his chances of having satisfying relationships, which increases his confidence and lowers his frustration.

A man, at his best, is refined and wild at the same time. He can be professional and polished while dreaming of the rugged outdoors. He can maintain a responsible life, but he will never be captivated by it. His heart will always yearn for something bigger than life even though he must master the rigors of his daily existence. He's always looking to the horizon. He can be relied upon, but he can never be fully tamed. A man without a dream in his heart is a dead man walking. The boxes on a man's waffle that are filled with adventure and wonder are inconvenient and disconcerting to those who love him the most, but they're what make him a man because they focus his heart. "Above all else, guard your heart, for it is the wellspring of life" (Proverbs 4:23).

The Worth of a Man

The estimated value of the chemical contents (inorganic compounds) of a 150-pound man:

- in the 1930s   98¢

- in the 1960s $3.50

- in the 1970s $5.60

Over 60 percent of the body weight is water, which would be free.[20]

The Worth of an Energetic Man

In th 1930s the worth of a man was assessed at 98¢. Now, with atomic power in view, this has all changed. Someone has figured that the atoms in the human body would produce 11,400,000 kilowatts of power per pound if they could be harnessed. On this basis of computation, a man weighing 150 pounds is worth $85,500,000,000.[21]

A woman of mystique is fully aware of her flaws and weaknesses, yet she's strong enough to admit them and not be embarrassed by them.

—JEAN LUSH

The Pasta Princess

Adam was created outside the garden and longs to conquer, but Eve was created inside the garden, and she has her own longings. Check out her creation:

> The LORD God formed the man from the dust of the ground and breathed into his nostrils the breath of life, and the man became a living being. Now the LORD God had planted a garden in the east, in Eden; and there he put the man he had formed (Genesis 2:7-8).

Adam was formed outside the garden, and then God planted a garden. Given God's track record of creation, it must have been some garden! It was perfect for man to live in:

> The LORD God took the man and put him in the Garden of Eden to work it and take care of it. And the LORD God commanded the man, "You are free to eat from any tree in the garden; but you must not eat from the tree of the knowledge of good and evil, for when you eat of it you will surely die" (Genesis 2:15-17).

Perfect, except…Adam was lonely! So God made woman:

> The LORD God said, "It is not good for the man to be alone. I will make a helper suitable for him." Now the

LORD God had formed out of the ground all the beasts of the field and all the birds of the air. He brought them to the man to see what he would name them; and whatever the man called each living creature, that was its name. So the man gave names to all the livestock, the birds of the air and all the beasts of the field. But for Adam no suitable helper was found. So the LORD God caused the man to fall into a deep sleep; and while he was sleeping, he took one of the man's ribs and closed up the place with flesh. Then the LORD God made a woman from the rib he had taken out of the man, and he brought her to the man (Genesis 2:18-22).

And Eve got quite the response:

The man said,

"This is now bone of my bones
 and flesh of my flesh;
she shall be called 'woman,'
 for she was taken out of man" (Genesis 2:23).

This is the equivalent to an "Oolala!" or "O Baby!" or "Wow, that's some hot mama!" You get the picture. Adam saw Eve and liked what he saw.

When single men are surveyed, nearly all make some mention of appreciating the beauty of women. Guys are not deviant for noticing women—it's an inborn trait given by God. It was only after the fall of man that this appreciation degenerated into ogling and addictions. Before the fall, as Adam gazed on Eve, it was all good—pure love.

For this reason a man will leave his father and mother and be united to his wife, and they will become one flesh.

The man and his wife were both naked, and they felt no shame (Genesis 2:24).

The garden was perfect; God thought Eve was perfect (He made her, after all!). Adam thought Eve was perfect. And even Eve was pleased with herself early on. After all, she was running around the garden naked with Adam with no shame.

Eve's Contribution

In the garden, Eve found herself. She knew her contribution. The garden needed tending. However, before the fall, we can't find any records of bugs or weeds, so tending was much easier! It was a case of the beautiful (Eve) creating more beauty (the garden). One of women's greatest roles in life is to bring beauty and order wherever they go. In one Gallup poll, men said one of the top three things they appreciated about women is that they were well organized. Because women process life like spaghetti, they can see all the loose ends that need to be connected. They can create order out of disorder.

In a recent survey women named their number-one desire as significance. Women want to know their lives count. They want the world to be a better place because they're in it. Emotionally healthy women intrinsically desire to leave the world better than they found it. They want people to be glad they were there.

Her Compassion

Although single men surveyed appreciated women's beauty and their organizational skills, the quality they admired most in women was their relationship skills. The respondents used many different words to describe it (kind, tender, empathetic, loving, nurturing, sweet, nice, a good listener), but all the descriptions fall into one main category: compassion. Waffle warriors appreciate that somehow women love them!

Her Character

And lest we forget, Eve was made in God's image. God encompasses all of the qualities of both males and females (and then some!). We are a reflection of Him. That is some great DNA! In addition, women were created from the "rib" of Adam.

There is a portion of a popular wedding ceremony that perfectly describes the significance of Eve's original creation:

> The woman God made was not taken from man's head to rule over him, nor from under his feet to be trampled upon by him, but from his side that she might be his equal, from under his arm that she might receive his protection, and from near his heart that she might own and command his love.

When women see their contribution, their compassion, and their character as good, we become women of influence, women who feel significant. We do make a difference! It's only as we fall prey to the lies of Satan and become discontent that trouble is created. Eve was living out her prefect destiny—then things changed:

> Now the serpent was more crafty than any of the wild animals the LORD God had made. He said to the woman, "Did God really say, 'You must not eat from any tree in the garden'?"

> The woman said to the serpent, "We may eat fruit from the trees in the garden, but God did say, 'You must not eat fruit from the tree that is in the middle of the garden, and you must not touch it, or you will die.'"

> "You will not surely die," the serpent said to the woman. "For God knows that when you eat of it your eyes will be opened, and you will be like God, knowing good and evil."

> When the woman saw that the fruit of the tree was good for food and pleasing to the eye, and also desirable for gaining wisdom, she took some and ate it. She also gave some to her husband, who was with her, and he ate it (Genesis 3:1-6).

The serpent told her that if she ate, her eyes would be opened and she'd be like God. Eve was discontent. She didn't think she was good enough as she was. She wanted to be better. Many women are self-deprecating today—and men don't like it. Many males surveyed said they hated hearing women put themselves down. It's one of the true turnoffs for a male (and males are not easily turned off!).

In one focus group, a man we'll call Brad said, "I hate hearing women put themselves down. It's a real slam to the guy they're with—like he doesn't have good taste being with her. What I find attractive is a woman who has confidence in herself."

Eve should have been *very* self-confident. Here's God's take on His creation:

> So God created man in his own image, in the image of God he created him; male and female he created them (Genesis 1:27).

> God saw all that he had made, and it was very good (Genesis 1:31).

The Bible says that after all the other days of creation, God saw that what He had made was *good*. But after creating man and woman, God said it was *very good*.

Eve thought she could improve upon what God created. She wasn't content with what God had done. She did not accept His assessment of her goodness. As a result, Eve wanted control. She wanted to be her own god. She couldn't leave well enough alone. And what were the results?

> Then the eyes of both of them were opened, and they realized they were naked; so they sewed fig leaves together and made coverings for themselves (Genesis 3:7).

The first result is shame. Eve felt bad about herself—so bad she covered up her body. Those fig leaves were probably the original "fat clothes." (Guys, all women have fat clothes, and to bring you up to speed, they're the clothes they wear when they're feeling bloated, ugly, and "fat." They're often worn during PMS. They're usually baggy, drab, and come with matching accessories, like a carton of Ben and Jerry's Chocolate Fudge Brownie ice cream.)

Then Adam and Eve acted ashamed and made some bad relationship statements:

> Then the man and his wife heard the sound of the LORD God as he was walking in the garden in the cool of the day, and they hid from the LORD God among the trees of the garden. But the LORD God called to the man, "Where are you?"
>
> He answered, "I heard you in the garden, and I was afraid because I was naked; so I hid."
>
> And he said, "Who told you that you were naked? Have you eaten from the tree that I commanded you not to eat from?"
>
> The man said, "The woman you put here with me— she gave me some fruit from the tree, and I ate it."
>
> Then the LORD God said to the woman, "What is this you have done?"
>
> The woman said, "The serpent deceived me, and I ate" (Genesis 3:8-13).

Remember the studies that showed when men fail, they blame some outside circumstance? Adam started that pattern in the Garden. He blamed Eve—*and God* for giving Eve to him. Now that's a cop out! If there's anything that irks a woman, it's men who won't step up to the plate and accept their responsibility. Guys who are willing to say, "I'm sorry" or "I blew it; please forgive me" will always have better relationships with women. At one of our conferences, a man handed us an article with the headline, "Men who say 'Yes, Dear' have better marriages." The headline was a bit misleading, but the gist of the article was that men who are willing to agree with women have better relationships with them. This concept should be a no-brainer, but some men are still unwilling to admit that they're wrong. Everything that goes sour in a relationship is the women's fault. When a guy chooses to maintain he's always right, he may keep his ego and pride, but he will become a very lonely man because no self-respecting woman will want anything to do with him!

But Eve wasn't much better. She didn't blame Adam, but she didn't seek his advice either. One of two things happened in the garden. Eve may have deliberately disobeyed the command. (It isn't clear whether or not the prohibition to eat from the forbidden tree was related to Eve, so she might not have known. On the other hand, it seems she had an awareness of the rule.) The other possibility is that Eve didn't seek out Adam's advice and opinion. Either way, she decided to make her own choice, regardless of the greater consequences for her, for others, and for the future.

And there *were* consequences:

> So the LORD God said to the serpent, "Because you
> have done this,

> "Cursed are you above all the livestock
> and all the wild animals!
> You will crawl on your belly
> and you will eat dust
> all the days of your life.
> And I will put enmity
> between you and the woman,
> and between your offspring and hers;
> he will crush your head,
> and you will strike his heel."

> To the woman he said,

> "I will greatly increase your pains in childbearing;

with pain you will give birth to children.
Your desire will be for your husband,
and he will rule over you."

To Adam he said, "Because you listened to your wife
and ate from the tree about which I commanded you,
'You must not eat of it,'

"Cursed is the ground because of you;
through painful toil you will eat of it
all the days of your life.
It will produce thorns and thistles for you,
and you will eat the plants of the field.
By the sweat of your brow
you will eat your food
until you return to the ground,
since from it you were taken;
for dust you are
and to dust you will return."

Adam named his wife Eve, because she would become
the mother of all the living (Genesis 3:14-20).

Eve became the mother of all living, but because of her discontent and desire to control, she was to endure pain in childbearing—and so do all women after her. I picture a long line in heaven as women complain to Eve about PMS, periods, and menopause and recount their own pain in childbearing. Thanks, Eve!

And in addition to this consequence, the text says: "Your desire will be for your husband, and he will rule over you."

No gals, this doesn't mean that we will have some hot, flaming, erotic desire for the man we marry. Rather, theologians explain this verse means we will desire our husband's role, and God said men would rule over us or be responsible for leading. Adam didn't step up and become a leader in the garden. He knew the fruit was off-limits. Either he didn't inform Eve, or he cooperated with her disobedience. He went right along with her plan of believing Satan and not God, and he refused to keep Eve's best interests in mind.

Let's look closer at the results of the fall.

Pain in childbearing. The childbirth process includes menstruation, which begins (for most girls) between the ages of 12 and 14 and ends with menopause between the ages of 48 and 58. So that's 34 to 46 years of monthly cycles with the bloating, cramps, and supply of feminine-hygiene products. Factor in PMS, which is an official malady (not something that's just in a woman's head). We try to cope with the mood swings and pain of PMS by joking about it.

You've heard or told a few PMS jokes:

- You know the difference between a woman in PMS and a terrorist? You can negotiate with a terrorist.

- You know the difference between a woman in PMS and a pit bull? Lipstick.

- You've heard of FedEx and Airborne Express. Well, there's a new delivery company in town. They have blue trucks with the letters PMS on the side. The company is very organized and efficient, except for seven days each month when they deliver what they want, when they want, and how they want.

The desire to control. The first part of the curse of the fall—pain in childbirth—is pretty well accepted. I can personally attest to this! However, it's the second part of the curse that I believe gives women a much tougher time in life. It's the propensity for discontentment—a woman's desire to control life—that can be the ruin of many good relationships.

I have often thought that we need to start a support group for recovering control freaks and perfectionists. You know, Control Freaks Anonymous. However, I am afraid it will never get off the ground because each of us would think *we* should be the one in charge!

Since the Garden of Eden, we women have had this problem of wanting control. It's "my way or the highway." Part of the curse is that we women have control issues. We naturally want to rule the universe. We tend to think our ideas are best, even when there is no moral or ethical reason to think so. We still want control over preferences. If you think I am kidding, just take a day and watch how often women, especially in the context of a home or comfortable work environment, second-guess men. How often have you heard your mother say to your father, "Why did you do that?" or "No, that's not the way it was" and then go on to correct him in front of family or friends? How often have you heard women criticize men for their methodology? Men do things differently than women, but that doesn't make them inferior or stupid.

Open Season on Males

Currently, we have a problem with male-bashing in our culture. Attacking the male species seems to be one of the few politically correct slams you can get away with. It's open season on the men.

In one set of surveys we took, we asked both genders to share the trait they appreciated most of the opposite gender. In a group of nearly 100, less than 50 women could name *even one* trait they appreciated about men. Seriously, most of the surveys came back blank on that question! On the other hand, nearly every man had numerous traits that he appreciated in women. Are men inferior? Definitely not! Have women been trained to undervalue the contributions of men? Or have our experiences with a few men jaded our view of all men? The longer a woman remains single, the more likely it is that she will be hurt by a male. Therefore, she will be more likely to have her own male issues to deal with.

There *Are* a Few Heroes!

Like many others, Bill and I were horrified as we learned of the deaths of the nearly 400 would-be rescuers at the World Trade Center disaster. We realized that the majority of these brave heroes were men. The passengers who overpowered the hijackers on Flight 93 were men. Throughout history, men have been doing heroic things, saving countless lives. We thought, too, about the soldiers sent far away to Afghanistan to find Osama Bin Laden. They too were mostly men. As we just filled out the papers to sign our oldest son up for the Selective Service, we were reminded once again to be grateful for "the guys."

What Do Women Want?

Some women in the survey were able to list traits of men they appreciated. Most appreciated were a man's strength and his ability to protect. Next was his ability to cope or to step back and be objective—to think like a waffle!

Gals, we can't have it both ways. We can't want men to be just like us and also expect them to step up and do the hard work, the rescue work, the dirty work. That's not fair. God created them with testosterone so they would be prepared to provide and protect.

The Princess and the Pea

When I was little, one of my favorite television specials was "The Princess and the Pea." A traveler came to a king, needing a warm and dry place to sleep. The king placed her in the nicest room with the nicest mattress. She couldn't get comfortable, so he commanded his servants to add another mattress. Still the traveler couldn't get comfortable. Over and over again they added mattresses, and still the young woman tossed and turned all night. In the morning, the servants removed the mattresses and found a tiny little pea. Upon learning this, the king and queen quickly realized the traveler must be a princess—a perfect match for their own prince of a son.

This is a fairy tale, but for the prince it was the beginning of a nightmare—the "nothing is good enough" nightmare. Women who have been the center of their daddy's world, who were doted on without sharing a growing level of responsibility, can become high maintenance. Nothing will be as good as daddy did it. She may have a difficult time bonding to a man because all men live in the shadow of her "perfect" daddy. She may also have been spoiled and may expect to be given royal treatment throughout life. She may feel that manicures, massages, a fancy wardrobe, and memberships to prestigious clubs are musts, rights, and requirements rather than privileges or perks.

If you were told over and over while growing up that you were "Daddy's little princess," you could actually begin to think you were the center of the universe and that the sun should rise and fall upon your whims. Well-meaning mothers and fathers can foster unhealthy self-love in their children.

One teen, while at a friend's for dinner, wanted everyone's attention lavished on her. She had been hurt by her biological father and had some abandonment issues to work through, but on the surface, it appeared she had the *attention-on-me* disorder. Whenever the conversation would drift from her, she would announce, "Focus, focus! Back to me." This was amusing at a dinner party, but not to her mother! Most women are not so bold as to say "Focus all eyes on me." But I have observed that women raised as "princesses" not only like attention but will try to control circumstances when they feel the focus is drifting from themselves or their agenda.

Another young woman announced to Bill in a premarital counseling session, "We don't want to have kids. I am the princess of the family. I am the only daughter, the only girl granddaughter, and the only niece. I have been the center of attention in my family, and I like it that way."

Bill turned to her fiancé and said, "Are you okay with this?"

The fiancé nodded sheepishly.

Bill looked him square in the face and said, "Man to man, I want you to remember this years from now when she wants all your attention, when she wants the world to revolve around her needs and not yours. Just remember, it's highly unlikely this trait will ever change. You knew about it, you accepted it, and you asked for this. Remember, you wanted it."

While some women will desire and manipulate until they get all the attention, others will constantly create a crisis to gain notice. We lovingly dress these gals up in T-shirts that sport the title, "Drama Queen." Love, to them, is a soap opera.

The Soap Opera Syndrome

The "soap opera syndrome" is most likely created if you grew up in a home with a lot of conflict. Your perception is that conflict is correlated with love. It doesn't feel like love unless there is a little bit of pain. The trouble with being a drama queen is that not many kings want that kind of constant crisis. Most men want to know life will be easier, not harder, if they date you. If a guy is constantly on pins and needles, wondering if the smallest comment will set you off, you will have a quick turnover of men in your life. Or you will find a man to include in your drama of conflict.

Women will often comment to me, "Why do I attract all the losers? I could walk into a room of 100 men and find the one loser of the bunch!" I often refer to this as the "loser magnet" or the uncanny ability to attract unhealthy men. This usually happens when women have been victimized. Subconsciously they think they don't deserve to be treated well.

Shonda traced her princess syndrome back to an unhealthy father who spoiled her and who was untrustworthy because of his alcoholism. She went to college and submerged herself in a women's studies program with professors who consistently promoted women and demeaned men. She married soon after college but found herself discontent with everything her husband

135

did. She told him what lane to drive in and how much butter to put on his toast. She questioned his parenting decisions and corrected him in front of company.

"I was ruining our relationship with my control," she admitted. "After our second baby, I was out of sorts. I wish I could blame baby blues or my hormones only, but it had become a pattern to harp, complain, nag, and criticize. My husband tried everything to appease me. But one day he exploded as he walked out the door and shouted, 'Will you *ever* be happy?'

"That was the first time I asked myself the same thing. *Would I?* I was married to a man who loved the children and me, provided for us, attended church with me...and I never thanked or praised him—or at least rarely did. No wonder I felt a distance growing between us."

Shonda could have saved herself and her husband a lot of turmoil if she would have learned early on that she didn't need to be in control of everyone and everything.

Life Feels Out of Control

All of us women, single or married, go through a midlife transition between ages 28 and 38. We ask, "Who am I? Why am I here on earth? What do I do with this ticking biological clock?"

Midlife can feel very uncomfortable for a single woman. She may feel like her choices are out of her control. She longs for more. If she doesn't directly seek to answer these questions through Bible study, small group interactions, mentors, and time with God, her personal pain lures her into less healthy venues of life. She may become depressed. Or she might have suppressed anger, expressed through a sharp tongue or a sarcastic wit.

Some women develop a cynical view of their role with men. *Men are like fine wine. They all start out like grapes, and it's a woman's job to stomp on them and keep them in the dark until they mature into something you'd like to have dinner with.*

These women either give up on men entirely and become male bashers, or they try to "fix" men. This is another reason for the "loser magnet" syndrome. She thinks she can create a new and improved model. There's a saying: A women marries a man hoping he will change, and he doesn't. A man marries a woman hoping she'll never change, and she does.

An unmarried woman may look to a man to help define her, imagining that if she were married, she'd be happy (or at least happier). She may hear her biological clock ticking and become willing to take *any* man so she can have a baby. This leads to a "desperate decision."

Catherine explains,

> My friend, Trish, who married a neighborhood jerk we both grew up with, said to me recently, "Isn't your mother worried about you?"
>
> I replied, "Why would my mom be worried about me?"
>
> "Well, you're thirty and not married. What's wrong with you?"
>
> "Nothing's wrong with me," I answered. "If any mom should be worried, it should be yours. Tom doesn't treat you very well, and now you have two kids to take care of. I don't want to settle just because I didn't take the time to discover who I was and I expect a guy to fill me in!"

Some women want to feel life is under control, so they *give up* control of their lives to a man.

"My friend Jenny is a mystery," said Kristine.

> She was a successful career girl. She was making close to six figures a year. She had a nice house and a new car. Then she met Jared, sold her house and her car, and quit her job. Then suddenly *he* has a house that's

being remodeled; *he* has a new sports car. Jenny has *nothing.* She's been living with Jared for nearly six years and there's no ring in sight. He's such a jerk. He even jokes about it. One day he said to me, "Did you hear? I have a surprise for Jenny."

"Wow, are you finally going to propose?" I asked.

Then Jenny walked up and Jared started laughing and Jenny said, "Oh, is he joking about asking me to marry him again?"

Kristine looked at me and asked, "How can a woman stay with a man who would joke about a subject so tender like that? Why is she staying with such a jerk? I don't think he'll ever ask her. Years from now he'll just get a younger version, and then where will Jenny be? She'll have no home, no car, no job, no money, no life."

Kevin sees this as a major issue in the single women he has dated. "It's like the women get too dependent. They start asking my opinion on everything. But it's not my life. How can I know what's best for her? I like a woman who is more confident and self-assured. Someone who has some sense of herself."

No One's Going to Tell Me What to Do!

Other women swing entirely the other direction and refuse to trust men they can't control. We see a pattern of women who marry Milquetoast men because they're easy to control. As they travel through life and responsibilities increase, these same women become angry that their men don't step up to the plate. They marry a spineless man, and then they suddenly expect him to grow a spine when life gets challenging.

From my experience as Director of Women's Ministry at our church and as an international speaker for women, I believe more than half of all women fall into this category. A woman is wounded early in life, so she decides she will never let it happen again. She meets a man who doesn't mind her emasculating him with constant correction, criticism, and control. As they marry and have children, her way is always the right way. This system may work for a few years until—bam! A crisis happens that she can't control. All of a sudden, the situation becomes *his* fault because he can't fix it. But he either can't or won't fix it because he has never been allowed to fix anything. He becomes more and more passive and pulls further and further away from her. She helped create this spineless man, and now she resents him for being that way.

The signs of a dominating, controlling female show up early in a relationship.

1. You throw an emotional tantrum if he doesn't give you enough time or spend enough money on you.

2. You belittle or correct him in public.

3. You take on responsibilities too early in the relationship. (You plan the social schedule, tell him what to wear, etc.)

4. You demand lots of phone calls and make lots of phone calls.

5. You're jealous of his time commitments: his work, his friends, his family.

6. You always want the details of the plan.

7. You become angry at surprises.

8. You force him into a "choose me over them" situation.

9. You tell people how they should think and feel.

10. You isolate your boyfriend from past relationships.

Women, do you see any of these signs in yourself?

Pack Your Bags, We're Going on a Guilt Trip

Some women attempt to control men through manipulation. By keeping the guy off center emotionally, she controls the power in the relationship. Men consistently report they're bothered with women who read something into every statement, action, or nonaction on their part. These men never know whether they're on solid ground or in the doghouse. Every day seems to have a new set of rules. Guys get weary of always feeling "wrong."

Women, it all boils down to this: Your security has to be in *Christ*—not your boyfriend or husband. No man will be able to read your mind and tell you what you want to hear. No man will be able to always know when he did or said something to hurt you. No man will be able to protect you from every hurt and inconvenience. To expect a guy to come running when you feel panicked, hurt, or frustrated is unrealistic. And if you do manage to weather the turbulent dating time, your man won't be able to meet the unrealistic expectations you will place on him in marriage. He may get discouraged or angry and leave. Or he may withdraw because you will constantly make him feel like a failure. He will tire of the hysteria and escape to safer emotional ground.

What are some signs to look for that may signal you're a woman with unreal expectations?

- Do you expect him to know how you are feeling?

- Do you expect him to keep you from harm?

- Do you expect him to come running if you hit a crisis or snag?

- Do you expect him to cater to you?

Some single guys are perceptive and spot the princess syndrome. Single women can tip their hand. One man said, "When she picked lint off my shoulder and told me to tuck in my shirt, I knew I had to end the relationship."

Many a good man will run in retreat from a woman who thinks she must be the center of attention. It might be a little like this joke:

> In her own eyes, Julia was the most popular girl around. "A lot of men are gonna be totally miserable when I marry."
>
> "Really?" said her date. "And just how many men are you intending to marry?"

As we learned earlier in the book, men like to go to boxes they can succeed in. If a man feels like he isn't a success around you, he may not want to stay around you. He will feel like a constant failure in your eyes. It's difficult for a man to stay motivated in a relationship in which he feels inadequate.

Coming to grips with the fact you may be a Pasta Princess is difficult. Ask yourself these questions:

- Did my father abandon me physically? (Did he leave you and your family? Did he fail to pay child support? Is he around but not involved or active in your life?)

- Did he abandon me emotionally? (Was he an alcoholic, drug addict, or workaholic? Was he emotionally distant or unavailable?)

- Was I abused (mentally, emotionally, physically or sexually)?

- Was I the center of attention?

- Did I usually get my way while growing up?

If you answered yes to even one of these questions, your chances of being a Pasta Princess are pretty high.

If you felt abandoned, you will want control so you won't ever feel abandoned or emotionally let down again. You may have issues of trust, wondering if you can trust men. You feel you can trust only yourself. If you have been abused, you might have serious trust issues—well-founded ones—so you will have to rebuild a circle of trustworthy males into your life.

Seeking professional counseling will help you recover and restore your ability to spot a trustworthy male instead of being a "loser magnet." If you keep dating men who mistreat you, you may have a problem. It's not just the men you date. Women who have been victimized behave and act differently from women who have not been wounded. Because of this victimization, they maintain the victim role. Counseling, however, can help a woman recover from her wounds, become more confident in Christ, and be more centered as a person so men who are victimizers no longer find her attractive.

How can you find good counseling that will help you overcome these trust issues and remove the "loser magnet" from your life? Good counsel will include the following components:

> **1. Identify who you are in Christ:** As you see yourself and your life from God's point of view, you will begin to value yourself more. As you value yourself more, you will naturally not put up with abuses from men of any kind. Also, you won't need to control as much because you will gain comfort knowing that God in His love is in control of you and your life. In surrender to God's love and His sovereign control, you will be freed from thinking you have to be god of your little world. Trying to control your world will shrink your world down to a size you can control—and that's pretty small. However, releasing control to God expands your world and the opportunities God can bring your way.

2. Identify the core issue: By discovering why you fear failure, have a hard time releasing control, mistrust men, or choose unhealthy men, you will be released to grow in areas that were shut down emotionally. Abuse can stop you from growing. For example, say you were raped at 16. Your ability to relate sexually to men may be that of a 16-year-old. You might be an adult, making decisions in this very mature area of your life with the emotional skills and viewpoint of a teenager. The Bible encourages us to grow in grace or come to maturity in Christ (2 Peter 3:18). Good counseling will help you identify core issues so you can "grow up" in those areas.

One woman who came to our office had been hurt by the bad choices of the men she had allowed into her life. At 16 she had been date raped; at 18 she married a drug addict and then got divorced. At 20 she remarried to a gambler who spent all her money. They divorced. At 26 she moved in with a man who ended up beating her whenever he drank, and he drank often. Then at 29 she married a man she met while doing a prison ministry. He promised he had changed, but he abandoned her when he was released. When we met her, she said, "No more! I don't have the time or energy for another bad relationship. I want to have a relationship, but I want to know what I'm doing to attract all these unreliable men!" Good for her! She's well on her way to having the ability to find healthy men attractive.

3. Identify new tools: Good counseling will provide you with new resources and tools to better equip you for healthy relationships. A counselor's goal should be to strengthen you so you don't need to come and see him/her anymore. Expect counseling to be hard. Look at it as a college course for life. Prepare to read many

books, practice new skills, and pray through barriers so
you can grow.

Too often, women don't want to pursue the hard work of
counseling. Instead, they fall into the "girls just want to have
fun" syndrome. They run to parties, bars, singles clubs, and
groups looking for a little fun. They rationalize the choices by
telling themselves they've earned it. However, what's really
earned is more heartache because the men that are attracted to
a "party girl" are known to be the most irresponsible! So in
having fun, she has set herself up for more heartache.

Why Change?

If you are a Pasta Princess, there is good news: You can
change! But there is also bad news: If you choose to remain a
Pasta Princess, you incur some risks:

It's all about me. Living at the center of your universe comes
at a high price. You could remain single and spoil yourself. Or
you could marry a man for his money and miss choosing a
healthier man who could meet your deeper emotional needs. Or
you could marry a weak man whom you can control like a
puppet and convince to meet your every whim. After a while in
marriage, you may begin to resent this weak man you married.
He may not be earning as much as you, or he might not be very
assertive and adventurous. He will seem like Milquetoast to you
when you long for "salsa," but you can't control the energy of a
"salsa" man or his aggressive, assertive behaviors. You may
develop wanderlust and fall into an affair.

Abuse me. Women who grow up in abusive homes tend to
marry abusive men. Sara was the daughter of an alcoholic, abusive father. He emotionally abandoned her, physically beat her,
and verbally abused her. Instead of dealing with the issue, Sara
began to date a series of men she could remake. Internally, she
desperately wanted to "fix" her dad, so she fell in love with men
that needed "fixing." Finally she married a man just like her

father. Ten years into the marriage and several children later, Sara finally pulled her head out of the sand and realized she had been living in denial of her own emotional baggage. Because she denied the impact of her baggage, she had repeated the very pattern she hated in the home she grew up in.

Avoid Sara's trauma. Own up to your past and get help for the pain in your heart. God can heal and redeem any past hurt. I (Pam) am a walking example of God's redeeming power. My own father was an alcoholic with a severe anger problem. He would regularly become verbally violent to every member of my family as he lashed out hurtful, stinging words.

My father was also constantly suicidal. I feared for my life every time I was in the car with my dad. He started drinking at breakfast and drank all day. He was a functioning alcoholic. He was brilliant at his job. He could perform his job better drunk than most people could sober, so people excused his behavior. As a child, when I approached Dad, I never knew if he was going to be lovey-dovey or give me the backside of his hand—or worse, his cruel, critical remarks.

I had a wonderful, creative, goal-setting, nurturing mother. She acted as a buffer through much of the trauma in our home. She often stood between me and the wrath of my father. Because Dad traveled, our home was happy and safe for five days a week and a potential hurricane for two. Mom made the most of the five days in our lives while she herself gained the strength to eventually stand up to my father.

As a teenager, I remember praying as I came home from a date. I begged God to not let my dad be passed out on the front lawn in his underwear. And it was even more embarrassing if Dad was still awake. In a drunken, slurring stupor, he would try to sit and talk with my date, usually with another beer in his hand.

But God had a plan for me. When I was a preschooler, my mother had a friend, Kathy, who was a secretary of a little church in our small town. My mother noticed Kathy had what she wanted—peace, joy, and patience. The fruit of the Spirit emanated from Kathy's life. My mother began to attend Kathy's church and always took us kids to Sunday school. Mom would then go home, but I would beg to stay for "big church." I felt close to God in that beautiful sanctuary with stained glass windows. And I felt safe.

In Sunday school, I memorized the twenty-third Psalm and earned a little white cross that glowed in the dark. On it was printed, "He Lives." One night when I was just eight, as my dad raged and my mom tried to talk him down, I lay on my bed and looked up at that little cross glowing in the dark. I prayed, *God, at church they tell me You had the power to rise from the dead. God, I believe You have the power to do anything. When I grow up, I don't want to live in a house like this with all this fighting. I want to live in a nice quiet house—like my pastor does. God, I think I'd like to marry a pastor.*

Shortly after that, I tried to earn a place on a quiz team at church. I always tried to earn any award I could because I thought that might make Dad happy and he might show he loved me. I was memorizing Matthew 5, 6, and 7 when I came across Matthew 7:7: "Ask and it will be given to you; seek and you will find; knock and the door will be opened to you." Sitting there on my bed, I prayed, *God, does this mean if I ask You to come into my life, You will? Please come into my life and be my Best Friend, my Savior and my Lord.* And I believe He met me there that very day.

I began to be transformed from the time I prayed that prayer. I was transformed from being a sullen child who cried at the drop of a hat into a happy carefree child. My circumstances didn't change—God was changing me. He was carrying out His promise to be the father to the fatherless (Psalm 68:5 KJV). If my dad didn't want to do the job right, God would. I treated God just like a Father, going to Him with everything in my life, reading His Word, and talking to Him all day, every day.

That lasted until high school, when I thought I was too cool for God. We moved to a new community, and I found it difficult to find a church that I felt at home in. I was too young to realize that most of the churches mom tried didn't preach from the Bible regularly. I fell back into the old patterns of trying to earn my dad's love. I tried to be perfect by seeking perfect grades, perfect looks, and perfect performances in dance and gymnastics. I became a cheerleader, a homecoming queen, and a college scholarship winner. I got all those awards, and I was still empty inside.

One day, a few years later, I returned home from college. Dad had been drinking, so of course he was arguing with mom. I looked at my brother and sister and said, "I don't know about you guys, but I'm tired of this. Do you want to go for a drive?" The answer was yes, and we left. We didn't know where to go, so we just drove around and eventually parked in a cornfield.

I said, "I don't remember a lot of stuff from church, but it seems like we should pray for Mom and Dad." So we did. Then we drove back home. I'm not sure what we thought would happen…maybe that somehow Mom and Dad were going to suddenly become like Ozzie and Harriet—the perfect parents. As we entered the house, we could hear Dad yelling. That was normal at our house. It was about midnight so we went to bed.

Then at about three A.M. we awoke to mom screaming for help. The three of us bolted from our beds into the pitch dark, looking for mom. I remember thinking, *Oh no, Dad's anger has escalated. We have to rescue Mom!* We raced from room to room to room and couldn't find mom. We could just hear her screaming for help!

Finally, my brother, who was a football player, burst into the garage, and there he saw that it was not my mom who needed rescuing but my dad. He was trying to hang himself from the rafters in the garage. Mom was screaming for anyone who could help Dad. My brother pulled Dad down, drug him into the house, and pushed him on to the sofa. I knelt on my dad's chest.

It took all four of us to hold Dad down while he kept yelling that he wanted to die. It was total emotional confusion. I looked at my siblings and Mom and said, "I think Dad needs us to pray." So we prayed for Dad and he calmed down a little. He was still thrashing a bit when I remembered the story from Sunday school about David, who played for the king when he acted crazy like this. "We should sing!" I proclaimed. So we sang every church song we could think of.

Dad calmed more, but was still upset. I remembered that Dad liked the song "Amazing Grace" because he'd heard it as a kid when they would go to make fun of the traveling evangelists that came to town. So we sang "Amazing Grace" over and over and over again. Dad finally passed out as the sun rose the next morning.

I pulled a blanket up over Dad and then looked at my mom, my sister, and my brother. They were exhausted. So was I. They headed to bed, but I went to diving practice hoping to find peace and solace in the water.

Later, as I drove home, I remember hoping I would see a family gathered who would say, "We can't live like this any-more!" and get some help. However, when I walked in the house, instead I saw a family who didn't want to talk about what had happened—especially my father, who was a very successful busi-nessman and who was now seated at the kitchen table doing his paperwork as if nothing had happened. But something had hap-pened to me that day on the drive home: God got in my face. In loving confrontation, God's Spirit whispered to my heart, *Pam, you have been treating Me like your earthly father. You think I am somehow distant, demanding, and unrelenting, but I am not like that! Dust off that Bible. Open it up. Find out who I am!*

Shortly after that, a friend who was appropriately named Grace invited me to a Bible study. At that Bible study, I was encouraged to have a daily quiet time. In one of those quiet times, a few days later, I came across the verse in Romans that says, "By him we cry, 'Abba, Father.'" I learned that Abba is what

Jewish children call their dads when they learn to talk, much like I had said "Da Da." I had a God in heaven who was my daddy and who loved me! He loved me unconditionally, just for who I was, simply because He created me and He wanted a relationship with me! I recommitted my life to Christ and God began transforming me in so many ways in a very short time. I quit looking to men—including my father—to fill my need to feel loved.

It's Worth a Risk

God's standard for romantic relationships may feel "risky" because it's so different from the norm. But why would people want the norm? Today the norm is a string of sexual partners with no commitment to a long-term relationship. When the relationship does lead to marriage, the norm is divorce, broken hearts, and broken families. Why settle for the norm? Take a risk! Trust God with your heart!

It felt risky when God led me to not date for more than six months because I had become addicted to the attention of men. I had been gathering boyfriends, often having three or four boyfriends at a time (they didn't know about each other, of course).

When I made a decision to accept God's way of relating to men, I quit using male attention to validate myself and academic awards to bolster my self-confidence. I was freed to pursue excellence just for the sheer enjoyment of a job well-done. I still received awards, but I no longer *needed* them to prove I was a worthy person.

As I began to spend time with God daily, He had me reevaluate all of my life: the way I chose men, the way I made decisions, how I dressed, what activities I participated in. This new process would have its ultimate reward nearly a year later when I met Bill and began enjoying a relationship with a man whom I loved. We were then free to marry and start a family dramatically different than the one I grew up in.

Right from the start, God asked me to completely trust Him for guidance in relating to Bill. One of the clearest examples was the week that God placed the question on my heart, What is the right time for you and Bill to kiss? At what level of commitment will you allow Bill to kiss you?

In all my other relationships "the kiss" had just happened. But in all my other relationships, a lot of other things "just happened," and it was obvious that living by my emotions hadn't been a healthy way to conduct relationships. I looked at the strongest marriages I knew—marriages that had weathered the storms of life. I saw couples who had placed God in the center of their love for each other. As I surveyed those couples, it seemed they were pretty conservative with regard to their first kiss. Their answers ranged from "when we started talking marriage" to "engagement." This was definitely a radical thought to me. But God began to speak to my heart and reveal the truth about me and my past relationships. I knew I was definitely wired hot. One kiss usually lead to many, and that lead to me feeling pressured sexually, even though I had managed to hang on to my virginity—it had been that important to me.

In my quiet time, I came across the verse, "Blessed are the pure in heart." That's when the Holy Spirit quickened another question to my heart, "How far back do you need to push your physical boundaries to remain pure in heart and thought towards Bill?" When I was honest with myself, I knew it was pretty far back, and kissing was definitely the line for me. But if I was that conservative, I was afraid I might lose Bill. Most women I knew were giving away their sexuality. Was I going to tell this great guy I wouldn't kiss him? How then would he know how much I really loved him?

One weekend, Bill and I sat overlooking the ocean, talking the afternoon away. We talked about all kinds of elements of our relationship. When we returned to Bill's car, Bill got out his "notebook." He had started a notebook of questions he wanted to talk to me about, and each time we went out on a date, the notebook came out. Bill was living a purposeful life, and he wanted his dating life to have direction too. Bill took a risk by running his dating life in an unusual manner—I admired that in him. I wanted a man who was bold, strong, and had a strong sense of values.

Bill said, "Let me see if we talked about everything I wanted to ask you today." I looked over his shoulder and read down the list of questions. We'd talked about all but one—kissing. But I didn't bring it up because I still wasn't 100 percent sure what I was going to say. That night after a very romantic dinner, Bill and I went for a walk along a creek, and then he drove me back to my friend's house, where I was staying.

"Pam, do you mind if I stop at my place to pick something up?" Bill asked. I said no, I didn't mind, so we stopped by his place. Once inside, Bill said, "I really did want to get something, but I also want to ask you something. May I kiss you?"

My reply was totally unplanned, but I believe God gave me the words: "Bill, I really, really want to say yes, but I really need to say no. I am wired really hot, and I have pretty much wrecked all my other relationships because of this and…well, I care too much for you to wreck this relationship. So even though I want to say yes, I am going to have to say no." Then I paused for a breath.

Bill offered a shocked and quiet "Okay." Then he drove me home and didn't say a word the entire 20-minute ride. Nothing. Not a word.

He walked me to my door and said, "Thank you, Pam. I'll pick you up for breakfast at eight." I frantically blurted out how much I loved the evening and how he was such a great guy and how I was really looking forward to breakfast. Then he walked away, and I walked into the apartment. All my friends were still up. I shut the door, leaned up against it, and burst into tears.

My friends jumped up and rushed to my side. I was so distraught, all I could get out was "Bill…" and then trail into tears. Then I got a chorus of, "What did he do?"

I explained that *Bill* didn't do anything; *I* did. I told them how God had led me so far in our relationship and how I had to turn down Bill's desire to kiss me.

One of my friends wisely said, "Pam, you've been telling us how wonderful and how godly Bill is. If this is really true, and we think it is, you have to trust Bill. And if God led you to this decision, you have to trust God." Then they gathered around me and we all prayed together.

The next morning, Bill picked me up for breakfast, and as we sat down, he reached across the table, took my hand, and said, "Pam, I want you to know why I was so quiet last night as we drove home. It was because I was embarrassed that you had to set this boundary to protect our relationship. Pam, I respect you for what you said, and I just want to tell you I've never respected or loved any woman more than I do you right now. Thanks."

At that moment I *knew* Bill was the one for me!

God had to rework me from the inside out, or I would have chosen a man just like my dad. God redeemed my life. My compassion to be in ministry comes from a redeemed "fix it" attitude. I no longer feel I have to be someone's rescuer—only God can do that. But I still long for them to be rescued by God. That is a healthy boundary. It's a safe place to relate to people from.

But God also had to redeem the "center of attention" syndrome I had developed. When my dad was sober, he realized he was not doing such a great job as a father, and he would try to buy us off by financially spoiling us. I believe this was from good intentions. My father really did love us, but his own pain and brokenness from his upbringing hindered his ability to express love in a healthy way. Had God not redeemed me as a young college student, I would have brought more of the "rescue me, spoil me, make the sun rise and set on me" attitude into our marriage. I was still something of a Pasta Princess especially that first year of marriage. God had to get my attention and show me that I was deflating, demoralizing, and discouraging a really great, godly guy with my unrealistic expectations. I am glad God painstakingly pointed out the Pasta Princess in me, or I might have lost the most wonderful man in the world! (Every woman should feel this way about the man in her life). I'm glad I realized being the daughter of the King of kings, a true "princess" of God, was better than trying to be the god of my own life and demanding people treat me like a princess. My husband has been known to tell men, "If you want to be treated like a king, treat her like a queen." That's been my payoff for choosing to give up control—and it's a rich reward indeed.

The Top Ten Reasons Why God Created Eve

10. God worried that Adam would always be lost in the garden because men hate to ask for directions.

9. God knew that Adam would one day need someone to hand him the TV remote. (Men don't want to see *what's on* television; they want to see *what else is on!*)

8. God knew that Adam would never buy a new fig leaf when his seat wore out and would therefore need Eve to get one for him.

7. God knew that Adam would never make a doctor's appointment for himself.

6. God knew that Adam would never remember which night was garbage night.

5. God knew that if the world was to be populated, men would never be able to handle childbearing.

4. As Keeper of the Garden, Adam would never remember where he put his tools.

3. The scriptural account of creation indicates Adam needed someone to blame his troubles on when God caught him hiding in the garden.

2. As the Bible says, "It's not good for man to be alone!" and the Numero Uno reason...

1. When God finished the creation of Adam, He stepped back, scratched His head and said, "I can do better than that."

WAFFLES
SPAGHETTI

Some answers women might use for the tacky pickup lines men use (not for real use—remember, men *do* have feelings too):

Man:	Haven't I seen you somewhere before?
Woman:	Yes, that's why I don't go there anymore.
Man:	Is this seat empty?
Woman:	Yes, and this one will be too if you sit down.
Man:	Your place or mine?
Woman:	Both. You go to yours, and I'll go to mine.
Man:	So, what do you do for a living?
Woman:	I'm a female impersonator.
Man:	Hey baby, what's your sign?
Woman:	Do not enter.
Man:	Your body is like a temple.
Woman:	Sorry, there are no services today.
Man:	I would go to the end of the world for you.
Woman:	But would you stay there?

Love does not die easily. It is a living thing. It thrives in the face of all life's hazards, save one—neglect.

—JAMES D. BRYDEN

Waffles and Spaghetti in Love

You wait anxiously for the phone to ring. You listen for his steps on your front walk. You look for reasons to cross her path. Falling in love, two hearts connecting—we yearn for that heart-fluttering feeling. But how do you know if your feelings are real? How do you know if this is a love that will last?

Heart to Heart, Hand in Hand, Shoulder to Shoulder

Working together, side by side, day in and day out is what marriage is all about. When we were dating, we spent our time playing together. And then when we were married, we spent our time working together. And we wonder why marriages suffer stress!

Before your hearts connect, see if your work ethics match. What are each of your plans for the future? Are these plans headed the same direction? How about education? Are you committed to helping each other get all the education needed to reach your dreams?

Theresa commented, "It's when Ken came out every day after work to help my parents finish their remodel that I fell in love with him. He really cared about my parents, their health, and their home. He could have been in his apartment with his feet up watching ESPN, but instead he worked hard. I wondered why he was so successful in his career, but now I know. And he's still concerned about family, friends, and being balanced too. I figured if he saw me in painting clothes and still loved me, he was the man for me!"

To see if your relationship "works," try these "working" dates:

- Volunteer to teach a Sunday school class together.
- Volunteer at a boys and girls club or youth recreation center.
- Volunteer at a rescue mission or soup kitchen.
- Go on a short-term mission trip.
- Help out some of your married friends with a home improvement project.
- Serve on the same planning committee for an event.

Resting and Relaxing Can Be a Key to Love

Work hard—play hard. Successful couples find ways to rest and relax together. Stress is a daily part of relationships. Knowing how men and women deal with stress can save your dating life! Too often, people in relationships "share" their stress in unhealthy ways. People can take stress out on the ones they love, which is wrong. But it's equally wrong to apply another person's "bad day" to yourself or your relationship. You might jump to conclusions and wonder, *What did I do? Why is he or she upset at me?* All along, the person we love may just be sad, hurt, or preoccupied. So how do men and women handle stress?

When stress hits, women need to traverse across all those noodles and emotionally connect with the people and situations involved. Since women are more "in tune" with the emotional and relational nuances of life, they report more anxiety overall.[1] It's generally well-known in the clinical domain that postadolescent females suffer a higher incidence of depression than their male counterparts. They also experience a higher incidence of anxiety disorders. In fact, "females have higher levels of neuro-chemicals linked to panic and anticipatory anxiety than their male counterparts."[2] Moreover, women produce lower levels of serotonin in their bodies, which raises their genetic vulnerability to depression. As a result women are prone to higher levels of depression-related anxiety than are men.[3] In short, women have more to deal with when it comes to managing stress. Not only do they seek solutions for the situations that need improving, they also have a flood of emotions to process.

For this reason, talking is a huge help to a woman who's stressed. As she talks through the stress of her life, the emotions associated with the circumstances dissipate. The clouds begin to clear as she expresses the emotional weather in her heart. Solutions begin to emerge and simpler approaches appear as possibilities. It's as if stress covers a woman with an emotional fog bank. Before she can navigate the course, she needs to clear the fog by talking her way through. Her conversational roadmap can include God, friends, extended family, and her boyfriend. The combination of people she talks with may change with each situation, but talking her way out of stress is the key.

Easy Boxes

Men, on the other hand, retreat to comfortable boxes to deal with stress. Every man has certain boxes in his life that are much easier on him emotionally than others. When he enters these boxes, stress melts away and he has an opportunity to recharge. Men do not get energized by constantly processing life. In fact, it drains them of energy. They get ready for the next challenge of life by disappearing into a stress-free box for a while. They emerge from that box energized and focused to conquer the next obstacle.

How do we recognize a man's easy boxes? It seems that God helped us women out a bit with this one. Men's easy boxes are generally shaped like boxes. A newspaper is shaped like a box. A TV screen is shaped like a box. A basketball court and a football field are shaped like boxes. A computer screen is shaped like a box. A refrigerator is shaped like a box. And the favorite of all men's safe, easy boxes—a *bed*—is, of course, shaped like a box! It may not be very romantic to watch a guy konk out on the couch, but try to remember that your man may like to "chill" on the beach, in front of the TV, or in the backyard hammock— and he'd count that time as romance!

Romance—Her Style

Men, if you're looking to romance a Pasta Princess remember her need to communicate with you. Find a great place to talk— no, to listen to her heart. Long walks on the beach or near a lake, strolls in the moonlight, a cozy corner of a coffee shop, or a lin- gering candlelit dinner for two will all do. In our case, Bill and I have found a wonderful spot at a nice fondue place that plays live romantic Italian music and lets us stay for hours and eat dinner nice and slow.

Another winner with women is to make romantic senti- mental connections. One friend of ours kept a torn ticket stub, a menu, a program, or some other kind of remembrance from every date he'd ever gone on with his fiancée, and he presented her with a scrapbook of their love for his wedding-day gift. Let me tell you, that guy has been married for years, and he's still living off all the points he made that day! Listen to the woman in your life; take notes after dates. If she says she collects some- thing or always wanted to try something—arrange it! If you forget, call her girlfriends—they will know every tiny hope or dream she's ever had!

Romance—His Style

To romance a man, keep it simple! Just tie together some of his favorite easy boxes. Bill loves sports, good food, and exercise. A perfect day for him would include those elements. Keep in mind, guys like to dwell in boxes they're successful in, so a day spent on one of his favorite hobbies, whether skiing or waxing his car, is a sure winner. If he feels he's looking good to you, he will feel good too.

True Heart

"I looked awful! Like death. Really, really bad!" Susan was chatting on the phone with her friend Carol. "I didn't really want him to see me, but where was I to go—we were on a boat! And here I am tossing my cookies overboard! Gary was so sweet. He got me all tucked in, and he stayed right by me. I thought it would get better once we got off the boat, but it got worse. How was I to know this would be the worst case of the flu I'd ever had? Gary took me home, and I climbed into bed with my sweats on. I didn't care. I felt so awful. Gary sat up all night checking on me, running to the store for medicine, doing whatever I needed. I tried to persuade him to go to work the next morning, but he called in and took a personal day. I slept 'most all day. I finally started to feel better that night so I sent him home. He hadn't gotten much sleep. I still looked bad. He stopped to check on me this morning. What a gem. If this was a test, he passed!"

To Susan, Gary wasn't only a gem of a guy—he was a good *friend* to her.

In Jim and Sally Conway's book *Traits of a Lasting Marriage,* friendship was listed as one of the key elements in a healthy, happy marriage. How healthy are your friendships? Look into your heart and ask: Is this a true friendship, or are we just in a habit of being together? Does the person you think you love act like a friend? Is he or she honest? Is he or she reliable? Does he or she keep promises? Do you two enjoy similar interests or do you just pretend to? Does he or she love you for "you" and not just for the idea of being in your life and enjoying its perks (a nice home, expendable income, and a good family)? How can you discover what your relationship is made of?

Dates for Discovery

In our surveys with singles, we heard some dating horror stories. Far too many women left dates with another guy—even their ex-boyfriend. One man thought he was out with a woman—only to discover his date was a cross-dresser! Another guy's date lit her cocktail straw on fire and then wrote her name with the ash stick on the white linen tablecloth. Another single man described his worst date as "a controlling femi-Nazi who endlessly berated masculine qualities while expecting queenlike treatment."

Many men realized early in a date that the relationship wasn't going forward, but the rejection still hurt. One man told us, "My worst date was getting the 'Dear John' talk before the main dish was served. I ordered prime rib—what a way to waste a good piece of meat!"

The women we surveyed weren't really impressed by some of the men they dated either. One woman lamented, "It's hard to be on a date when all the guy wants to do all night is play Nintendo—alone!" Another woman had to eat with her date's cat sitting on the table next to her plate. Still another had a date that talked about his mother all night. Even worse, many women complained that their dates talked about themselves all night—or didn't talk at all!

Being "stood up" was a pet peeve among women, guys, so at least call! However, those gals might be glad their dates didn't show because a few who did drank so much they embarrassed them or put them in danger. The very worst dates for women were ones that ended in a date rape or a "stalking" relationship.

One of the worst dates we heard about happened to a woman who worked very hard to take precautions that should have kept her safe. She met a man at her health club. She and friends were going out, so she invited him to join her group. They each drove themselves to the event. She participated in several more dates with him in the group, always being careful to drive herself. She never gave her home number, just her cell phone number. She never gave him her home address. However, after many group dates, she drove to a central meeting place where her date picked her up. They then drove together a short distance to a dinner dance.

At the dance, she noticed that he made some snide comments about women. But the major faux pas came when he hit her on the back of the head to get her to leave the dance floor.

"I think it's time for me to get home" she replied because she was anxious to get away from such rude behavior. As they waited for the car, he started joking about her ethnicity, so she shot back a comment. The valets were joining in what she thought was a simple round of teasing. When he got in the car, he said, "You better learn some respect."

She replied, "You better learn not to push women to get them off the dance floor."

She continued to describe the horrific saga to me: "Then he clocked me. He hit me right in the face!" In self-defense, she swung back at her date, a six-foot, four-inch body builder—and she prayed.

"He turned up the radio really loud. Then he'd turn it down and start swearing at me. Then he'd turn up the radio, and then turn it down and reel off another line of expletives. I was afraid I'd never make it back to my car alive. I prayed so hard. Finally he pulled up next to my car and I ran to get inside. Then he started backing up his car like he was trying to run me down. I got in the car. I was so scared. I drove off and got my mom on the cell phone. My dad called all his friends in law enforcement, hunted down the phone number to the guy's parents' restaurant, and went to tell his parents what he'd done.

"I was afraid he might stalk me, but I think the police and my dad scared him. He quit my gym, and I never saw him again. I did get a short apology call on my cell. But that experience really shook me, and I didn't date anyone for a long time."

How can we minimize the risk for the nightmare date? Be smart. Be safe:

1. Don't give out your home number or address.

2. Drive your own car to and from dates.

3. Go on group dates until you *know* vital information about your date and have confirmed the information by visiting his work or meeting his/her coworkers and friends.

4. Get character references. These don't have to be formal referrals, but try to meet people who can vouch for his or her character and have known him or her for many years.

5. Meet at neutral ground—not at either one or your homes.

6. Find out about his or her family.

I Want to Get to Know You!

How can we discover that "dream" of Mr. Right or Ms. Right? Before you tie the knot, try these dates to discover what's inside that Mr. or Ms. Right you're dating.

It's a party: Cohost a dinner party or open house—a fancy one with lots of details. This date will require lots of planning, decision-making, and time stresses, so it's the perfect way to work together for a fun payoff. Remember, most of marriage is working together. Be sure to invite a wide variety of friends and family so you can also meet everyone who is important to the one you love.

The kid connection: Invite your nieces, nephews, or kids from your neighborhood to join you on one of your dates. To get a true picture of how the one you love relates to children, be sure and make the date a long one—perhaps a day at Disneyland, a zoo, or an amusement park. It will be a perfect testing ground for patience if you invite a child who is in diapers and a rowdy preschooler who is at his or her best when hungry and tired!

Home to mom: This is the traditional test when the relationship gets serious, but don't wait until the date has been set and the ring has been bought to introduce your sweetheart to your family. A fun and not-so-threatening way to spend the evening is to pull out a board game—try the Ungame or Trivial Pursuit—so conversation can be less like a police interrogation.

The soup kitchen date: Volunteer to serve in a soup kitchen or to pound nails with Habitat for Humanity. Go someplace with no running water where you sleep on the ground and go without a shower so he or she can see you at your worst. If love can last this, it can last anything.

The remodel or move: Offer to help a friend move, remodel, or build anything. Shop together at Home Depot. Try to choose a project that neither of you likes at all. If you are both bored stiff and can make it enjoyable, chances are you can survive the whirlwind of parenthood and home ownership.

Sunday morning: Attend church together, go to brunch, and talk over each of your spiritual journeys. How similar are you in the areas that really count? Chat about your views about God, morality, and politics—all those things that people say you never should talk about in polite conversation!

The great adventure! This date is hard to plan. Try rock climbing, a day biking in the mountains, or any activity that puts you both out on the edge and out of your comfort zone. You want to see how the other person reacts under pressure. When the chips are down, does the one you love still lift you up?

A Test Neither of You Can Pass

"Jen, I think we should take our relationship to the next level—let's live together!"

"Aah, I don't know. I'm sure my parents would freak!"

"Yeah, well, I don't want to end up divorced like my folks—my dad has been married three times. I want to see if we have what it takes to be married. I feel like I want to be with you always."

"So are you saying you want to marry me someday?"

"Oh, let's just play that by ear. Maybe living with me will drive you crazy."

"I don't know. I really love you. I love being with you. But I guess I always pictured walking down the aisle and having you carry me over the threshold of our new home after the wedding. I know it sounds old-fashioned."

"I'm just not ready for that kind of commitment."

"Are you committed to me, though?"

"Of course; that's why I want us to move in together. It's practical. You stay over all the time. Why have two places?"

"Well, it would save money, I guess."

"Definitely. And I love being with you. We don't need a ceremony to know we're in love, do we?"

"I guess not. What is a marriage—just a piece of paper, right?"

Wrong!

Should We Live Together?

How do you know you're in love? How do you know know if this is Mr. Right or Ms. Right? How do you know how far to progress sexually and at what commitment level? These seem to be grand mysteries today. Often couples today are opting for a live-in, cohabiting arrangement. According to the U.S. Census Bureau, cohabitation increased 533 percent from 1970 to 1992. Many states are even seeking to legitimize these domestic partnerships with laws giving them the same status and privileges as married couples. But is living together really the same as marriage? Before packing your bags and moving in together, consider these startling facts:

Children *are* affected. Forty percent of all cohabiting couples also have children living in the household with them. Twenty-seven percent of all births are to couples cohabiting rather than marrying. These kids are at risk. Eighty-four percent of non-parental abuse of children is committed by the mother's boyfriend. According to the *Journal of Marriage and Family,* girls living in a home with a boyfriend (not a stepfather or father) are at a much higher risk for sexual abuse.

This is not a safe option for a single woman. During a one-year period, 35 out of 100 cohabiting couples experience physical aggression. Domestic violence is twice as likely among live-in couples as it is among married couples. In one study by the *Journal of Family Violence,* 48 percent of couples living together experienced domestic violence, compared to19 percent of married couples and 27 percent of those who were divorced or separated. There seems to be a correlation: less commitment means more violence. The marriage license does seem to be a shield of protection for many women—probably because the man in her life valued her enough to commit to her in marriage.

Cohabitation sets you up for divorce. Those who live together prior to marriage are twice as likely to divorce if they do get married. And the longer the cohabitation, the more likely divorce is, according to sociologists at the University of Wisconsin. Those who live together separate more often if they do marry, and they also regard the relationship as a less important part of their life. It seems cohabitation trains couples to disregard the love relationship—just the opposite of what most couples would cite as their reason for living together.

Studies show that other problems usually accompany a live-in relationship. According to a UCLA study, cohabiting relationships are also more likely to be plagued with adultery, alcohol, and drugs. Those who live together prior to marriage are more likely to commit adultery both while living with their partner and if they marry. In addition, one study found that cohabiting women were more jealous than married women and had a higher emotional dependency on the male live-in partner. Many developed a pattern of few friendships, no job advancement aspirations, and few outside interests.[4]

Cohabiting couples, when asked to rate the quality of their relationship, give much lower grades than married couples. Women in these relationships feel less secure economically and emotionally and have a much higher rate of depression. Three out of every four cohabiting couples surveyed said they thought their relationship was in serious trouble.[5]

Why does cohabitation or living together set a relationship up for failure? Several studies suggest that those who refuse to commit to marriage do so because they're very individualistic. This is a nice way of saying they're selfish. Those who cohabit are less likely to express personal character traits that foster a good relationship: sacrifice, humility, flexibility, empathy, and the ability to delay gratification. In the nearly 20 years Bill and I have worked with couples, we have seen that those who cohabit usually also have unhealthy priorities. These priorities can become plagues after the wedding (if the relationship even makes it that far).

For example, money often becomes more important than the relationship. The job wins out over the spouse, and earning money overshadows the children. A pattern of poor decision-making was established when the couple decided not to live a life that pleases God and not to be committed enough to their relationship to marry. Finally, the drawback few people talk about but Bill and I have seen over and over again is that those who cohabit prior to marriage are more likely to be discontent or have problems in their sex life. Trust is the most important factor a woman needs to experience total sexual fulfillment, and trust is broken rather than built in a live-in relationship.

Cohabitation is a pathway to a broken heart that has become very popular in our modern world. In a study reported in *Adolescence*, 24 percent of males and 18 percent of females actually cohabited. But astoundingly, 71 percent of the males in that study and 68 percent of the females were totally open to cohabitation despite the evidence of its ineffectiveness.[6] If you are intent on being in a relationship, marriage is more than a piece of paper—it's a ticket to a happier, more fulfilling life together.

Sex or No Sex, That Is the Question!

Why all the fuss? Why not just do what feels good? Why all the rules that make us feel guilty for no reason?

Boundaries exist for a very good reason! Sex was designed to enhance life, but sex outside of marriage steals joy from a couple's hearts, from their relationship, and from their future. No wonder they feel bad!

Why wait? The current Surgeon General of the United States says monogamy is the only real answer for the spread of sexually transmitted diseases (STDs). A wise recommendation, considering that as of June 1999, the Center for Disease Control had nearly 775,000 reported cases of AIDS, and more than half of those people have died of the disease. Dr. Michael Coplen warns that "AIDS is the greatest human threat since nuclear war."[7] It's estimated that one to two million Americans are currently infected with HIV, and the number is currently doubling every ten months!

One in four Americans will get another form of STD, many of which are incurable. Some leave the recipient unable to bear children.

Some may ask, what about condoms as a preventative?

A panel of experts that was headed by the National Institutes of Health and included the Center for Disease Control, the Food and Drug Administration, and the U.S. Agency for International Development admitted in a report released in July 2001 that *there was no scientific evidence* that the use of latex condoms provides significant protection against most sexually transmitted diseases (STDs), including such widespread STDs as human papilloma virus, chlamydia, gonorrhea (for women), genital herpes, chancroid, syphilis, and trichomoniasis.

The report further found that condoms did not provide any protection for women against HPV, an STD that can lead to cervical cancer, which in turn kills more women in the U.S. than die from AIDS each year. The same report found that condom use offers limited protection against HIV/AIDS (85 percent risk reduction or 15 percent failure rate) and against gonorrhea for men only (25 percent to 75 percent risk reduction).[8] Condom use means you are playing Russian roulette with your life.

Add to this the risk of unplanned pregnancy. There are now more unmarried women giving birth in America than married women. And life is harder on these single mothers and their children. Half of all single mothers live in poverty. Kids in single-parent homes and blended families are twice as likely to drop out of school or get pregnant during their teen years.[9]

Is abortion an option? Not when you consider that a fetus has a heartbeat at five weeks, and most women are just barely aware they might be pregnant at that point. And consider the aftermath of abortion. The child is dead, and according to a study by the University of Minnesota, there are long-term emotional consequences for the woman:

- 81 percent report preoccupation with the aborted fetus.

- 73 percent reported flashbacks of the abortion itself.

- 69 percent reported feelings of "craziness" following the abortion.

- 54 percent recalled nightmares relating to the abortion.

- 72 percent of the subjects had no religious affiliation and yet in retrospect 96 percent say they believed abortion was the taking of a life.[10]

Abortion victimizes all involved, and the consequences can be long-term.

Sex outside marriage makes you unable to make a clear decision. When you share an intense sexual experience, you may feel in love. But rather than being in love with the *person*, it's easy to be in love with *love* or with that intense sexual moment. Because endorphins are released and adrenalin is produced, sex produces a "high." Even if the person you are seeing has numerous flaws and incompatibilities, the intense sexual experiences may blind you to those weaknesses.

"I was just so curious about sex," said Christy, a respected businesswoman. "Why was it such a big deal on TV? Why did my friends say it was so great? I just had to know. So when Clint came into my life and found me sexually attractive, I let my guard down. Once we had sex, I felt it didn't matter that we continued to. After all, I'd already lost my virginity. Sex became more and more frequent until that was what defined our relationship. We quit going out and all Clint wanted to do was stay in, watch movies, and have sex. Suddenly I realized that he really didn't have any goals. He was even kind of lazy. I was a successful career woman, and he was going nowhere. Suddenly he wasn't as good of a lover as I thought he was because I didn't respect him. I didn't belong with him. Not only did I need to kick him out of my bed, I needed to kick him out of my life!"

Trent knew exactly what Christy meant, only he came to the realization over a year after the wedding! Sex with Allison was steamy and risky because she loved having sex in public places. She said provocative things while at dinner with friends. All his friends envied him—until after the wedding when she began to flirt with all those friends and with other men too.

"I was so blinded by the sex. I didn't really check up on her past relationships," Trent said. "I thought it didn't matter since she seemed to love being with me. I found out after we married that she had a string of broken relationships and was 'the other woman' in several marriage breakups. I met her when Trish and I were having marital problems, and she seemed understanding, compassionate, and caring. I mistook her attention as commitment, but now I realize she really doesn't know what that means! I come home and find a babysitter and a note most evenings. Usually it says something like:

Baby cried all day, just had to get out. Don't wait up. I'm out with the girls.

Sex builds an unrealistic foundation for a relationship. When sex enters a relationship, more important relationship builders are often ignored. Marriage is mostly about building a life together: working together, parenting together, building a financial future together, and serving one another on good and (more often) on not-so-good days. When sex becomes the primary activity or even a common way to spend time, verbal communication skills don't get the honing they will need after marriage when the responsibilities of life mount up. Before saying "I do," couples need to talk about career choices, financial plans, in-laws, and children. Sex distracts from the vital issues.

Sex before marriage can wreck sex after marriage. Our office is filled weekly with couples who want a satisfying sexual relationship in marriage but who have short-circuited their sexual response to each other by having sex prior to marriage. For some couples, sex inside of marriage isn't exciting because it isn't taboo or forbidden. They built their premarital sex life around the thrill and excitement of the illicitness of their sex. Without the rush of being "caught" or "bad," sex for them isn't good.

If you had sex before marriage, you didn't exercise self-control. We are seeing numerous marriages broken by this pattern of self-indulgence. When a man isn't willing to wait for sex before marriage, he may not be willing to wait for it while his wife is pregnant with their child or after the baby is born.

As one woman told us,

> I just didn't put two and two together. Tarren kept pressuring me to have sex before we married. I didn't want to lose him, so I gave in. After we were married and I got pregnant, he became impatient with me

when I felt sick. He became more and more distant from me during the pregnancy. He told me he was working extra hours to make more money for the baby. One night, a few weeks before the baby was due, I called his office, and his secretary answered. It was 11 P.M.! He said they were working, but I had my doubts.

When I went into labor and couldn't reach him on his cell phone, on his pager, or at his office, I was panicked and heartbroken. But nothing was as hard as the day my mom had to bring me and the baby home because Tarren said he had to work. When we walked in, most of the furniture and all his things were gone. And so was he—without a note. I had a new baby and no idea where his father had gone. I just didn't see his pattern of impatience and selfishness before we married. I mistook his pressuring me for sex as passion—that he wanted me, needed me. He just needed to please himself.

Sex outside of marriage distances you from God. Because God's will is for sex to be inside the context of marriage, a decision to have sex before marriage means you are deciding against God as a couple. You have started a pattern of disobeying God together, which can lead to disobeying God in other areas of life. Before you know it, your life is a whole lot different than you had planned. Couples who attend church weekly, pray daily, and are involved with friendships that believe in long-term marriage are couples who *have* long-term marriages. Also, these marriages give their sex life the highest possible passion rating. It seems the more passion a couple has in their relationship with God, the more passion they have in all areas of life, including in bed. Why would you want to short-circuit your entire lifetime of sex for a few moments of premarital pleasure? Instead, fan the flame on your relationship with God and watch how He sends lifelong passion your way after marriage.

On Different Wavelengths

Our society has fooled people into thinking they're in love because they're having sex! Research is plentiful that shows that sexual arousal produces romantic attraction.[11] In other words, if you are aroused while spending time with someone of the opposite sex, you will conclude that you are falling in love with that person. You will most likely decide to further the relationship because you believe you are made for each other.

The thrill of an emotionally charged, sexually passionate relationship is seductive. In the long run, sex without commitment is agonizingly destructive to the relationship.

It appears that the main criteria for deciding the extent and value of sexual involvement is the emotional commitment of the couple. A researcher uncovered that "the more emotionally involved a person was in a relationship, the more likely increasing levels of intimacy were regarded as appropriate."[12]

Confusion results from the fact that females quite often attribute a higher level of commitment to a relationship than do males.[13] According to a study of college students, males expect sexual intimacy sooner. Females tend to tie sexual intimacy to love and commitment (dating one person only). Love appears to justify sexual intimacy for females.

In any given relationship, the male may perceive that the couple is at a lower commitment level than the female. Because of this misperception, women give sex to receive the love they think is already present in the relationship, while men give love to encourage more sexual activity.[14]

This pattern of emotional misunderstanding between the genders is repeated over and over. With every misunderstanding comes a new emotional wound. A *Redbook* magazine survey revealed that those who experienced intercourse by age 15 or younger had more sexual partners in their lives and were more likely to rate their marriage and marital sex as bad.[15]

In another study, it was found that 54 percent of college students had some sexual experience with another child prior to adolescence, and 85 percent had a sexual experience with another teen by age 16. If childhood genital contact had taken place, subjects were more likely to have engaged in premarital intercourse during young adulthood and had more intercourse partners than subjects with nongenital childhood experiences.[16]

Breakup rates for those who have sex before marriage are alarmingly high. The intimate nature of sex causes the termination of a relationship to be traumatic for two reasons:

1. Repeated hurts from repeated breakups with sexual partners can erect a wall around the heart that isolates the individual from intimacy.

2. An individual becomes emotionally locked into a relationship that is negative because of a strong commitment based on sexual involvement.

The authors of *Why Wait?* tell us, "Sex forms an almost unexplainable bond. It locks people into relationships. The longer it goes on, the harder it is to break it off."[17]

The implication is that sexual arousal can lead to "feeling in love," which can lead to sexual activity before marriage. These premarital experiences can be bombshells that explode your chance at a lifetime of sexual compatibility. This happens because one or both of the partners may develop nagging doubts about whether he or she has chosen the right partner. Doubts linger as each wonders if the marriage happened because of true love or because the heat of the moment had them trapped.

We recently saw a Valentine's Day TV program that featured a man who studies relationships. He noted that as he travels to college campuses, he's finding that young women are very disillusioned with love in general because it seems the romance is gone. Few go out on dates, fewer still have men who plan romantic events or give romantic gifts and gestures. It seems that relationships have dissolved into friendships with the side perk of sex. The result is a lot of casual sex and very little romance and caring. Sexual promiscuity has led to a lack of love and very little passion.

On the other hand, sexual purity can lead to greater passion and pleasure for a lifetime. Tim and Beverly LaHaye surveyed over 3000 people and found that wives who had experienced no premarital sex experienced greater marital sexual satisfaction than did those who had experienced sex prior to marriage.[18]

How Much and When?

The Bible gives some simple and clear guidelines that can help build a healthy relationship and maximize the satisfaction of your sexual life. The first principle draws a definitive line. The clearest statement is in 1 Thessalonians 4:3: "It is God's will that you should be sanctified: that you should avoid sexual immorality." In this verse, God draws the line at sexual intercourse. The word for sexual immorality refers specifically to any sexual intercourse that occurs outside of a marriage relationship. A broad use of the term would include any action or behavior that is part of the sexual act (so foreplay and oral sex would fall under this definition). An individual who is concerned about pleasing God in his/her life must commit to avoiding sexual intercourse until marriage.

But then the Bible modifies this commitment in a very fascinating way. Hebrews 12:14 calls us to "make every effort to live in peace with all men and to be holy; without holiness no one will see the Lord." God asks each of us to set our sexual standards high enough to maintain holiness in our hearts. Holiness (including sexuality) is not based on rules; it's a matter of the heart. Avoiding intercourse isn't the key issue; rather, the question becomes, How far back do I need to push our physical boundaries to protect both our hearts and our relationships with God? Each person needs to ask the question, What standards do I need to have in my relationships with the opposite sex to maintain holiness in my own heart?

The Payoff

We're very glad, 23 years into marriage, that we waited until after the "I do." Bill and I both came from homes where the marriage wasn't healthy. My own parents eventually divorced. Bill and I wanted to enjoy love God's way. We decided to wait until Bill proposed before we kissed. Prior to our rededication to Christ, we'd both been in relationships with other people who wanted more sexually than we wanted to give, and we had felt pressured. We had maintained our virginity in high school, but we both knew we were wired hot. Our sexual drive was not something to be taken lightly or a game to be played.

The day Bill lowered on one knee, sang me a song he had written, and proposed to me was the day we first kissed. We had a short engagement because we wanted to maintain our purity. Because our energy wasn't distracted by sex, we developed some very strong communication and relationship skills that have served us well. We have had 23 very happy and sexually fulfilling years together.

Insights for a Happy Ever After

"Happily ever after" can happen, but only if you first ask yourself some simple but important questions:

What traits do I want in the person I would someday like to marry? List Scripture verses that describe the person God would want you to marry someday. What qualities must this person have? Honesty? Integrity? Faith? Financial security? Empathy? A sense of humor? Christian singles list these top-12 traits:

1. Growing relationship with God

2. Caring (empathetic, sensitive, kind, understanding)

3. Sense of humor

4. Wisdom, intelligence, and education

5. Attractiveness (a good fit)

6. Good listener and communicator

7. Fun, lighthearted, and happy

8. Loyal and trustworthy

9. Down to earth, easygoing, and flexible

10. Spontaneous and adventurous

11. Loving and romantic

12. Responsible, goal oriented, hardworking

What are the top 10 to 20 qualities you are looking for? Date that kind of person. And look at the list again—are you those things? Quality attracts quality.

How will I know if the person I would like to date has those traits? Below is a chart I encourage singles to use so they can discern if a person has the traits he or she is looking for. This chart will also help you identify "loser" traits or red flags early.

How Can I Decide?		
Attributes	**Green Light**	**Red Light**
Character traits I want in the person I marry someday.	How can I tell the trait is there?	How can I tell the trait is NOT there?

How will I handle my dating life? Will I drive myself to the date? Pay for myself? Pay for the date? What kinds of gifts will I accept and at what level of commitment?

Watch for dates or gifts that raise the intimacy level too early in the relationship. If you are given expensive gifts, you might feel an underlying pressure to go to the next step in a relationship before you are ready.

What are God's physical standards for my relationships? Read our comments on 1 Thessalonians 4:3 and Hebrews 12:14 (p. 174). Use the continuum below to mark the limit of your physical contact for each stage of your relationship: marriage, engagement, serious dating.

hold hands	hugs	a kiss	kisses	make out	petting	foreplay	inter-course/ oral sex

(We recommend you move the line back as far as you need to to maintain a pure heart and mind.)

Who are two people I can ask to hold me accountable for my standards? Choose leaders, mentors, best friends, or family members who intimidate you a bit! Also, choose people who can observe your life closely: a roommate, a neighbor, or a friend in your social circle. Tell them your dreams and desires in the area of relationships, and ask them to hold you accountable for your choices.

What are the consequences if I go against my own conscience? Will I set new, higher boundaries? Will I change the places I go on dates? Will I ask for more accountability? Will I get counseling if I continue to violate my own conscience? If you continue to violate your own conscience or place yourself in unhealthy relationships or dangerous situations over and over again, it may signal a deeper issue or problem.

Good Counsel = Great Love

If God is leading you into a more serious relationship with someone, then deliberately answer the question together: Are we right for one another? Use the "Dates to Discover Your Dream" in the appendix so you can study the Bible together, discuss key issues, and pray. If that goes well, enlist pre-engagement counseling from a pastor or professional marriage and family therapist. Good counsel will include personality testing and readiness-for-marriage assessment (the PREPARE/ENRICH test measures your ability to resolve conflict—the most vital predictor of the success of the marriage). Counseling should also include practical questions about your views on money, sex, children, and families of origin. Pre-engagement counseling will help you feel confident about making a decision to marry or not to marry. If you become engaged, pay for your wedding dress, and rent the church *before* you receive counseling, you might feel pressured to go forward with the marriage even if you sense it isn't right. Every session of premarital counseling you attend ups your likelihood to succeed in marriage!

It Pays to Date God's Way

If you honor God, God will honor you. The evidence seems clear: If you want a lifetime of great sex in marriage, you need to delay it until after the wedding ceremony. But the choice is yours.

Some of you may have lost your virginity, but even so, you can regain your integrity by deciding to choose God's standard for your *future* sex life. This decision will give you the opportunity to discover a quality relationship that will provide the elements necessary for a lifetime of love.

The Bible is full of examples of those who chose integrity. Moses refused to be called a Pharaoh's son and instead chose to identify himself with the people of God. After a lengthy stint at the backside of a desert shepherding sheep, Moses led his nation out of captivity and now lives in history.

Daniel refused the king's food and instead chose to eat according to God's laws. He also refused to bow to an idol and was thrown in a lions' den only to be miraculously saved. He was then elevated by God to leadership of the world's most powerful nation of his time.

It will take a lot of self-control and self-motivation to run your relationships according to God's plan, so keep the payoff in mind:

- No good thing does he withhold from those whose walk is blameless (Psalm 84:11).

- My shield is God Most High, who saves the upright in heart (Psalm 7:10).

- For the Lord is righteous...upright men will see his face (Psalm 11:7).

- His children will be mighty in the land; the generation of the upright will be blessed (Psalm 112:2).

- He holds victory in store for the upright, he is a shield to those whose walk is blameless (Proverbs 2:7).

- The integrity of the upright guides them, but the unfaithful are destroyed by their duplicity (Proverbs 11:3).

- In my integrity you uphold me and set me in your presence forever (Psalm 41:12).

- Righteousness guards the man of integrity (Proverbs 13:6).

- And when you and your children return to the LORD your God and obey him with all your heart and with all your soul according to everything I command you today, then the LORD your God will restore your fortunes and have compassion on you and gather you again from all the nations where he scattered you (Deuteronomy 30:2-3).

• Trust in the LORD with all your heart and lean not on your own understanding; in all your ways acknowledge him, and he will make your paths straight (Proverbs 3:5-6).

• His master replied, "Well done, good and faithful servant! You have been faithful with a few things; I will put you in charge of many things. Come and share your master's happiness!" (Matthew 25:23).

Running your relationships according to God's plan may or may not mean an "I do" is down your path, but it does mean God will guide you and bless you along the way.

Twenty Free or Nearly Free Ideas for Great Dates

Romance doesn't have to be expensive to be great. The best romance is often free or nearly free because it's usually accompanied by a lot of creativity!

1. Have a candlelight picnic in an unusual location, such as a rooftop, a park bench, or overlooking the ocean.

2. Snap photos of each other all over the city. If finances permit it, take them to a one-hour developing location. You may want to frame your favorite and give it to your sweetheart with a note. The others can be sent as postcards to each other all spring.

3. Walk or bicycle to an inexpensive ice cream shop or a fancy coffeehouse.

4. Drive in the mountains, arriving in time for a sunset or moonlit stroll.

5. Go to a park, push one another in the swings, and talk. Take turns listing A to Z the positive traits of the one you love.

6. Walk the mall. The goal is not to buy, but to test perfume and cologne along the way.

7. Be young again: have a squirt gun fight or fly a kite. Play "parent" for a day: Take a niece or nephew to the zoo. Take a younger sibling to a sporting event. (On a survey single women completed for us, a man who interacted well with children was seen as "sexier" because he seemed more sensitive.)

8. Write clues on dime-store Valentines and place them around town, and then take your love on a car rally or treasure hunt. The date consists of gathering clues and small romantic treasures like poems, chocolates, and other small treats.

9. Be poetic: check out a poetry book and read a few classics aloud to one another. Write a song or a poem and perform it for the one you love. Even an original version of "Roses are Red" can be a treasure if it's from the heart.

10. Reenact a portion of a great romantic drama. Shakespeare's *Romeo and Juliet* is a great place to begin.

11. Question it: Interview some couples who have been married happily for many years. What are they glad they did? What habits have helped them stay in love?

12. Anticipate the future. Do the "Dates to Decide" in the back of this book. Consider buying a book to help prepare for the next season of love. Invest in pre-engagement counseling or watch a relationship video.

13. Have a theme date: Try a living room luau or an evening in Venice complete with Italian music and pasta.

14. Rent an old-fashioned romantic movie. The movies made in the 30s to 50s are a good place to start. Hot flicks of today are often remakes of yesterday's classics. The original can be more wholesome but just as romantic.

15. Work out together. Go for a jog, do aerobics to a video, or visit a gym.

16. Bake something extravagant together.

17. Play a board game together. Classics like Scrabble or the Ungame are good conversation starters.

18. Put on your special song and waltz around. Find some new romantic music, choose an "our song," or take a dance lesson.

19. Play twenty questions. Each of you think of ten questions you'd love to know the answer to. Try questions like, "If you introduced me to a stranger today, what one thing would you say I do that you really appreciate about me?"

20. Go to a church or an outdoor cross and pray together. Take turns praying and thanking God for one another.

Remember, it's not the expense of the date but the thought that counts!

Question: How is being at a
singles bar different from
going to the circus?

8

Answer: At the circus, the
clowns don't talk.

The Social Life of
Waffles and Spaghetti

Always a bridesmaid, never a bride," Charee's mother sighed as she patted her Harvard-law-degreed daughter on the back, as if to console her. Later, in the car after the wedding, Charee confessed to her friend, Sandi, "I've come to hate weddings! I hate the looks of pity I get from relatives. I hate the awkward silence after the question, 'So, when are you going to get married?' I hate the line of people waiting to ask that question and having to answer it over and over and over again."

"Me too!" Sandi agreed. "How about this one? 'Oh, dearie, you aren't married? A pretty little thing like you? What's wrong?' I always feel like asking, 'Why does something have to be wrong?'"

Charee rolled her eyes and added, "I hate the one, 'Oh, no one has scooped you up yet?' Like I was ice cream!"

"I hate how they make me feel inferior, just because I'm not married," Sandi replied. "But I really hate the way I feel when I get home from these things. I peel off the most recent bridesmaid's dress I'll never wear again, slip into my pajamas, and climb into bed—alone. Then it hits, the scariest question of all. *What if they're right? What if all the really good ones are already married? What if I never find Mr. Right? Does that make me Ms. Wrong?"*

"I really am happy being single," Charee said, "until someone tells me I shouldn't be. Sure, I'd like to be married someday. But only if it's the right guy. Life's too short to be married to the wrong man."

Is There Anyone of Quality Left?

Clint wandered to the car in the dark after that same wedding. He had stayed as long as the reception lasted. The wedding had so many beautiful young women in it and at it—yet none seemed to click with him. He didn't think he was being too picky—a guy has to have some standards. Some of the single women there were so wild, others seemed so insecure, and still others would barely say two words to him. *Is something wrong with me?* Clint wondered. *I have a good job. I drive a nice car. I even help old ladies across the street. What is there not to like about me? Maybe I don't look like a movie star, but neither do some of the women I met tonight. Are there any good women left out there?*

And what do they want from us men? Do I pursue them? Or should I be laid-back? How can I feel so together at work and still have so many questions when it comes to relationships?

Questions of the Heart

Some of the most pressing questions singles raise—such as those posed by Charee, Sandi, and Clint—are pretty deep.

- Is there really only one perfect match—one soul mate for each person?

- What's the difference between having standards and being too picky?

- Are all the really great ones already taken?

- What's the best way to meet the person who's right for me?

- Should I take matters into my own hands, or should I wait for God to bring him or her to me?

- Does God want me to acknowledge He's sovereign in this area, or does He want me to take responsibility for my own life and choices?

- How do I know God's will?

- How does one really know he or she is in love?

Whew! Quite a list! But actually, if you look at the questions again, you will find there is one pivotal question. If you answer this one, all the rest come into focus. The pivotal question is, Can God's will be discovered?

Can God's Will Be Discovered— or Will I Ever Find Mr. or Miss Right for Me?

There is ample evidence from the Bible that God's will *can* be discovered. The Scriptures use many phrases to assure us of God's leadership, including "He leads me beside quiet waters," "guide me in your truth," "your word is a lamp to my feet," and "seek and you will find." Of this one thing you can be sure: God wants you to know His will even more than you want to receive it!

The question is not, Can I find God's will? but rather, *How* can I find God's will?

First, if you want God's blessings, then live a life He can bless. Having a mate is just one kind of blessing. Proverbs 18:22 says, "He who finds a wife finds what is good and receives favor from the LORD." However, check out what the apostle Paul recommends in 1 Corinthians 7:6-9:

> I say this as a concession, not as a command. I wish that all men were as I am. But each man has his own gift from God; one has this gift, another has that. Now to the unmarried and the widows I say: It is good for them to stay unmarried, as I am. But if they

cannot control themselves, they should marry, for it is better to marry than to burn with passion.

God says singleness can be a gift! Okay, so how do we know if that gift is *ours?* And if we feel we don't have a gift to be single, how do we discern who our gift in marriage is? How do we know we're not choosing someone else's present?

To discern God's will, start with the known. In the Bible, God provides several verses that explicitly say, "This is God's will for you."

A Life that God Blesses

There are only a few statements in the New Testament that clearly say, "This is God's will" or "This pleases God." When we are obeying those statements, all the decisions we make while obeying them agree with God's will. There is freedom in obeying the basic responsibilities God has given us.

God blesses a life that is saved. First Timothy 2:3-4 says, "This is good, and pleases God our Savior, who wants all men to be saved and to come to knowledge of the truth." God blesses a person who has decided to believe in Him and come to Him through Christ, admitting that he or she is imperfect and needs the Savior, Jesus Christ. Want to find God's best? Start by finding God Himself.

God blesses a life that is Spirit filled. Ephesians 5:18 says, "Do not get drunk on wine, which leads to debauchery. Instead, be filled with the Spirit." God blesses a life that is in step with Him.

God blesses a life that is sanctified. Romans 12:1-2 explains,

> Therefore, I urge you, brothers, in view of God's mercy, to offer your bodies as living sacrifices, holy and pleasing to God—this is your spiritual act of worship. Do not conform any longer to the pattern of this world, but be transformed by the renewing of your mind. Then you will be able to test and approve what God's will is—his good, pleasing and perfect will.

You will be able to see God's will when you think more like Him and less like yourself, so commit your thought life to God. He explains it is good, pleasing, and perfect to live a life that is "holy" as a living sacrifice. A sacrifice was the best of the best animals in the Old Testament, and that's what God wants. He sees *you* as the best of the best because He created you and redeemed you. As you live out your life, act as if you are taking care of God's very best.

Author Josh McDowell made a necklace for his daughter that has three golden hearts and three golden question marks. The three questions are ones that will guard your heart and, in the process, guard your life: Does this show respect for God? Does this show respect for others? Does this show respect for myself?

God blesses a life that is sexually pure. First Thessalonians 4:3 makes it clear, "It is God's will that you should be sanctified: that you should avoid sexual immorality." Here's a hard one, especially for singles. God will bless you only when you run relationships His way. And His way means no sex outside of marriage.

God blesses a life that says, "Thank You!" First Thessalonians 5:18 commands, "Give thanks in all circumstances, for this is God's will for you in Christ Jesus." You got it—God blesses a positive attitude! Instead of seeing what you *don't* have, try thanking God for what you *do* have. Instead of going to a group function and saying, "I hope I meet someone," choose to say, "I hope I help put someone else at ease." Instead of saying "There's no one for me," try saying, "How can I help create a positive social atmosphere for my other Christian single friends?" Instead of worrying about how others are receiving you, try receiving others by loving and accepting them unconditionally. Take your eyes off yourself. That's the kind of life God blesses. How do we know? He confirms it in many places including Philippians 2:3-4: "Do nothing out of selfish ambition or vain conceit, but in humility consider others better than yourselves.

Each of you should look not only to your own interests, but also to the interests of others."

God blesses a life that is suffering for right. First Peter 3:17 reminds us, "It is better, if it is God's will, to suffer for doing good than for doing evil." And 1 Peter 4:19 adds, "So then, those who suffer according to God's will should commit themselves to their faithful Creator and continue to do good." This one's a little tougher to put in perspective. Here's the deal: Everyone will suffer. We live in a broken, imperfect world. There is pain. There is frustration. There is inconvenience. There are hassles. Life is hard, so choose your suffering. It's better to do right and have the suffering that comes from pleasing God more than man. It's silly to make wrong choices and have the suffering compounded by natural consequences and God's discipline. For example, it's better to take some ridicule over high sexual standards than to give in and suffer the consequences of a sexually transmitted disease such as AIDS.

God blesses a life that seeks Him. Psalm 119:2 says, "Blessed are they who keep his statutes and seek him with all their heart." Proverbs 8:17 notes, "I love those who love me, and those who seek me find me." Deuteronomy 4:29 adds, "But if from there you seek the LORD your God, you will find him if you look for him with all your heart and with all your soul." God blesses a seeking heart. When you are looking for God and His best for your life, your heart takes you places you wouldn't go naturally. For example, consider how Bill and I met.

I grew up as the daughter of an alcoholic father. The result was a vacuum in my life that I thought attention from men could fill. I desperately wanted men to like me and love me. I was so desperate for love that at one time I had three boyfriends. They all lived in different parts of the same city, and I knew them from different contexts of my life. The charade came crashing down when all three came to the same car show where I was performing with a dance company. From backstage I saw them all three in the front row, each waiting for me to finish so they could take me on a date! Yikes!

One of those guys eventually won out, and we dated for a couple of years. I found myself feeling pressured to please him even if I was going against my own value system. About this time, my father tried committing suicide by hanging himself in our garage. We got him down in time to save his life. The day after this incident, I was driving home from college classes when God began to whisper to my heart, *Pam, you have been treating Me as if I am like your earthly father—distant, demanding, unrelenting— but I'm not like that. Dust off your Bible and find out who I am.*

So I did. Shortly after that, I came across the verse that says, "By Him we cry, 'Abba, Father'" and I realized that I had a Daddy God in heaven who loved me and wanted a relationship with me, not for what I could do, but just because I was His. A huge wave of acceptance and unconditional love swept over me.

Within a few weeks, a friend from my swim team named Grace invited me to a Bible study. I had been praying, asking God to send me someone who could help me understand Him better.

At the Bible studies, I was encouraged to spend time with God daily in His Word, so I did. And the more I spent time with God, the more truth He showed me about myself. I realized I was addicted to men and needed to go cold turkey—dateless—until I could relearn what a healthy man looked like and what healthy relationships were all about. I broke up with my boyfriend who was pressuring me, and I turned down all kinds of dates. It got easier because soon I got a reputation for turning guys down. Then my real insecurity showed. I no longer felt desired by men. God used His Word to remake me from the inside out. He began to help me have a healthy self-image based not on what people thought of me but on what He thought of me.

This caused me to make a lot of changes and gave me an intense desire to grow even more. Everyone at church could see how fast I was growing in my new relationship with Christ. I soon began to want to tell others about Christ and what He was doing in my life. I became involved in a Sunday evening Bible study held just off the college campus. A few months after I rededicated myself to Christ, I went through the dorms, inviting everyone to come to this Bible study. I showed up with more than 20 of my friends that night.

During this time I was also being discipled by a mentor, Tina. At one of these meetings, Tina asked if I was coming to the next Sunday night Bible study. Although I attended these studies faithfully, I explained that my boyfriend was coming to town and taking me out for my birthday. I didn't think he'd want to come to a Bible study. Then Tina began asking the hard questions: "Pam, didn't you make a commitment to being at the Sunday night Bible studies? Don't you keep your commitments? Where do you think Jesus would want you to go?"

I tried rationalizing my choices, and then she asked point blank: "Pam, who's more important, Jesus or John?"

Ouch! I knew Jesus was far more important, but I sure hadn't been answering Tina that way. That's when I decided to not only go to the study but to invite my boyfriend. He didn't really want to go but reluctantly complied. However, when we got back to my place, I found out he just wanted to take my virginity for my birthday. And I had been hoping for a watch or necklace! I could clearly see we were on different dimensions spiritually. To be fair to both of us, I told my boyfriend of my growing faith and suggested we break up—which we did. In so doing, I found a tremendous freedom in not having to define myself by my boyfriend. I learned of an upcoming leadership conference sponsored by Campus Crusade for Christ and approached Tina about it.

"It's for leaders, Pam." Tina told me.

"Where do you think Jesus would like me to go?" I smiled.

"Pam, going to a conference like this means you're willing to share your faith on campus—but then I guess you're already doing that, aren't you? And it means you'll be asked to lead a Bible study for a few girls."

"No problem, " I responded.

"Well, it costs $75."

"Who do I make the check out to?"

That conversation took place in June. Two weeks later, I was home to be with my mom for the summer. Things had gotten so bad with my father's drinking that it was no longer safe for any of us to live with him for fear of our very lives. My mom made the decision to move back to Idaho and I offered to help her pack. All along, I kept telling her I couldn't stay all summer—that I had to go back in August for the leadership retreat. I had made a commitment, I told her, and she had raised me to always keep my commitments. So even though she was in pain, she agreed to send me back to college early.

My dad heard that I was home, and he called and tried to talk me into skipping the conference so I could see him instead.

He tried bribery: "I'll buy you a new car."

He tried guilt: "Do you love your mother more than me?"

But I told him the same thing I told Mom: "I have to go to the conference. I gave my word, and you raised me to keep my promises."

So I was off to a leadership retreat at Campus Crusade for Christ headquarters. I'll never forget one evening soon after the conference began. I had just spent a wonderful time in the Word near a stream, and I reentered the conference lobby. I sat on a sofa, waiting for my friends. In walked a handsome athlete with curly hair and a beautiful broad smile. He sat on a sofa across from me and asked, "So what did God say to you?"

I wanted to say, "You're talking to me?" But I knew he was because no one else was in the lobby yet. I was amazed that such a godly and gorgeous guy was talking to me about spiritual things and asking my opinion. He listened—he really listened! Six weeks later, after a second leadership conference, we started writing back and forth. A few months later, we started dating at still another leadership conference.

On the first night of that Christmas conference, Bill asked me for a date on the last night. However, the next day, Bill told me he couldn't concentrate and that he needed to express his feelings to me. He sat me down, grabbed my hand, and said,

"Pam, I really like you, and I want to spend time getting to know you." I thought, *He's gorgeous, he's godly, and now he's showing me that there will be no games! Can life get any better than this!*

It did less than one year later, the day I married Bill.

Seeking God step-by-step ensured that I was at the right place, on the right day, at the right time, to meet Bill—God's choice for me. When God is leading your life, you will be at the right place on the right day. God knows you need a social life, and He knows whether being married or single is best for you. That's why seeking God is the key ingredient to discovering the plan God has for you.

God will confirm the call to matrimony or the single life, whichever it is. Bill and I decided we didn't want to play games with each other's hearts. We decided to separate for the next summer to seek God. I was going to an Institute of Biblical Studies in Colorado for six weeks; Bill was headed back home to work. We decided we wouldn't write or even call for those six weeks. We'd just seek God and ask Him to lead us. Bill came by to say goodbye to me and then started his two-hour drive home. Although he felt God was impressing him to marry me, he argued about the timing.

"God, you don't understand," he said. I am only 20 years old. I haven't even finished college."

After he'd argue with God, Bill would feel all torn up inside. But then he'd say, "Okay, fine. I'll marry Pam," then he'd be at peace.

Then he'd start arguing with God again. "But God, I know how things go. I'll get married. I'll never finish college. We'll have kids. I'll get a job I hate, and I'll never get to live my dream—and I'll resent Pam." Bill's stomach would ache. Then he'd say, "Okay, fine! I'll marry the girl!" And he'd have peace again.

Again he'd pick up the argument, "God, I'm only 20. I only own two pairs of pants. One has a rip in the knee. I drive a green Vega with a blue back door!"

He'd feel tense and anxious again until he said, "Okay, fine, I'll marry the girl!" Once again he'd get the peace that God offers when He leads.

Now some of you may be saying, "I seek God, and I don't have a story like this." That doesn't mean you never will. It simply means you will have your *own* story. It's critically important that we keep our thankful attitude as we seek God. God has not provided a set of magic steps to happiness. Rather, He has called us to a redeemed, healthy lifestyle that He blesses—whatever that might look like.

God says He knows "the plans [he] has for you, to give you a future and a hope" (Jeremiah 29:11). He doesn't say you have no future without a spouse or that you'll lack hope until you have a mate—God is bigger than that. God does not necessarily promise a mate when you seek Him. What He does promise is an abundant, meaningful life.

One day, I had a heart-to-heart talk with a dear single friend about the "grass is always greener" syndrome. She told me she was envious of my great marriage and wonderful kids. I told her I envied her for all the exciting things she gets to experience—traveling the world, kayaking in Alaska, biking through Europe, being a missionary to Russia, and of course her expendable income. For many years, I didn't even *have* an income, and hers was six figures! Her comment to me was, "It's easy to forget the blessings you become accustomed to." Wise woman.

How to Develop a Healthy Social Life

The singles we have known over our 20 years in ministry seem to have one common trait. They don't focus on what they can get from life. They focus on what they can *give*. Gary and Sheryl went to two different churches, but they saw the same need. Gary noticed that it was difficult to gather older singles who were serious about their relationship with Christ. There seemed to be just a handful in each church. Sheryl noticed that singles in her community needed more healthy social options.

Sheryl went to each pastor in her community and asked for names of singles between the ages of 26 and 40.

When Sheryl met Gary's pastor, he told her Gary had come to him wanting to do something similar and offered to call Gary and set up a meeting. Gary and Sheryl met with a few others over lunch and a new ministry was born.

Over the next three years, the group grew to be several hundred strong, and Gary and Sheryl stayed at the leadership helm together. One day, Gary looked over the planning table and thought, "We're great as a team—maybe we're meant to be a team for life."

Within a year, wedding bells rang as hundreds of singles and married friends gathered to wish Gary and Sheryl well in their new life. That was nearly 20 years ago, and they're still happy teaming together in marriage. *Purpose* brought them together.

Where Do Healthy People Hang Out?

In most communities, there are many options for meeting other singles. Which places are safe, and which are unsafe? How can you know where to go and whom to hang out with? Are there guiding social principles for meeting people and forming relationships? Let's look at how God forms relationships.

God Knows Us by Name; We Should Know Others by Name

"Then those who feared the LORD talked with each other, and the LORD listened and heard. A scroll of remembrance was written in his presence concerning those who feared the LORD and honored his name" (Malachi 3:16).

"Are not two sparrows sold for a penny? Yet not one of them will fall to the ground apart from the will of your Father. And even the very hairs of your head are all numbered. So don't be afraid; you are worth more than many sparrows. Whoever acknowledges me before men, I will also acknowledge him before my Father in heaven!" (Matthew 10:29-32).

"You give me your shield of victory, and your right hand sustains me; you stoop down to make me great" (Psalm 18:35).

God is personal. He knows not only our name but also every hair on our head. We are the apple of His eye, and we are safe and secure in His hand. We should seek to follow His example of personal treatment of people. The more impersonal we treat our social life, the farther we drift from the heart of God.

God Values a Good Reputation; We Should Know a Person's Reputation

"Then you will win favor and a good name in the sight of God and man" (Proverbs 3:4).

"A good name is more desirable than great riches; to be esteemed is better than silver or gold" (Proverbs 22:1).

"A good name is better than fine perfume" (Ecclesiastes 7:1).

"And Jesus grew in wisdom and stature, and in favor with God and men" (Luke 2:52).

God proclaims that a good name, a good reputation, a track record of good character is to be highly valued and sought after. As you navigate your social life, you will run into less pain if you hold people to a high accountability in their dealings with you. Get to know their friends and family early. Meet his or her pastor, small group leader, and coworkers. And if you notice any half-truths or people aren't telling you the whole story about someone, put some distance between you and the other person. Life is too short to be in a relationship that's not based on honesty.

There are many ways to meet people socially, including the internet, chat rooms, single matchmakers, video dating services, personal ads, internet matchmaking sites, singles groups at church and in the community, work, and personal and career conferences. The higher the accountability of the persons making the connections, the safer the meeting becomes. We noticed that those matchmaking websites that had the résumé and personal contact information of the site's developer often had higher accountability for the people using the sites. For example, they required references and established rules of conduct. People who are worth knowing will offer to give you background information and other personal contacts so you can get to know them, their life, and their world. If someone is too aloof, too independent, that should be a yellow flag—no matter how you met him or her.

Inner Character Quality Is Valued Higher than Outward Appearance

"But the LORD said to Samuel, 'Do not consider his appearance or his height, for I have rejected him. The LORD does not look at the things man looks at. Man looks at the outward appearance, but the LORD looks at the heart'" (1 Samuel 16:7).

"My shield is God Most High, who saves the upright in heart" (Psalm 7:10).

"Blessed are the pure in heart, for they will see God" (Matthew 5:8).

Yes, God tells us that our body is His temple, but too often single people begin to worship the temple, rather than God who dwells in the temple. God is more concerned about a person's heart than his or her sex appeal. We have male friends who would be awesome providers and great fathers, and who are wonderful Christian leaders, but because they don't look like the cover of *People* magazine, their greater traits are overshadowed by their average looks. And in the same regard, we have female friends who would be super teammates in life and are wonderfully tender, compassionate, quality women, but they have just an average appearance so they get overlooked in this media-driven age.

We *do* believe that physical attraction is an important part of life. When God made Eve, Adam was stunned by her beauty. As a result, part of the decision-making process in relationships involves some sexual energy and chemistry. But superficial sexual attraction can make you "feel" in love, when you may be experiencing nothing more than a hormonal rush. Keep a balance between personal character and sexual attraction.

Romantic connections happen because of adventure and mystery. A man meets a woman who is mysterious to him, and he immediately becomes attracted. A woman meets a man who is strong and spontaneous, and her heart is stirred. In contrast, when a man meets a woman who is too "safe," he may view her as a sister. When a woman meets a man who is so "stable" he lacks drive, she views him as a brother. There are no sparks, no flames, no excitement.

The problem is that adventurous, mysterious people who lack character are disastrous to live around. They break hearts and wound souls. The only treasure you end up with is a storehouse of disappointment. Look for people of character who know how to live on the edge—people who are stable enough to be trusted but unpredictable enough to be exciting.

As you seek God, expect Him to make you that kind of person. The same God who says, "seek peace" also says, "take up the full armor of God." He is the Lamb of God and the Lion of Judah.

God creates competitors who have compassionate hearts. The truly attractive are those who have courageous character, and they're worth waiting for!

Meet People in a Way that Keeps You in Ministry

"But seek first his kingdom and his righteousness, and all these things will be given to you as well" (Matthew 6:33).

"For the Son of Man came to seek and to save what was lost" (Luke 19:10).

"'My food,' said Jesus, 'is to do the will of him who sent me and to finish his work'" (John 4:34).

Keep first things first. God's priority is that we seek His will first before anything else. God has bigger plans for you than just finding a mate. There are people to influence, worlds to build, and challenges to overcome. If there was one lie we could keep singles from believing, it would be the "I'd be happy if I were married" myth. There are plenty of unhappy married couples.

Some are unhappy because they didn't seek God's guidance when choosing their mate. Others were driven by sexual passions and misread sex as love. Still others quit seeking God and "settled" for someone because they mistakenly believed God was not providing anyone for them.

Socialize to Stay Other-Centered, Not Self-Centered

> If you have any encouragement from being united with Christ, if any comfort from his love, if any fellowship with the Spirit, if any tenderness and compassion, then make my joy complete by being like-minded, having the same love, being one in spirit and purpose. Do nothing out of selfish ambition or vain conceit, but in humility consider others better than yourselves. Each of you should look not only to your own interests, but also to the interests of others (Philippians 2:1-4).

Secure, successful singles look for what they can give, not what they can take. Successful singles enter a room thinking, *Each person here has a story. This is like a great library. I'm sure there are some interesting books here.* So they listen.

Successful singles think their own life can be a great story of God's grace. They take care of their emotional baggage in healthy ways by participating in self-help groups, counseling, and mentoring relationships. They don't expect their friends to play counselor, especially early in a relationship. They seek out ways to grow and assume others can be helped by their story, so they get involved.

Successful singles see what they can bring to the single circles. They use their gifts, talents, and time to create more opportunities and connections for everyone—not just for themselves.

There Are Fish in the Sea like You

Let's take at look at some options of meeting singles:

Natural Circles

These include your work, your working networks, your church, your family's friends, your friends, your friends' friends, classes, sports, and organizations that interest you naturally even if you don't meet anyone there.

Natural circles are places you would go as a natural course of your life. These are benefits of natural circles:

They don't take any extra time. You'd be doing all these activities anyway.

You have a frame of reference for the people you meet. Someone you know knows the people you meet.

The people you meet fit naturally into your life because they have been running in the same circles.

The focus of these relationships is bigger than just "meeting someone."

Natural circles also have some disadvantages:

- These circles can become ingrown. For example, if you have followed the show *Friends*, you probably noticed that everyone on the show has dated and slept with pretty much everyone else. If you don't keep growing as a person, your world can become very, very small.

    One of the negative side effects of a small circle of relationships is that it can become easy to feel angry with your friends as they marry and you don't. Bill and I have had some of our single friends say some hurtful things to us and to other married friends and family in their world. Statements such as, "You don't value my friendship" or "You never have time for me" can be unfair, especially as your married friends begin to have children and experience more and more family responsibilities. Burning bridges with your married friends might be self-defeating. They might just work with, go to church with, or be related to someone that would be just right for you. At the very least, your married friends can be an ongoing circle of support because they have known you for so long.

- You can slip into a depression as you feel your world shrinking. Bill and I have seen attractive, talented, positive singles slide into a dark depression because they didn't keep working on expanding their friendship circles.

- Your current natural circles might have been built on your married life. If you are recently divorced or a widow(er), most of your friends could be married.

Assertive Circles

Assertive circles cause you go out of your way to meet people. Our friends Tony and Susan know the benefits of assertive matchmaking. Susan's mother was proud of her hard-working daughter living abroad to raise funds to support her family in the Philippines. She wrote a personal ad describing her daughter's strengths. Tony's buddies in the states wrote up a personal ad touting Tony's attributes and then wrote Susan a letter as if Tony wrote it! Susan wrote back! Many letters, tons of phone calls, and a few months later, Tony flew halfway around the world to propose. They have been happily married for more than ten years.

The Advantages of Assertive Circles

They expose you to a broader variety of people than you would meet normally. Pastor Jim Rives gives advice on a singles' website that offers a cruise with teaching and seminars by strong, nationally recognized Christian leaders and entertainers including Kathy Troccoli. Other singles' sites also give some helpful advice about the dating process: pray, don't pay as much attention to the pictures as to the written profile, keep friendship in mind, don't lie, remember God is watching you, and let your spirit and not your body run your relationship.

Some websites also sponsor conferences and events that offer you a safer place to meet in person someone you've met over the web. Others offer surfing options that limit the field or "match" for you based on a set of criteria. Others offer on-line viewing of videos. Others offer questions for individuals to answer so the profile feels more like having coffee and less like reading an ad.

Many Christian sites keep track of marriages that have resulted, and as time passes, more research will be available on the marital satisfaction and divorce rates resulting from this type of meeting. Many sites are affiliated with good, reputable Christian networks, and this promotes some level of accountability. Others offer personal matchmaking, not just random ads, and this does two things: It saves you time and adds to the accountability—someone else knows the person. The sites that match the criteria we discussed earlier include pages on the leadership of the site: its founder, its pastor, the counselor, and the matchmakers. The more that was revealed about the people behind the sites, the closer the sites seemed to match the safety net of God's principles.

Neil Clark Warren's site, *eharmony*, was launched as a result of his extensive research over decades that led him to one irrefutable conclusion: Mate selection is *the key* to a brilliant marriage. Therefore, his site only connects people who match in over 29 human compatibility dimensions such as common values, beliefs, attitudes, personality, temperament, behaviors, and skills. Dr. Warren spent years in divorce analysis and has written numerous books helping singles make wise choices on mate selection. In addition, *eharmony* helps guide the subscriber in early conversations so the most vital information is learned quickly. They claim emotionally unstable people are identified and screened out. Warren explains, "Eighty-five percent of what matters is what's inside you: your beliefs, your principles, and your values. Fifteen percent has to do with the wrapping." And as a society, he said, we spend far too much time on the 15 percent.

You avoid feeling like you are doing nothing to meet people. Bill and I were invited to speak at Park Church in downtown Chicago. An offshoot of Moody Bible Church, this church plant targeted the population that lived in downtown Chicago, which was primarily single, upwardly mobile professionals. The congregation was nearly 90 percent single! We were impressed as we walked into the foyer of the church because there were table after table of ministry opportunities. These singles had created a healthy place to mature in Christ and navigate the single social life in a healthy manner. There was every kind of small group, social interest, outreach, and mission opportunity you could think of! What better way to really get to know a person than to take a missions trip or river-rafting trip with someone?

You can be reasonably confident that other people want to meet you. As Carl said to us, "I never know how strong to come on with women. Are they already in a relationship, wanting to be left alone, or do they want to meet me but are just shy or reserved? At least when I used a matchmaking service I knew the women wanted to meet me because it was a two-way response."

It just might work. The popularity of the movie *You've Got Mail* romanticized e-mail. E-mail definitely does have its advantages. You can e-mail whenever you are thinking of a person, night or day, so the time constraints that formerly ruled the process of getting to know someone have been eased by technology. Letter writing also has the advantage of the recipient being able to savor the words, reading them over and over again. And e-mail is an inexpensive way to shrink the miles if you are dating someone from whom you are separated geographically.

And if you meet someone in a chat room...then what? What if you want to learn more about a person? One couple we know met in a ministry-related chat room. They began to e-mail back and forth. However, they maintained some vital boundaries. Early on, they each asked a few friends to e-mail character references and personal letters to the other. Phone numbers were exchanged so that they could each call the other's references. When those references checked out, they exchanged personal phone numbers and a calling relationship started. Then they agreed to meet at a Christian conference for singles, each bringing a few friends with them. Following the conference, they each asked their pastor to be available to talk to the other and give their insights. When that went well, they traveled with family to see where the other worked and lived, and to meet the other's friends and family. They used e-mail to do Bible study together. Finally, they began pre-engagement counseling—all before either of them decided to move near the other. Eventually, Diane moved, they completed pre-marital counseling, they married, and they have created a happy life together.

The Disadvantages of Assertive Circles

It can be quite expensive. Methods for meeting people can be free or can cost thousands of dollars. As with any other investment or purchase, do your research and check up on the options and their successes. Get personal recommendations from others who have used them. Some may cost more because there is higher selectivity and accountability, and that may be worth every cent for your safety.

The potential for disappointment is higher because the focus is usually on meeting the right person to marry. In our travels, we meet many leaders. One recently confessed, "It was bad enough feeling rejected because I was still single, but it felt worse after I spent thousands of dollars and still felt rejected. Then I had therapy bills on top of that! I came to the conclusion that I had wasted years of my life chasing marriage. I only started feeling happy when I started chasing God with the same intensity. I threw myself into ministry and went back for more education. It was when I served on a leadership council for a ministry that I started dating the man whom I later married."

The potential for getting distracted from God's purpose for your life is heightened because the focus is usually on meeting the right person to marry. "Clubbing" may expose you to many singles, but rarely have we seen the relationships that have developed from these liaisons become very positive. Usually, they turn into relationships that range from a one-night stand to a volatile relationship fraught with drama.

The great Canadian physician Sir William Osler was lecturing one day on alcohol.

"Is it true," asked a student, "that alcohol makes people able to do things better?"

"No," replied Sir William. "It just makes them less ashamed of doing them badly."

The potential for deception is higher because people are intentionally putting their best foot forward. It may take a lot of effort to get the full picture. That's why chat rooms hold all kinds of unknown dangers. Who knows who those people "really" are? They may not even be the age or the sex they claim to be! They might not even be single!

Chaerise was a frequent chat room attendee. CharlieZ28 seemed funny, charming, and personal. Soon their chat room conversations expanded to e-mail correspondence. Then one day, her parents found a note in Chaerise's room. CharlieZ28 had sent money for a plane ticket, and she'd gone to meet him. When she arrived, she was surprised to learn "Charlie" was more than 20 years older than she was. Still, the couple moved in together—and soon Chaerise discovered she was pregnant. Then "Charlie" began to beat her. Chaerise endured the beatings even when he hit her when she was pregnant a second time. "Charlie" began working less and less and drinking more and more. Chaerise had to get a job to earn enough for food and diapers. One day, two police officers came into the café where she was a waitress with the news that "Charlie" had shot himself and their two little girls. They were all dead.

Some sites say that if you provide untrue or inaccurate information, they will unsubscribe you—but how can they possibly check out the 500 to 10,000 people a day they are claiming join their site? In most of the disclaimers, the sites say they are not responsible for anything that happens to you as a result of being on their site. Many sites also list the things they don't want members to do: stalk, spam, sell to others, track down geographical address, send obscenity—so one might be lead to believe all these could happen if you are on the sites. Many of the sites claim to have twice to three times as many men as women members.

Could this be because a computer is shaped like a square (waffle box)? Or is it because there might be some men who hide behind their computers instead of developing good relationship skills? Some Christian sites don't appear to be much different than other sites. In fact, when surfing, if you type in the keyword *single* and then *Christian single*, a majority of the sites appear on both lists. Some give mixed messages. There may be endorsements from a leading respected government leader on the same page as a bikini-clad model. Some sites allow surfers as young as 16!

Common Sense Makes the Most Sense

Jim Conway lost his wife, Sally, after years of marital happiness. He initially found the single world a frightening place. He decided the safest route back into the single social circle was to simply have coffee. Coffee was safe. Jim and his guest would each drive to the appointed Starbucks and drink a latté. If the conversation went well, coffee could last an hour or more. But if it was obvious the relationship had no future, both quickly finished the cup and escaped graciously and quickly. While going out to dinner might involve dressing up and an investment of several hours, coffee was more of a business meeting where each stopped in just as they were. It didn't involve the romantic trappings of candlelight, music, or lengthy conversation that can make a single feel awkward or pressured. Coffee was just the safer route.

I (Bill) frequently receive calls or get into conversations where the single person complains about the singles' spectrum and the lack of "others like me." I encourage them, "Keep your boat in the water."

Giving up too easily is a common mistake. If they don't discover Mr. or Miss Right, they throw in the towel and quit dating altogether. They pull away, fearing another rejection, but their fear of rejection keeps them from meeting new people. Their world gets smaller and smaller…one day they might wake up and not have any single friends at all. They have dry-docked their relational boat. Just as boats are made for water, people are made for relationships. Wise singles will keep sailing even though they will encounter all kinds of singles' squalls and storms. They will keep sailing in the sea of relationships by creating more and more social connections and ministry service opportunities until one of two things happen. They may decide that solo sailing is a nice pursuit and that they don't need a mate to feel complete. Friends and ministry companions are enough. Or they will pull into a harbor and discover someone sailing a vessel that is just right for them. They realize they would have never met that person had they kept their relational boat safely in dry dock.

Raise the anchor and keep sailing!

SPAGHETTI
WAFFLES

A marketing director for a prominent computer manufacturer was devising a new advertising campaign for his company. While researching consumer response to his product, he asked "Naval ships are commonly referred to as 'she' or 'her'. What gender would you assign to your computer? Give four reasons to support your answer."

A large group of women reported that the computers should be referred to in the masculine gender because:

1. In order to get their attention, you have to turn them on.

2. They have a lot of data, but are still clueless.

3. They are supposed to help you solve problems, but half the time they are the problem.

4. As soon as you commit to one, you realize that if you had waited a little longer, you could have had a better model.

The men, on the other hand, concluded that computers should be referred to in the feminine gender because:

1. No one but the Creator understands their internal logic.

2. The native language they use to communicate with other computers is incomprehensible to everyone else.

3. Even your smallest mistakes are stored in long-term memory for later retrieval.

4. As soon as you make a commitment to one, you find yourself spending half your paycheck on accessories for it.

The test of the morality of a society is what it does for its children.

—Dietrich Bonhoeffer

Waffles, Spaghetti, and Kids

For the most part, single parents have the same parenting issues to deal with as two-parent families, including discipline, motivating children, chores, and homework. The difference is you might not have much (if any) help with your children. Knowing what you have to offer, either as a waffle or as spaghetti, will help you know what else your child might need from people of the opposite gender such as grandparents, aunts or uncles, coaches, and teachers.

Being a man or a woman does impact your parenting. When Bill and I occasionally saw one of our little boys get hurt, our reactions were similar and yet different. We'd both run to the aid of our son with many different thoughts in our heads. Mine might sound like this:

Let's see if he's okay. Looks like it. No broken bones. He's breathing. There's a little blood and a scraped knee. "Okay, buddy, you'll be all right." Need to help him balance this. It's all right to express emotion, but I don't want him to be a wimp. If he's a wimp, he'll be made fun of at school and his self-esteem will take a hit. Then he will make poor choices...maybe even get into drugs or drinking. But then again, if I don't allow him to express emotion and he becomes a tough, nonemotional male, he'll miss out on the depth of relationships. His kids and wife will feel emotionally distant from him. He could end up divorced or disillusioned and depressed. I want more for him than that.

In the midst of this I will usually say something like, "Honey, it's okay to cry, but you're all right. Let Mama pray for you. Hey sweetie, think you'll be all right by the time you get married?"

He laughs and nods his head, wipes his tears and stands up. *Whew! Seems like I did okay this time. Give me wisdom, Lord!*

Bill's response would depend on what box he was in at the time. He likes to describe them as multiple-choice boxes/responses:

a. **Tough guy box:** No blood, no broken bones and he's breathing means, "Okay son, suck it up, you'll be all right!"

b. **Sympathetic dad box:** "Wow! That must hurt, son. Let Dad give ya a hug and help you up."

c. **Macho man:** Let Mom respond, and yell from the garage, "You okay, son? Sounds like it! Hey, come here and I'll show you the scar from when I ripped open my knee on a sprinkler head."

To Bill, it's an isolated incident. But I attach all kinds of meanings to one small second in time. My mind runs all the possible scenarios like a computer program. Maybe that's why studies say, "During the first year of their lives, children tend to laugh and smile more at their fathers, but are more likely to turn to their mothers for reassurance when threatened or in distress."[1] Why is this? One study of boys and girls says this:

At a physiological level, girls and boys were equally affected by the sight of the child smiling or crying. Their heart rate tended to slow down when it smiled, and they became physiologically aroused when they saw that it was crying. But it would have been impossible to tell that they shared the same gut reaction from the way that they behaved. The girls looked much more interested while the boys pretended to ignore the baby's distress, a sex difference which was much more marked among the older than the younger children.[2]

Could it be we are telling boys and men that only mom can help in distress? Maybe mom doesn't let dad jump in because he nurtures differently. Different isn't necessarily bad, different can be just different—thus complementary.

The Power of a Waffle

When both parents are involved in child rearing, their roles are not interchangeable. "...fathers tend to be more physical when they play with children, while mothers favor conventional games like peek-a-boo, and also provide them with more intellectual stimulation by reading to them or encouraging them to manipulate objects."[3]

Children tend to turn to Mom for comfort and reassurance, but Dad's role is just as vital. A child's relationship with Dad is the most important factor in determining how he or she will react to the rest of the world. For example,

> An experiment carried out on six-month-old boys found that those who had most contact with their fathers were least disturbed when a stranger of either sex picked them up. Similarly, a recent American study shows that the less frequently babies of both sexes are dressed and bathed by their fathers, the longer they cry when they're left alone with an adult they don't know.[4]

Nor is social development the only area in which fathers make a significant contribution:

> The rocking, talking and touching that fathers provide in response to their children's signals teaches a baby that it can affect other people by its actions, and encourages its intellectual curiosity. As a result, research shows that the more contact a child has with its father, the more advanced it's likely to be. This effect is more marked for boys, though other aspects of a father's behavior can also have a direct effect on a daughter's intellectual development:[5]

Dad definitely makes a difference! So what's a single mom to do? If possible, work out a relationship with the father of your child for your child's sake. It might not be easy or comfortable, but it can be worth it. It's especially vital if you have a son. There comes a time in a young man's life when he will look to Dad for guidance and help in learning the ropes of manhood. And the love of a father will keep his teen daughter from seeking love elsewhere. So if at all possible, try to help your children stay connected to their biological father.

However, sometimes this just isn't possible. Maybe Dad doesn't want anything to do with the children. Or perhaps Dad is so dysfunctional that more harm than good will come from his time spent with the children (as often is the case with men who abuse drugs or alcohol). If this is the case, pray and ask God to show you how to create a strong, positive, committed male influence in your child's life.

When Joan was six, she called her biological father, who had remarried. Her dad said to her, "Don't ever call here. I don't want anything to do with you or your mother. I have a new family now, and I don't need or want you to call." Then he hung up—and he held true to his word: he never talked to his daughter again.

Joan's mom wisely approached her own father and asked if he'd step in and play Dad in Joan's life. He came to dance recitals, soccer games, and other activities important to Joan. He called and talked to her regularly and took her out on "dates." He was positive and encouraging. But he died when Joan was 14. She was devastated. Again, her mom prayed, and she approached a family in her church. She took Sue and Jim to dinner, explained that her daughter would soon be dating, and asked if Jim would step in and serve as a surrogate father. Would he be willing to meet the young men who wanted to date Joan? Would he and his wife come to Joan's high school events and be a part of Joan's life?

Jim had been a great father. His grown kids were successful, well-adjusted, and secure. How could he not say yes to helping Joan? He knew his input may help spare her from looking for love in all the wrong places. Joan's mom, Sue, and Jim worked together to set healthy boundaries. Sue was always home when Joan and her dates came, and Sue was in the same room when Jim called Joan or Joan stopped by for advice.

Kelly was a single mom but not by choice. Her husband left her and her three sons one day and was never heard from again. Kelly immediately sensed a need for male input into her sons' lives. She searched out healthy coaches and enrolled her sons on their teams. She encouraged her sons to join the Boy Scouts and to take music lessons—from a man. She also put her children in a Bible class taught by a man. She talked to the pastor and youth pastor of her church and asked if they would mind going out of their way to greet her boys on Sundays and ask them about their week. Both agreed to look for opportunities to talk with the boys naturally. When the boys reached high school, she asked their youth pastor if he'd come to any events where a "dad" was required, including Senior Night during football season when the fathers are given a gift on the 50-yard line.

Kelly's determination to ensure a male presence in her sons' lives cost her extra time and effort—but the results of having three mature adult sons was well worth her trouble.

The Influence of a Good Spaghetti Dinner

What does the care of a mother look like? It's easily recognizable. One study explains,

> Most mothers seem to have a standard way of touching their newborn babies, beginning with the arms and legs and then stroking the back and stomach. They also tend to hold their babies so that they can look into each other's eyes. When holding or feeding the baby, they bring its face to within about a foot of their own, which happens to be the distance at which a newborn baby's eyes focus best. More significantly, even adults without children consistently hold babies at a distance at which the baby's—though not necessarily their own—eyes are best in focus. Mothers also pitch their voices higher when talking to their babies, and we know (though mothers may not) that babies are more responsive to high-pitched sounds.[6]

God intended children to respond to Mom's voice. Mom plays a powerful role in the life of a child. Because she integrates life and emotionally connects to those closest to her, Mom provides the first primary trust relationship with a child. The more bonded a child is to Mom those first few weeks and months, the stronger his or her ability is to trust others.

Dr. Brenda Hunter, in her book *Where Have All the Mothers Gone?* examines studies by numerous specialists in the mother-child bond. Dr. Jack Raskin, child psychiatrist at Children's Orthopedic Hospital and at the University of Washington states no psychological event is as important as the bonding that occurs between the mother and child during the first few moments of life.[7] Psychoanalyst John Bowlby points out that this attachment to mother is the "foundation stone of personality." Bowlby explains that the mother-child attachment is evident throughout childhood and only weakens as the teen years progress because more adults become important to the child.[8]

Maggie Scarf builds upon the preponderance of evidence gathered since WWII. Studies that follow children who have been institutionalized because they have no mother, or children who are tossed from foster home to foster home, show these children are often permanently impaired. Scarf says that when these basic relationships are disturbed and the mother is absent, especially during the first four to five years of life,

> The child experiences acute psychological pain. This anguish has three distinct stages: protest, despair, and finally detachment. When the child reaches the last stage...he no longer cares. And if this separation from mother is too long, the process may never be reversed. Some children literally die from the absence of this protective and absorbing emotional bond.[9]

However, this primary nurturing relationship isn't instantaneous. Recent surveys have shown that only about half of women feel an immediate sense of love for their babies. Four out of ten first-time mothers recall that their predominant emotion on holding their baby for the first time was indifference. In the huge majority of cases, however, this is replaced by love and affection within a week of delivery. And it should be said that an early lack of affection is often linked to some understandable cause such as difficult labor, unusually large doses of painkillers, or depression that existed before the child was born.[10] If you are a single mother and you don't "feel" especially thrilled to be a mom each and every day, hold on. The feelings of love will return. In many cases, all you need is a nap or a brief break from your 24/7 responsibilities.

Hints for Raising a Waffle

When Bill and I were newlyweds, Bill was in youth ministry and he was discipling a group of four freshman football players. One day they were at our apartment for Bible study. I was in our bedroom, studying, and the noise from the kitchen and living room kept getting louder and louder. Soon I heard a loud *crash* as if something had broken. I dashed out to see a football being flung across the living room to a wide receiver directly in front of my glass shelves!

I gasped. Then coughed. The air smelled like a locker room. And there was so much gas in the room, I was afraid if I lit a match, we'd all go up in a blaze of glory! I threw my hands over my face like a gas mask and headed in, ducking under the football passes and grabbing Bill's arm. As I arrived in the kitchen, I was greeted by a belching contest. I took my hands off my face long enough to whisper in Bill's ear, "Can I talk to you for a minute?" He was laughing and said, "Sure."

"Honey! What's going on?" I asked. "Can't you get them to stop?"

"Stop what?"

"Honey, those are glass shelves. Someone might get hurt if they broke—"

"Oh, that won't happen, Brian has great hands!"

"What!" I could see I was losing on that front so I tried a different tactic. "Bill it smells in here! And those boys are *belching!*"

"Okay, okay, I'll take care of it—but Pam, they're just being guys," Bill said. My Bill, who I thought was a totally refined man straight off the pages of *Gentleman's Quarterly,* was condoning—or at least tolerating—this barbaric behavior!

Disgusted, I threw up my hands, turned on my heels, and headed straight back to my feminine haven. On my way I muttered, "Then I never want to have boys!!!"

By now in the book, you may have guessed it—I am the mother of three sons, and *I love it!* I have a whole new appreciation for male contributions to society. In fact, I have become nearly helpless when my males are away from home. Their brute strength carries all my groceries and my books, moves my furniture, and builds whatever I think needs building. In fact, last year when they were all away from home on a father-son trip, I thought, *Wow, I have the house all to myself! I'll reorganize and decorate!"* I promptly bought a computer armoire and two bookcases that required some assembly. How hard can it be? It's just following directions, right? *Wrong!*

First, the young man at the store loaded the three heavy boxes in my van, and on the way home I realized I didn't have anyone home to unload them! I had to borrow my friend's two sons who lived up the street. After all the boxes were inside and I began to assemble them, I quickly realized I wasn't strong enough to move the pieces, hold them, and put them into place. It took me five days to assemble three pieces of furniture my men could have whipped together in a matter of hours!

I have come to depend on my guys to set the VCR and my radio alarm and to program my computer. Yes, the fuel for these handsome men is costly—three athletic sons can really put away the food—but it's so worth it to have four knights in shining armor to rescue Mom at the drop of a hat! They all love being servants and heroes—and in today's world, we need a few more heroes.

But Boys Need Help Too

Boys are much more likely than girls, however, to have discipline problems at school and to be diagnosed with attention deficit disorder (ADD). Boys far outnumber girls in special-education classes. They're also more likely to commit violent crimes and end up in jail.[11]

Michael Gurian, author of *The Wonder of Boys,* says one of the new insights we're gaining about boys is a very old one: boys will be boys. "They are who they are," says Gurian, "and we need to love them for who they are. Let's not try to rewire them."

Indirectly, boys are benefiting from all the research done on girls, especially the landmark work by Harvard University's Carol Gilligan. Her 1982 book, *In a Different Voice: Psychological Theory and Women's Development,* inspired Take Our Daughters to Work Day along with best-selling spin-offs like Mary Pipher's *Reviving Ophelia.* The traditional, unisex way of looking at child development was profoundly flawed, Gilligan says. "It was like having a one-dimensional perspective on a two-dimensional scene."

Other researchers are studying mental illness and violence in boys. While girls' horizons have been expanding, boys' have narrowed. Boys are often confined to rigid ideas of acceptable male behavior no matter how hard their parents tried to avoid stereotypes. The macho ideal still rules. "We gave boys dolls and they used them as guns," says Gurian. "For 15 years, all we heard was that [gender differences] were all about socialization. Parents who raised their kids through that period said in the end, 'That's not true. Boys and girls can be awfully different.' I think we're awakening to the biological realities and the sociological realities."

But what exactly is the essential nature of boys? Even as infants, boys and girls behave differently. A recent study at Children's Hospital in Boston found that boy babies are more emotionally expressive; girls are more reflective. (That means boy babies tend to cry when they're unhappy; girl babies suck their thumbs.) This could indicate that girls are innately more able to control their emotions. Boys have higher levels of testosterone and lower levels of the neurotransmitter serotonin, which inhibits aggression and impulsivity. That may help explain why more males than females carry through with suicide, become alcoholics, and are diagnosed with ADD. The developmental research on the impact of these physiological differences is still in the embryonic stage, but psychologists are drawing some interesting comparisons between girls and boys.

For girls, the first crisis point often comes in early adolescence. Gilligan and others have found that until then, girls have an enormous capacity for establishing relationships and interpreting emotions. But in their early teens, girls clamp down, squash their emotions, and blunt their insight. Their self-esteem plummets. The first crisis point for boys comes much earlier, researchers now say. "There's an outbreak of symptoms at age 5, 6, 7, just like you see in girls at 11, 12, 13," says Gilligan. Problems at this age include bed-wetting and separation anxiety. "They don't have the language or experience" to articulate it fully, she says, "but the feelings are no less intense."

That's why one of Dr. Gilligan's students, Judy Chu, is studying preschoolers. For girls at this age, Chu says, hugging a parent goodbye "is almost a nonissue." But little boys, who display a great deal of tenderness, soon begin to bury it with "big boy" behavior to avoid being called sissies. "When their parents drop them off, they want to be close and want to be held, but not in front of other people," says Chu. "Even as early as 4, they're already aware of those masculine stereotypes and are negotiating their way around them." But now some researchers think that process is too abrupt. "When boys repress normal feelings like love because of social pressure," says William Pollack, head of the Center for Men at Boston's McLean Hospital and author of *Real Boys*, "they've lost contact with the genuine nature of who they are and what they feel. Boys are in a silent crisis. The only time we notice it is when they pull the trigger." No one is saying that acting like Rambo in nursery school leads directly to tragedies like Jonesboro or Colombine. But researchers do think that boys who are forced to shut down positive emotions are left with only one socially acceptable outlet: anger.

Scientists have known for years that boys and girls develop physically and intellectually at very different rates. Boys' fine motor skills—the ability to hold a pencil, for example—are usually considerably behind girls. They often learn to read later. At the same time, they're much more active—not the best combination for academic advancement.

"Boys feel like school is a game rigged against them," says Michael Thompson, coauthor with Kindlon of *Raising Cain*. "The things at which they excel—gross motor skills, visual and spatial skills, their exuberance—do not find as good a reception in school" as the things girls excel at. Boys (and girls) are also in academic programs at much younger ages than they used to be, increasing the chances that males will be forced to sit still before they are ready. The result for many boys is frustration, says Thompson.

Boys want and need attention, but often just don't know how to ask for it. In a recent national poll, teenagers named their parents as their number-one heroes. Researchers say a strong parental bond is the most important protection against everything from smoking to suicide.[12]

Give Them Words

Because women are much more verbal than men and because women can tap into their emotions easier than most men, one of the biggest favors a parent can do for a son is to raise his vocabulary, especially in the area of learning to express his emotions. One of our three sons was especially nonverbal. His typical answers were vague: "I dunno," "Okay," "uh-huh," "whatever…" But more than anything he'd just shrug his shoulders when asked, "How do you feel? " or "What's wrong, honey?"

Zach had a sensitive heart. He was the one to try to comfort a crying baby, the first one on the scene when a small toddler fell. He spotted the symptoms of my migraines before anyone else in my family, always asking if he could help me. But he couldn't express his own emotions even though he could spot emotion in others.

Knowing that his future wife would want more than grunts and moans, I went to the local teachers' supply store and bought a poster that had rows of circles on it, each circle with a face that depicted a different emotional state. Under each face was a word describing that feeling such as discouraged, stressed, and pensive." Each time I saw Zach's emotions change, I took him to the poster and asked him to point out how he was feeling. Of course, I had to give definitions and descriptions of the words to help him choose an emotion. (Later I discovered a magnet that had many of these faces on it with a movable frame that said, "Today I feel . . ." So each day Zach would move the frame as he came in from school.)

We began playing games to help him learn to express his emotions. I asked him questions: "If how you are feeling right now was an animal, what animal would it be?"

At first, I'd get the typical "I dunno." For example, when he was having a tough time with homework one night, I asked a multiple choice question, "Is it like a bobcat that wants to attack, or a kitten that is mad and cornered, or a cheetah that wants to run away fast, or something else?" I'd act out all the choices with full sound effects. "It's like the cheetah, Mom!" Zach would say, excited because someone was emotionally connecting with him.

"So you feel like running away?"

"Yeah, I guess so."

"Why do you want to run away honey?"

"I dunno."

"Is it because you don't want to do this? Or because you are afraid you aren't going to do it right? Or—"

"That's it, Mom. I don't think I can get it right."

Then we went on to have a good talk about school, about doing the best we can, and about rewards. I pointed out to him that each person in our family has different strengths and weaknesses and that none of us is perfect.

Zach felt freed up emotionally, and the nightly homework struggle we'd been having suddenly came to an end.

Other questions I asked included, "What kind of car would show how you are feeling?" "What kind of food—burnt toast?" Or I would compare a feeling he was currently feeling with something he'd gone through in the past. For example, one day when Zach was eight and taking piano lessons, he sat frozen on the piano bench. I walked through the living room and casually said, "Zach, practice, buddy."

He just sat there. I went over and put my hand on his shoulder. "Zach, play this one. I love this one." I flipped back to a very familiar tune that I knew he had mastered weeks before. Zach shook his head no.

I sat down on the bench next to him. "Zach, you can do this one. I know you can. You've done it lots before."

He shook his head, tears rolling down his cheeks. "Honey, what's wrong? What is it?"

Zach just sat frozen and silent, tears rolling down his face. "Zach what is it? I asked again. "You can do this. Here I'll do it with you." I placed my hand on his and lifted it to the keys. Zach violently pulled his hand back, slamming my hand hard against the wood of the bench.

"Zach!" I said. "You could have hurt Mom or yourself. You don't have to practice right now, but you do have to practice sometime. What you do need to do is tell me what is going on in your head right now."

"I'm stupid!"

"You're not stupid. Why would you say you are?"

"I'm stupid."

"Zach, I'm not going to argue with you. But what I want to know is why you are feeling like you are stupid."

His shoulders shrugged. This went on for a few go-rounds, me saying he wasn't stupid, Zach shrugging his shoulders and wiping his tears. I tried being compassionate, tough, and concerned. I even tried walking away and being as stubborn as he was. "Fine, Zach, sit there. But you will sit there until you practice or until you tell me what's wrong."

I glanced at the clock on the wall. What was supposed to be a half-hour practice session had turned into an hour-and-a-half dead-end argument. I felt like I was beating my head on the wall of Zach's heart. I walked back into the living room, sat down next to Zach, and turned him by the shoulders so we sat face-to-face. I took his chin and held it in my hand.

"Zach, I'm going to be very serious right now. Someday you are going to grow up. You are a smart, talented young man that will someday have a job, get married, and have kids. Zach, if you shut down your emotions, if you won't share what's going on inside you, then your wife will always have her feelings hurt. Right now, my feelings are hurt. I thought you trusted me to help you with your feelings, but you won't share with me. Zach, if you grow up without talking to your wife or your kids, you will be very, very lonely. No one will really know what a really great guy you are down here." I tapped on his heart, "Zach, let us into your heart."

Zach sobbed out loud. "But I will never be as good as Brock at piano, so why should I try?"

"Is *that* what's going on?" I asked. "You think you have to be as good as Brock at the piano? Zach, I don't even care if you end up playing the piano. We just have every son take piano for one year so they can be exposed to music. You never ever have to compare yourself to any of your brothers. You can play any instrument you want. Zach, one thing you can't do, Honey, is stuff your emotions, especially if you are feeling like this."

"Like a failure," Zach sighed.

"Oh, Honey," I said as I wrapped my arms around him, "you will never be a failure as long as you share the wonderful Zach that's in here." I tapped on his heart again. "You have a great heart. You don't have to be anyone other than yourself. Promise me that anytime you feel frozen, you will tell me. And to make it easy, if you feel like you're frozen, like you want to try but are afraid you might fail, just call it your 'piano feeling,' okay?"

"Okay, Mom."

Still to this day, six years later, Zach will whisper to me, "Mom, pray for me. I have that 'piano feeling' again." His confidence has grown; he rarely gets that "piano feeling," but when he does, he now has the ability to articulate exactly what it is. Recently he said, "Mom, I'm excited about going to high school. I think I would like to be someone who helps other people…you know, like Dad does. Maybe I'll be a counselor—a Christian counselor. I want to help people with their emotions and feelings. I want to help them so they don't feel afraid of life. Mom, they have classes for that in high school don't they? Psychology? Right?"

Hints for Understanding Your Noodling Daughter

The best thing you can do for your daughter is to listen to her. I (Pam) was always amazed when our next-door neighbor, Shannon, would come over to play with my youngest, Caleb. Shannon chatted and chatted, following me from room to room, barely stopping to breathe. As the parents of sons, we're not used to that many words.

Because we have not raised a daughter, we can only share from what we have seen in the young women we have worked with in our ministry. What is obvious from our observation is that girls need to talk their way through life. They process life verbally. They figure out what good friends are like by talking about their experiences. They learn how to respond to hurts, disappointments, and opportunity by talking. They guide their own emotions through interaction.

Physical touch is also important to daughters. Kind, encouraging, appropriate touching releases endorphins in the body. Endorphins are chemicals in the human body that make people "feel" better. When a daughter has loving, respectful physical contact with a parent, she "feels" better about whatever she's doing. By demonstrating consistent affection, parents help their daughters associate good feelings with good activities. For example, when endorphins are released during a conversation with you, conversations with you feel good to your daughter. When decisions are accompanied with reassuring touch, decision making is seen as a good thing. When conflict is worked out and concludes with a hug, resolving conflict will be seen as a positive. Reinforce positive elements in your daughter's life by accompanying them with good touch. One family expert captured the essence of great parenting with these words: "The child should spend a substantial amount of time with somebody who's crazy about him [or her]."

Differences in Parenting

What if Mom, the spaghetti, has a different opinion than Dad, the waffle, on what is best for the kids?

Bill and I have a regular weekly meeting to go over family business, scheduling, and other matters that arise. By staying close and communicating often, there are fewer parenting disagreements that come up. But sometimes there *are* disagreements, and when those happen, we try to use the same communication tools that we would use to talk over any other issue. There is one difference: Bill brings an advantage in our family of all boys—he was one!

However, because I can often see all the baggage and strings attached to any decision, I will share them with Bill to get his opinion on the topic from a male perspective.

Having some resource people of the opposite sex will help you parent your child. My (Pam's) parents divorced when I was 18, my sister was 16, and my brother was 15. Wisely, my mother moved to be near her parents so Bret would gain time with his grandfather. However, she also gained other resources: fathers of Bret's friends, coaches, and a pastor—all who were available to offer perspective. Then I met and married Bill, and my mom gained my husband as an ally in helping to positively influence

Bret. It's important to have mentors who can give you insight into your children. It's even more important when you're a single parent because you don't have a built-in sounding board—you have to build them in yourself.

Understanding a child of the opposite sex can be a challenge. A few years ago, when Brock was a freshman, he was captain of the J.V. men's volleyball team at his high school. One day, I picked him up from practice and noticed he was upset. Bill and I have stressed anger management and self-control with our boys, so it's rare when any of them show visible reactions of anger. But Brock got in the car and with a clinched fist slammed his own leg and said, "I am so mad!" He went on to explain that during practice there was a contest. Players were matched up into teams of two, and the winning team won a big chocolate chip cookie. Brock, the best player on the team, was paired with a poor player, and he lost the contest.

I tried my mother's logic first, "Honey, you know it was just a motivational tool. He still knows you're a great volleyball player."

"Mom, I know coach knows I am a committed player. It's not that."

"Well, you aren't letting this attack your self-image as a player are you? It was just a game."

"Just a game!" Now Brock was agitated at me! "Mom, you just don't get it!"

"Well, tell me then!"

"I wanted to win."

"Honey, I'll get you a cookie!"

"Mom! It's not about the cookie!"

"Then what is it about? Your fragile male ego?"

Brock shot me a glare, and I knew I was right and it was the wrong thing to say! The next day, wanting to cheer Brock up, I brought him a chocolate cookie after practice with a card that said, "I think you're a winner!"

Brock opened the card and said, "Mom, thank you so much. Your heart is in the right place, but you still don't get it. Ask Dad about it—I think he could explain it better. I don't want to hurt your feelings. Thanks for the cookie, Mom."

So I asked Bill after explaining the entire cookie incident. He told me, "Pam, it *was* about ego. For a teen boy, winning is everything. Winning reflects his self-image. Teen boys are always jockeying to be at the top of the pile. Brock, being a good athlete, saw a chance to be recognized as a winner, and he wanted it—"

"But it was just a cookie! The coach and all the players already know Brock is the best on the team. Brock even knows it. What's all the fuss over a cookie?"

"It's not the cookie—it's the winning. He probably would have even given the cookie away—and that's just it—"

"So should I be worried about Brock being angry that he didn't win? He looked really steamed. You should have seen him!"

"I'll talk with him again and remind him of our standards of self-control, but you don't have anything to worry about. He's normal. He has terrific self-control and composure on and off the field, so I'm sure even Brock has realized he overreacted. But expect to see him that competitive again. It's one of the reasons he's MVP of every team he plays on. He's competitive. He gives 110 percent and I wouldn't want to change that. It's cookies now, but it'll be bonuses and perks later on in business."

"You're right," I admitted. "I want him to fight for what's right. I don't want to take the heart out of him. When he gets married and things get tough I want that competitive spirit to kick in and help him fight *for* his marriage and family. When college and his career come and life isn't handed to him on a silver platter, I want him to be assertive and motivated."

"Now you're getting it."

I shared my conversation with Bill the next day with Brock. "Mom, you're right in that I need to control my temper—

always. But Dad was right-on about the cookie. I want to win in life. And Dad is right—I want to channel that winning spirit into things that are good for my future and my future family."

"I'll make you a deal, Brock."

"What?"

"You keep competing 100 percent, but keep your self-control. And I'll keep buying you chocolate chip cookies and cheering you on—okay?"

Cheering them on—that's your goal as a single parent. You want your children to believe you are on their team. One day, Caleb was playing third base when he was knocked down to the ground by a line drive. The coaches ran to the field, and I was on their heels. We all wanted to know if Caleb was okay. When I reached him, he was still on the ground, struggling to breathe.

"Caleb, can you breathe? Caleb, can you breathe?" I asked in a self-imposed calm that barely covered my panic.

Caleb nodded his head in the affirmative. Then he raised up on his elbows.

"Caleb, do you want Momma to pray for you?"

He shook his head no, jumped up, dusted himself off, ran back to third base, and finished out the game.

It was the final inning, so after the game, I ran Caleb to the hospital just to make sure he was all right. While waiting for the doctor, I asked Caleb about the incident.

"Caleb, honey, usually when you are afraid or hurt, you want Momma to pray for you. How come you didn't want Mom to pray today?"

"I did," Caleb answered, "but you never asked."

"Sure I did." Then I recounted the course of events.

"Oh, I thought you said 'play for me'!" Caleb replied.

Caleb was so convinced I was on his team, he thought I was going to don his uniform and be his sub! May your children and mine always be so convinced of our love for them!

Courses for Waffles:

1. You Too Can Do Housework

2. PMS—Learn When to Keep Your Mouth Shut

3. Get a Life—Learn to Cook

4. How Duct Tape or Flowers Can Fix Almost Anything

5. How to Put Down a Toilet Seat (formerly called, No It's Not a Bidet)

6. The Remote Control—Overcoming Your Dependency

7. The Weekend and Sports Are Not Synonymous

8. Surviving the Rhetorical Questions (formerly titled, Honey, Do I Look Fat?)

9. Coming to Compromise: We Forget Birthdays—You Forget Sports Stats. We're Even, Right?

10. Timing Romance: How to Give a Compliment During a Commercial Break

A Few Classes for Spaghettis:

1. Silence, the Final Frontier: Where No Woman Has Gone Before

2. You Too Can Shop in Less than Four Hours

3. Man Management: Minor Household Chores Can Wait till After the Game

Advanced class: Superbowl: A Sacrament, Not Just a Game

4. Communication Skills I: Tears—The Last Resort, Not the First

5. Cooking: Bran and Tofu Are Not for Human Consumption

6. Compliments: Accepting Them Gracefully

7. PMS (Poor Me Syndrome): Your Problem…Not His Sessions; PMS: Happened Since Puberty—Deal with It; Gaining Five Pounds vs. the End of the World: A Study in Contrasts

8. Dancing: Why Men Don't Like To

9. Classic Clothing: Wearing Outfits You Already Have

10. Telephone Translations: Formerly titled Me Too = I Love You (And Other Men-Speak)

Extra Credit classes:

For women:
 Are You Ready to Leave? A Definition of the Word "Yes"

For men:
 75 Ways to Say I'm Sorry

Hot heads and cold hearts
never solved anything.

—BILLY GRAHAM

God Loves Waffles and Spaghetti

Why are men and women so different from each other? How did men and women come to see life from different points of view? The simple answer is that God made us this way.

At the very beginning of the Bible, God proclaims the height of His creative work when he says, "Let us make man in our image...So God created man in his own image...male and female he created them" (Genesis 1:26-27). Each of us carries in himself or herself a portion of the image of God, who has all the characteristics of men and women in their perfect state. In His divine love, God has chosen to share His life and joy with us by creating us in His image.

If this is true, the obvious question is, Why isn't the plan working better? Why are men and women so clueless about one another? Why is there so much conflict and disappointment in relationships? The answer is also found in Genesis. Adam and Eve chose to follow their own ways rather than the instructions of the one who made them. God gave the first waffle and the first spaghetti a choice so that His relationship with them would be freely chosen and sincerely pursued. God wanted not robots but people—living, breathing, feeling, thinking, acting people. So he gave them a choice, and they chose poorly. And so do we.

Ever since that fateful day in the Garden, relationships have been awkward. Notice the strain that was immediately caused in Adam's relationship with God.

> But the Lord God called to the man, "Where are you?"
>
> And he said, "I heard you in the garden, and I was afraid because I was naked; so I hid" (Genesis 3:9-10).

And we have been afraid ever since. We are afraid of intimacy and we are afraid of being alone. We are afraid of success and we are afraid of failure. We are afraid of not being noticed and we are afraid of being the center of attention. And so we hide. We hide from opportunity. We hide from friends. We hide from healthy interaction with the opposite sex, and we hide from God.

The variety of creation mixes with the corruption of the human soul and makes some very interesting results. Our needs are much more intense and sensitive than they were ever intended to be. Our needs were intended to make our relationships rich and satisfying. Men were created with the ability to meet some of a woman's needs, and women were created with the ability to meet some of a man's needs. And then it happened. The fall of mankind made these needs fragile, unpredictable, and relentless. They are never fully satisfied and always looking for as much attention as possible. This is easiest to illustrate by looking at the most common needs men and women experience.

Questions of Security

Security is the typical woman's most pervasive need. She longs to know that life is safe. She wants to be assured of physical safety, financial safety, social safety, and emotional safety. She doesn't mean to be unreasonable about this, but it's a constant need for her to know she's secure around important people in her life. To build confidence, she continually asks questions in her heart to confirm that her security is intact.

The strategy for giving answers to these questions is simple in concept and complicated in practice: *Look for a woman's need for security first, and the related issues become manageable.* Always address the security first! A man who keeps this in mind will find that most issues can be discussed with a woman in a sane and logical fashion. If, however, he doesn't get this one right, he'll be left with an intricate web of conversation to try to untangle. The issue will become so layered and will change so many times that he will get lost in the discussion. The interaction will be completely void of the kind of logic men understand. He will conclude that women are illogical, irrational, and unreasonable as she beats him to a pulp with her overpowering skills of conversation. He thinks she's being impossible when in truth she's checking to see if her relationship with him is secure. Because this desire to have security is a pervasive need in her life, she asks internal questions that motivate her behavior:

Question #1: Am I More Important than Money?

She knows that money is important, and she deeply respects those who make and manage money well. But inside her heart she wants to know that she's more valuable to someone than his or her money. When her friends are willing to spend money on her, she gets the message and the message feels good. When her parents spend money on her, she gets the message and it feels good. And when a man spends money on her, she gets the message and it feels good. It may appear that she's spoiled, but money is merely the vehicle that delivers security to her heart.

Some might ask why. This is an emotional need, and emotions do not run on logic. They're designed to be expressed, and that is really all they do. When emotional needs come to the surface, they demand expression and often complicate our lives. The key is to acknowledge these needs with compassion. When emotional needs are acknowledged and compassionately accepted, they are fulfilled and quickly soften.

In romance, a woman asks this question on a regular basis. When a man deliberately spends money on a woman to communicate to her that she's valuable to him, he reaches straight to her heart. When, on the other hand, he spends money on her to manipulate her or to get something from her, she feels ripped off and used. She feels no more important than a dishrag.

Question #2: Are You Being Sincere?

"Pam, you look great!" I said, thinking I was saying the right thing. I had noticed Pam was feeling self-conscious, and I was hoping to help her feel better about herself.

Her response was, "You're just saying that so I will be easier to be around. You don't really mean it."

It drives me crazy when women do this. We men don't always know the right things to say, and we're hoping that what we say will be accepted. Not only do women want men to have good intentions, they also want us to be sincere at all times. We men should not take this too personally because women also expect this from each other.

Sincerity connects to security because it's linked to trust. Because everything in a woman's life is connected to everything else, trust is an all-or-nothing prospect for her. If a woman trusts you, she trusts you with everything in her life. If she doesn't trust you, she trusts you with nothing. When she opens her heart in one area, all the other areas of her life follow. If she's confident that you're sincere, she will believe you are telling the truth. If you're telling the truth, you can be trusted. If she thinks you are just flattering her with your words, she will feel she's setting herself up to be hurt.

I don't believe that women have this struggle intentionally. They're often aware that they're overstating the need for sincerity but they can't turn it off until they're confident your responses are from your heart.

Sincerity isn't just about words, however. The gifts we give also must be delivered with sincerity. Often it's when we have the least money that our friends will believe we have the most sincerity.

Question #3: Do You Notice Me?

Every woman wants to be noticed. She wants to believe that she's special in her own way. This is another reason that conversation is important to her. She wants to believe her words are important and attractive. She's captivated with people who are interested in the way she thinks.

She especially wants you to notice if she's stressed. However, most men need some clues to know just how stressed she is!

My husband, Bill, has trained my sons to respond appropriately to my stress, but I have to help them. One day I was running late to catch a plane. Bill and I had a tight schedule. I was speaking at a retreat, and he was preaching at church. We were to rendezvous at our home at about 2 P.M. My retreat ran late, so I called Bill's cell phone and said, "Honey, I'm running late. Can I ask you to do a few things for me?"

Bill responded with, "Well, Pam, I have some good news and some not-so-good news. The good news is, I love you. The bad news is I'm 30 minutes away from our house, waiting for the tow truck to pick up Brock's car. So there are a few things I need you to do for me."

Now my list had doubled and my time was cut in half. I walked in and only Zach, our 15-year-old son, was home. I ran in and rattled off my dilemma and all the things I wanted him to do to help. (Mistake #1: Never assign verbal lists to young men. Write each task on individual square sticky notes!) I ran into my office and then my bedroom, frantically gathering what I needed. As I passed through the living room, Zach was still slowly moving toward accomplishing task number one. I wanted to scream at him, but he didn't cause this stress, and even if he did, he didn't cause my reaction. I needed to choose my emotional response. So I chose to clue Zach in.

"Zach, remember how Mom and Dad explain the way men and women process life? I'm spaghetti, and right now the spaghetti pot is boiling over and there's going to be a pasta explosion! My noodles are ready to fly all over the place!"

"Oh, sorry, Mom," Zach answered. "Why didn't you tell me it was that pasta thing?"

Then he said what Bill has trained him to say and did what Bill trained him to do. He walked over, gave me a hug and said, "Mom, what can I do to help you right now?" I felt loved because I knew Zach noticed.

Too often we set men up for failure. We expect them to notice our thoughts even if we haven't shared them. We expect them to just "know" what we want for gifts or what we want romantically. This is unfair. They will be better at noticing if we give them the information they need. We'll get our feelings hurt less often if we communicate with them.

Another way that we express our need to be noticed—and test men unfairly—is by fishing for compliments.

"Do you notice anything different about me?" we ask.

Doesn't this question send chills up and down your spine? Guys have had more opportunities to crash and burn on this question than any other. We even see great people in the Bible fishing for compliments. In the Song of Songs 2:1-2 King Solomon's bride prods him with the following words, "I am a rose of Sharon, a lily of the valleys."

The rose of Sharon and the lily of the valley were the most common flowers growing on the hills around her parents' farm. What she's saying is, "I'm just a plain country girl. There's nothing special about me. How could you, a king, choose someone like me who lacks any real beauty?" To say the least, she's feeling insecure. If Solomon agrees with her, he might as well make reservations for the doghouse!

But his response is remarkable. "Like a lily among thorns is my darling among the maidens." Oh my goodness, how did he come up with that on the spur of the moment? He looked her in the eyes and said, "Compared to you all the other women in the world are thorns and you are the single flower!"

We know her heart melted because her response is, "Like an apple tree among the trees of the forest is my lover among the young men." When is the last time you saw an apple tree in the forest? She's letting him know that there has never been a man like him before because he hit the target of her heart dead center.

When a guy notices, there is a big payoff.

Questions of Simplicity

Women ask questions of security because everything in their entire life is connected. Everything impacts everything else, so she's more prone to feel that things are out of control. Men have a corresponding characteristic in their lives. Because men compartmentalize life and have a problem-solving bent to life, they're drawn to the boxes where they think they can succeed. In fact, men only like to go to boxes where they can perform well. If a man is good at communication, he likes that box. If he's not good at conversation, he prefers to avoid it. If he's good at making money, he gives his career lots of attention. If he's good at projects, he fills his life with projects. If he's lazy, he will look for ways to be lazy, and so on.

As a result of this pursuit of success, men like to keep life as simple as possible. The simpler life is, the fewer boxes he has to deal with. It's an emotional need in a man's life to seek simplicity. When things get complicated, he becomes unmotivated. He begins to detach himself from some of his boxes so he can simplify life to a level he can deal with.

So what are the questions men ask to keep their lives simple enough to succeed?

Question #1: Will Life with You Be Filled with Admiration?

Because men love to succeed, they drink up compliments like babies devour milk. The cousin to compliments is flirting. When a woman flirts with a man, the box he happens to be in at the moment ignites with enthusiasm. She may think she's playing a game, but he knows that the way to a man's heart is not food, it's flirting. Food fills his stomach, but compliments from the woman he loves fill his soul with confidence.

Think about it. One of the most common phrases in our world today is "You' the man!" Men love to hear it, and men love to say it to one another. It makes them laugh, and it makes them stand a little taller.

It's frightening to the typical man how the compliments of a woman will energize him. It's equally unnerving how her negative assessments set him back. I have reluctantly come to the conclusion that God made a man to be responsive to the words of important women in his life. Their compliments give him confidence, their flirting makes him feel sexy, their suggestions motivate him to change.

Another preacher had just finished his sermon, and he was greeting people at the door as they were leaving. One young lady in the congregation enthusiastically shook his hand and while holding on to it said, "Pastor, I believe you are one of the truly great preachers in our country."

On the drive home, his wife noticed that he was introspective with a rather contented smile on his face. She couldn't help but ask about his obvious satisfaction. He explained to her what had happened and what the young lady in the congregation had said.

The two of them rode in silence for another 15 minutes when she asked him, "What are you thinking?"

He hesitated, broke out in a sly smile and said, "I was just wondering how many truly great preachers there are in this country."

She took a quick look at him, leaned over and whispered in his ear, "One less than you think."

Question #2: Will Life with You Be Free from Complications?

Men are drawn to success like moths to the light. Because a man loves to be thought of as a hero and to do the things he's good at, he gets overwhelmed when life becomes too complicated. This usually causes either frustration or confusion for the women who know him. While the man is focused on the areas he can succeed at, she's processing her entire life. She sees her needs, the needs of her family, her financial needs, her vacation plans, and her hopes for her best friends all at the same time. While he's trying to simplify his life, she's feeling like he's blind to many of the important areas of life. This being the case, there are a number of things that a woman can do that will cause her male friends to want to spend more time with her.

Avoid unrealistic expectations. It's natural for a man to want women to be happy with him. He likes it when a woman he loves is happy with his input and performance. He feels very good about himself when she smiles and says, "Thank you." Her appreciation motivates him more intensely than he ever wants her to understand. If, on the other hand, her expectations are beyond his ability, his available time, or his financial potential, he instantly feels like a failure and loses motivation to do *any* of what she has asked of him.

Avoid interpreting men's statements and actions as if they have a deeper meaning. Since men love simplicity, they would never dream of harboring complicated thoughts. When they are quiet, it's because they're not thinking about anything. They sit the way they do because it's comfortable for them. They are often naive in relationships and lack the understanding of the complexities of interpersonal interaction. They do not look for ways to complicate their friendships. When you read into his actions, he becomes confused, wondering how you could have ever come up with your conclusion. It only takes a few of these misunderstandings before he loses interest in spending more time with you.

Clue him in to unreasonable arguments. Each man likes to be an expert in a few areas of life, and he loves to be asked for his opinion. He falls into this problem-solving mode as easily as a new car starts when you turn the ignition key. When a conversation starts between a man and a woman, he immediately assumes the problem-solving role. This is an awesome trait when a logical answer is required. But when the conversation is for the purpose of visiting or releasing emotional energy, there is no answer to be sought because there is no real problem. Often a woman just wants to talk because she is feeling more emotions than she can calmly control. If a man will listen calmly, she will release the emotions and reconnect to the stability of her life. If he will not listen calmly but works hard to finish the conversation with questions such as, "What are you talking about? Is this conversation going anywhere?" the emotional stress builds up inside her.

Because a man falls into this role so easily, it's helpful for him if the women in his life will clue him in before they start talking. If she says, "I can tell I am pretty emotional, and I just need you to listen to me," he knows how to succeed, and he will be more willing to interact. If she assumes he understands her needs and she just starts talking, he will assume there is a problem, he will start to form answers, he will miss the point, he will get confused by her anger at his sincere attempts to help her and the turmoil will intensify.

Stay amused with their easy boxes. Men need easy boxes to relax in. They are a little like rechargeable batteries. When you put a battery into a flashlight or some other electronic device, it wears down as it powers the device. When it wears down, it needs to be put in the charger. While it's in the charger, it appears to be doing nothing. It's not active, and it's not working to make anything happen. But it's getting recharged. When men produce in life, they wear down. When men engage in conversation, they wear down. When men dispense advice, they wear down. As a result, they need to recharge their batteries, and it frustrates most women to watch men recharge. The women who encourage these easy boxes where men can comfortably recharge cause men to want to be their friends.

Question #3: Will Life with You Be Lived in the Present?

Men like to live in one box at a time, so they tend to focus on the present. They don't remember details of their past as readily as women because they don't create as many emotional attachments to the events of their past. Men want to preserve the dignity of the present.

A man hopes the past won't haunt him forever. Every man makes mistakes. He puts his foot in his mouth and often offends others. He says things he wishes he hadn't said, and he doesn't say things he wishes he had.

Men long for success in the same way that women long for security. Men want to do everything in which they can succeed and very little of what they fall short in. They are attracted to everything women do that make them feel successful. Women want to feel safe in all areas of their lives, and they are attracted to everything men do to make them feel secure.

Don't Just Talk About It, Be About It

How do men and women ensure that these needs don't get out of their control? Human history is replete with stories of people of both genders who have given their hearts to another only to be disappointed or devastated. We have taken the most important needs of our lives and entrusted them to fallible, inconsistent, selfish people.

God has a better way to get these needs met. He has offered to let each of us have a personal relationship with Him that will meet these needs more effectively than any other.

God offers to every woman in the world the security she longs for. She is so valuable that God gave His only Son to die in her place. You never have to worry about God not being sincere because He always tells the truth. He is the one person who always notices you. He thinks you are special and has given you everything that pertains to life and godliness. When you ask Jesus to come into your life, He adopts you into His family. He listens to everything you want to say to Him. He is never too busy to stop and pay attention to you. He has promised to give you the desires of your heart if you delight in Him (Psalm 37:4). Jesus will meet the security needs of your heart if you give Him a chance. Then you can have relationships with other people that enhance your life rather than make you vulnerable to others. But He will only give it to you *if you ask.*

God offers every man the opportunity to have the simple life He longs for. When you ask Him to come into your heart, He begins a new adventure with you. He tells us, "Come to me, all you who are weary and burdened, and I will give you rest…for my yoke is easy and my burden is light" (Matthew 11:28-30). He will forgive you for all the mistakes of the past so that each day can be lived in the present. He can remove your sins as far away from you as the east is from the west. This is equivalent to a never-ending distance. If you travel on the equator due west you will never begin traveling east. On the other hand, if you start at the South Pole and you head due north, you will begin heading south as soon as you pass the North Pole. The point is God wants to meet you in the present, not make you feel bad about your past. Also, when you invite Him into your life, He adopts you into the family and He becomes your greatest fan in life. He will simply love you. He will simply guide you into your purpose in life. He will simply take you on the greatest adventure you have ever encountered. But He will only do it *if you ask.*

The Secret Ingredient

The secret ingredient in a recipe is always that special something that makes the food taste so good, so out of the ordinary. When people sense there's something special in a recipe, they probe a little and ask, "Hey, what's in this?" Bill and I have been asked that question for more than 22 years. People have asked us how we stay in love, how our lives stay fresh and strong. People ask us for the secret ingredient all the time.

You see, true intimacy involves risk—a risk to open ourselves up and share; a risk to connect our life to another and share; a risk to care, to connect, to accept one another; and a huge risk to sacrifice and serve. Where can this strength and courage to plunge in and risk to build a relationship come from? It is a strength that is more than any one person can carry off—it requires supernatural strength. The strength God can give to a relationship isn't really so secret because God wants us to know Him and the strength He gives. How can a person tap into God's strength? How can you receive God's love for your own life? Read God's statement of love for you, and simply receive God's gift of love in prayer.

God's Statement of Love to Us

• *I love you and have a plan for you.*

I came to give life—life in all its fullness (John 10:10 NCV).

I came so they can have real and eternal life, more and better life than they ever dreamed of (John 10:10 THE MESSAGE).

For God loved the world so much that he gave his only Son…so that whoever believes in him may not be lost, but have eternal life (John 3:16 NCV).

• *I know you are imperfect, so you are separated from My love. Our relationship is broken.*

All people have sinned and are not good enough for God's glory (Romans 3:23 NCV).

…we've compiled this long and sorry record as sinners…and proved that we are utterly incapable of living the glorious lives God wills for us… (Romans 3:23 THE MESSAGE).

And when a person knows the right thing to do but does not do it, then he is sinning (James 4:17 NCV).

It is your evil that has separated you from your God. Your sins cause him to turn away from you (Isaiah 59:2 NIV).

- *I love you. I, who am perfect, paid the price for your imperfection so I could restore our relationship.*

But Christ died for us while we were still sinners. In this way God shows his great love for us. We have been made right with God by Christ's blood [death]. So through Christ we will surely be saved from God's anger. I mean that while we were God's enemies, God made friends with us through the death of his Son. Surely, now we are God's friends, God will save us through his Son's life (Romans 5:8-10 NCV).

Christ had no sin. But God made him become sin. God did this for us so that in Christ we could become right with God (2 Corinthians 5:21 NCV).

Christ himself died for you. And that one death paid for your sins. He was not guilty, but he died for those who are guilty. He did this to bring you all to God (1 Peter 3:18 NCV).

The greatest love a person can show is to die for his friends (John 15:13 NCV).

- *To initiate this new relationship, all you need to do is to accept My payment for your imperfection. I cannot make you love Me; that is your choice.*

I mean that you are saved by grace, and you got that grace by believing. You did not save yourselves. It was a gift from God. No! You are not saved by what you have done...God has made us what we are. In Christ Jesus, God made us new people… (Ephesians 2:8-10 NCV).

If you use your mouth to say, "Jesus is Lord," and if you believe in your heart that God raised Jesus from death, then you will be saved (Romans 10:9 NCV).

And this is eternal life: that they know you, the only true God, and Jesus Christ, the One you sent (John 17:3 NCV).

To accept God's love for you, talk to Him and tell Him whatever you feel necessary. Let Him lead the decision-making part of your life. Here is a sample prayer:

Jesus, I am sorry I have chosen to live apart from You. I want You in my life. I accept the payment of love You gave for me by Your death on the cross. Thank You for being my Best Friend and my God.

Bill and I have seen in our own lives and in the lives of countless others that the source and strength to love springs from the love God first gives us. We sign all of our books with the same verse that sums up the secret of all relationships: *We love because he first loved us* (1 John 4:19).

SPAGHETTI
WAFFLES

What Gender is Santa Claus?

I think Santa Claus is a woman. I hate to be the one to defy sacred myth, but I believe he's a she. Think about it. Christmas is a big, organized, warm, fuzzy, nurturing, social deal, and I have a tough time believing a guy could possibly pull it all off!

For starters, the vast majority of men don't even think about selecting gifts until Christmas Eve. Once at the mall, they always seem surprised to find only Ronco products, socket wrench sets, and mood rings left on the shelves. On this count alone, I'm convinced Santa is a woman.

Surely, if he were a man, everyone in the universe would wake up Christmas morning to find a rotating musical Chia Pet under the tree, still in the bag.

Another problem for a he-Santa would be getting there. First of all, there would be no reindeer because they would all be dead, gutted, and strapped on to the rear bumper of the sleigh amid wide-eyed, desperate claims that buck season had been extended. Blitzen's rack would already be on the way to the taxidermist. Even if the male Santa *did* have reindeer, he'd still have transportation problems because he would inevitably get lost up there in the snow and clouds and then refuse to stop and ask for directions.

Other reasons why Santa can't possibly be a man:

- Men can't pack a bag.

- Men would rather be dead than caught wearing red velvet.

- Men's masculinity would be threatened being seen with all those elves.

- Men don't answer their mail.

- Men would refuse to allow their physique to be described, even in jest, as anything remotely resembling a "bowl full of jelly."

- Men aren't interested in stockings unless somebody's wearing them.

- Having to do the Ho-Ho-Ho thing would seriously inhibit their ability to pick up women.

- Finally, being responsible for Christmas would require a commitment.

I can buy the fact that other mythical holiday characters are men:

- Father Time shows up once a year, unshaven and looking ominous—definite guy.

- Cupid flies around carrying weapons.

- Uncle Sam is a politician who likes to point fingers.

Any one of these individuals could pass the testosterone-screening test. But not St. Nick. Not a chance.

Discussion Questions for Small Groups

The more you speak the truth, the more strength the truth gains in your life. By being a part of a small group that discusses this book, you will gain friendships, wisdom, and encouragement. Please use the questions below as small group discussion prompts, topics for lunch discussions with a friend or friends, or even topics to discuss on a date.

Basics for good discussion groups:

- *Be personal.* Greet each person as he or she comes. Try to provide an icebreaker question (the answers to these can be written on their name tags to enhance dialogue).

  - What's the worst pickup line you have heard?

  - How do you answer the question, "Why aren't you married?"

  - If you were going to write a book for singles, what would you title it?

  - What qualities do you look for in a best friend?

- *Be early.* Have the room set up for easy conversation. Simple drinks (coffee, tea, water) and food are nice. Set up chairs in a circle. Fresh flowers and soft instrumental music are nice additions.

- *Be prompt.* Begin and end on time—childcare is often an issue. Feel free to end the meeting, but allow couples who want to stay to do so.

- *Be available* between sessions for quick questions, prayer, and encouragement.

- *Be a leader.* Don't put anyone on the spot, and try to keep everyone involved. You may need to say things like, "That was a great response—any one else have any input?" Then look the more reserved people eye-to-eye. To handle someone who dominates the group, you can say, "Before Gary shares, does anyone else have an answer/idea?" Or simply don't look at the dominator until you have scanned the crowd for other answers and input. If the person is very dominating, pull him or her aside individually and privately and say something like, "Joe, you are so quick thinking and your input is very valuable, but because you are so confident, others who are more reserved may not be sharing as much. Could you do me a favor, and help me draw them out? Maybe count to five in your head before responding, or if you sense another group member might have something to share, look their way. I sense you are a natural leader, so I could use your help on this." Most people feel complimented and will respond positively.

- *Be creative.* Go on a fun group date to a theater or miniature golfing. Have a group picnic or end-of-series dinner party. Give door prizes and funny awards, or host a game show. Fun ideas will model creativity in relationships. Give your group plenty of time to interact.

• *Be spiritual.* It's always appropriate to open and close a gathering in prayer. You can pray, invite them to pray with one or two others, pray conversationally as a group, or ask for a volunteer to pray.

• *Be assertive.* If a group for singles doesn't exist in your area, call several pastors, ask for names of singles in their church, and tell them you want to create a community-wide group for singles and would like to talk with a few key singles from their congregation. Invite them to an informational meeting, and ask them to bring a few friends if they'd like. Ask the group if they'd be willing to meet for ten weeks. Use this book and the small group questions as a small-group training guide to get to know each other better. You may decide as a group to invite friends and lead them through this material. (The group becomes group leaders.)

Chapter 1: Male and Female He Created Them

"Let us make man in our image, in our likeness....So God created man in his own image, in the image of God he created him; male and female he created them" (Genesis 1:26-27).

1. What are some apparent differences between the genders that you noticed as a part of your life before you read this chapter?

2. Aside from the obvious anatomical differences in our bodies, how are men and women different?

- in the way they use their time

- in the way they use their money

- in the way they parent

- in the way they approach their careers

- in the way they want to use free time

- in the way they approach God

3. In what ways do you relate to the analogy that men are like waffles, women are like spaghetti?

4. What are the benefits you can see of God creating us male and female?

5. What new information did you learn in this chapter that you think will benefit your life?

Chapter 2: Don't Overcook Communication

1. How will what you learned in this chapter impact the way you communicate with those of the opposite sex?

2. What changes do you think you should make to better relate to those of the opposite gender?

3. Why do you think conversing with the opposite sex can be such a challenge?

4. What are the most difficult kinds of topics or kinds of conversations to have with the opposite gender? As a group, can you think of any way to make these kinds of conversations easier or work out better?

5. What kind of words should we use when talking with one another? Read the verses below and see if you gain any wisdom on your vocabulary and use of words in your relationships:

- Philippians 4:8

- Ephesians 4:29

- 1 Thessalonians 5:11

- Ephesians 5:4

- James 1:19

6. Think of a conversation you had with a single person of the opposite sex that you think went well. Why do you think that conversation was successful?

Chapter 3: Waffles and Spaghetti at Work

1. What were the most revealing insights you gained on the way men and women approach achievement?

2. What has been your biggest obstacle in dealing with the opposite gender in the workplace?

3. What has been the nicest surprise in dealing with the opposite gender at work?

4. What new insights did you gain from this chapter that will help you in your work relationships?

5. How has what you have learned about the opposite gender so far made a difference in your work environment?

6. How important is understanding each other's view of career and family to a dating relationship?

7. What kinds of questions should singles ask to see if their careers are compatible enough to create a future together?

Chapter 4: Relationship Ready

1. How do you pick yourself up after a hurt or rebuff in a relationship?

2. How do you discern if someone isn't ready for a dating relationship? How can you tell if they might be carrying some baggage from the past that hasn't been dealt with?

3. What have you done in your own life to overcome past hurts, bad habits, or negative patterns that you might have grown up with?

4. When in a relationship should you discuss sensitive issues from your past?

5. As a group, come up with five questions every single must ask in order to avoid falling in love with someone who is unhealthy emotionally.

Chapter 5: The Waffle Warrior

(Group facilitator: You might want to assign both the Pasta Princess and Waffle Warrior the same week and then divide the group into smaller groups by gender for more candid conversation. The questions below are for a coed group conversation. You might choose to have part of the meeting together, and part of the meeting in smaller gender-specific groups.)

1. Discounting the opposite gender is a common malady in today's society. As a group, brainstorm together and see how many answers you can get to these questions:

   • What are positive qualities of the male species? How do they benefit life?

- Women: What did you learn about men that will help you relate to them better?

- Men: What did you learn, or what were you reminded of about your gender that will help you as you navigate relationships with women?

2. Men go to boxes to escape pain; some boxes are not healthy choices (abuse, alcohol, addictions, anger). Do you have any boxes you escape to that aren't healthy? How do you battle the temptation to go into unhealthy boxes?

3. How about the boxes you (men) escape to that are healthy—what adventures do you long to go on?

4. Women: How will you handle a man you might meet that may not choose healthy boxes to escape to?

5. How will you encourage the men in your world to keep a sense of adventure?

Chapter 6: The Pasta Princess

1. As a group, brainstorm the answer to this question:

- What are the best qualities of women as a gender? How do they benefit life?

- Women sense their worth easier when they pursue their character, compassion, and contribution. Which of these areas do you need to look more closely at? Your character? Your compassion? Your contribution?

- Which area would you like to send more time developing?

2. Did you recognize any signs of being controlling as you read the chapter?

3. After reading this chapter, what changes or adjustments do you want to make that you think will improve your relationships?

4. Men: What did you learn about women that helps you value them more? What did you learn that will help you as you relate to women?

5. Women: What were you reminded of about the female gender that men might need to be informed about or given grace for if they don't understand?

Chapter 7: Waffles and Spaghetti in Love

We are called in Hebrews 3:13 to "encourage one another daily, as long as it is called Today, so that none of you may be hardened by sin's deceitfulness." The word "encourage" is made up of two Greek words—*para,* which means "alongside," and *kaleo,* which means "to be called." The word literally means, "called alongside to help." When you encourage, you are committing yourself to be alongside to help in whatever way you can. Sometimes it means cheerleading, sometimes it means confronting, and sometimes it means romancing. The amazing thing about encouragement is that it's the primary work of the Holy Spirit. In John 14:16, Jesus promised His disciples, "And I will ask the Father, and he will give you another Counselor to be with you forever." The word "Counselor" in this verse is the Greek word *paraclete* or "one who is called alongside." The Holy Spirit is in our lives to encourage, and when you encourage your friends you are making it easier for the Holy Spirit to do His work.

1. How does this information impact the way you look at your love life?

2. Sex and dating is a topic about which singles have widely diverse views and standards. What do you think God considers the right context for sex in a relationship?

3. How do you deal with people who have very different views?

4. How do you find other singles who might have similar views to yours about sex, dating, living together, and marriage?

5. As a result of reading this chapter, what changes do you want to make in

   • your view of the role of dating in your life

   • your sexual standards and physical relationship boundaries

6. Studies show that as a relationship progresses, women may attribute more commitment to the relationship than do men. How can you better ensure you are equally committed?

7. There are many resources to strengthen relationships and to help you decide if this is the right person to marry. When in a relationship should you consider the following resources?

   • healthy married couples (mentoring/ modeling)

   • Bible studies to do together

   • books to read together

   • counseling (pre-engagement and premarital)

8. Leader: Give the group time to write out the top five qualities they will look for in the person they want to someday marry. Ask members if anyone

would like to share their list. (It's great if everyone will, but some might feel shy, so let it be a volunteer question.)

9. What safeguards will you put in place to ensure you live out your relational goals and standards?

Chapter 8: The Social Life of Waffles and Spaghetti

1. Ask the group to name the four guiding principles of a social life. Then ask, How will this information impact the way you meet and relate to people?

2. Review the seven characteristics of "A Life that God Blesses." Which area(s) do you feel strongest in? Which do you either want to make changes in or learn more information about?

3. In your experience, what has been the best place(s) to meet interesting, like-minded people? What has been the worst?

4. When you enter a new social group, how do you discern if this group is a good fit for you?

5. Why do you think some singles pull back from new social interactions, or what would make a single just quit socializing with the opposite sex?

6. What is your personal recommendation for developing a more interesting social life that God would be pleased with?

7. Finish this sentence: One new way I might try to expand my social circle is...

8. As a group, plan a social event that will produce a lot of conversation and interaction. The best way to get to know people is to lead with them.

Chapter 9: Waffles, Spaghetti, and Kids

1. Why would this book need a chapter on children?

2. Talk about the homes you grew up in. What role did gender play in who did what at your house?

3. After marriage, how does a couple know they're ready for kids?

4. When single parents date, when should their kids meet?

5. Questions for single parents:

   • What can you do to maximize your strengths that will benefit your children?

   • What new idea do you want to try to connect your children in a positive, safe way to good role models who aren't your gender?

   • What new insight did you learn that will help you relate better to your children of the opposite gender?

6. For the entire group:

   • What do you see in young girls and boys that gives a glimpse of what they will be like as adults?

   • As a society, how can we teach children to value the opposite gender?

Chapter 10: God Loves Waffles and Spaghetti

1. The Bible explains we are "wonderfully made," and it's clear God gave inborn personality traits. What did you learn about personality that you think will help you in your relationships?

2. What is your romantic personality style? Based on your personality, describe a "perfect date"

that someone would plan to make you feel loved or appreciated.

3. The key need of a woman is security; the key need of a man is simplicity. How does this information impact the way you relate to the opposite sex in all types of relationships?

4. Have you been looking to the opposite sex to fill a need that was only meant for God to fill? How does it impact relationships when you place unrealistic expectations on your relationships with the opposite sex?

5. If we have an accurate view of God, it can often help address our need for security and simplicity. Below is a short list of attributes of God. Which questions of security or simplicity are foremost on your heart and mind? What character trait of God might help meet that need in your life?

God is...

A Father	True	A Bridegroom	All powerful
A Refuge	A Friend	All knowing	A Shield
Victorious	A Shelter	A Sanctuary	Almighty
Gracious	A King	Most High	Joy
Peace	Hope	Love	Good
Gentle	Patient	Kind	Light
A Savior	A Helper	A Redeemer	Faithful
	A Comforter	A Healer	Just
		Holy	

These are just a few. Write down an area of weakness that you think has a negative impact on your relationships. What strength of God's could you draw on to fortify that area? For example, if I am overly angry at the slightest offense, it is likely that the issue is more about me and the hurts I carry than about another person. Because I struggle with anger, I can look to God my *peace* for help and comfort. By learning all about the peace of God, I can gain clarity and plan how to better deal with my anger. By memorizing verses about peace, I have a new recording to play in my head when I sense the old recording of anger is about to go off!

6. Read the verses below. What encouragement do they give that can help you address the security and simplicity needs in your life?

   • 2 Corinthians 3:5

   • 2 Corinthians 12:9-10

7. If you'd like, share an area of weakness that you'd like the group to pray for you about. If anyone in the group has a verse about God's ability to give strength for that area, have them either read the verse to you or write it down. You can take it home and memorize it or use it as a springboard to cross-reference it and find other verses.

8. Can anyone in the group share a time when a weakness of yours was causing stress in your relationships and God provided an answer to address the need?

   As a closing to the group take turns affirming (encouraging) one another by having each group member thank a "chosen" group member for a contribution they made, a personality quality they appreciated, or some wisdom he or she shared that left a positive impression or impact. Put each person in the "chosen" position. Have someone in the group record the group's statements on a note card. Give the card to the "chosen" person so they can have it as a daily encouragement to help remind them of the positive truths about themselves. (This card is especially nice to have after a dating breakup!)

You may decide to have a dinner out together or some other celebration to bring closure or transition to your small group time.

Dates to Decide

We recommend couples who are in a serious dating relationship read *Single Men Are Like Waffles, Single Women Are Like Spaghetti* and then complete the Bible study and discussion questions below together, using separate sheets of paper to give you enough space to fully respond. Do not wait until you're engaged; rather, use these questions when you first start discussing marriage. Of course, if you are already engaged, this study will be a terrific addition to your premarital counseling.

Chapter 1: Male and Female He Created Them

1. Consider the home you grew up in: What gender roles were on display? For example, what was your mom's role? Your dad's? Do you agree with how they ran their marriage? Your family? What changes, if any, do you want to make when you marry?

2. Read the verses below. Write the key thought(s) next to each verse and then discuss what you see are God's principles for making marriage relationships work.

- John 13:34-35
- Romans 12:10
- Romans 12:16
- Romans 15:7
- 1 Corinthians 1:10
- Galatians 5:13
- Ephesians 4:2
- Ephesians 4:32
- Ephesians 5:21
- Colossians 3:13
- 1 Thessalonians 5:11
- Hebrews 3:13
- Hebrews 10:24-25
- 1 Peter 1:22
- 1 Peter 3:8
- 1 Peter 4:9
- 1 John 3:11

3. How can you tell if someone has a servant's heart and attitude? In what ways can you see this attitude in the one you love? (Note: If you *can't* see it, then this is a huge red flag warning, *danger ahead!*)

Chapter 2: Don't Overcook Communication

1. Read James 1:19. God's priority is for you to be a good listener. On a scale of one to ten, ten being the best, how would you rate your listening ability? How would you rate your boyfriend's/

girlfriend's? What one suggestion might improve the way you two communicate or listen?

2. Read the verses: Psalm 141:3; Proverbs 4:24; 6:16-19; 8:6-8; 10:11-12; 13:3; 15:1,4; 16:1,13,24; 21:23; 24:26; Ephesians 4:29; 1 Thessalonians 5:11; James 1:26. What should you say or not say in conversation? Each of you make lists:

• What I will say to you:

• What I will never say to you:

3. Discuss the elements of your list, make any additions or adjustments, sign the bottom, and give the list to your dating partner/fiancé as a pledge to say only what is edifying and will build them up.

Chapter 3: Waffles and Spaghetti at Work

1. What did you learn about the way men and women approach achievement?

2. What are your goals in the following areas?

• Family

• Finances

• Career

• Material possessions

3. How do you think couples should divide the roles of parenting, home and family responsibilities, and work? (Who should do what around the home, the yard, for the family, etc.?)

4. Each of you write a paragraph describing how you envision your life together as a married couple five years from now, ten years from now,

and 20 years from now. Where will you be living (in the city, suburbs, country)? Where do you see work and children fitting in? How about vacations, travel, and holidays? Will you live close to either set of parents?

5. Each of you write out your own definition of success. How will you know when you have achieved it?

6. Read your definitions to one another. Are they similar or dramatically different? If they are different, how will you decide what course to follow? How do you think major decisions of life should be decided?

7. Is your decision-making process similar? If your goals, your vision for your future, and your decision-making process are dramatically different, further counseling is recommended.

8. Now, be practical. Create an estimated budget of what you would need to live on.

9. Each of you create a debts and assets sheet so you know exactly what you have to work with.

10. If you already have children and families, talk about how you will make financial decisions. Will you do everything jointly? Have some joint and some independent money at each of your own discretion? How much will you keep in savings? How will you make investment decisions?

11. Complete this sentence: "To me, money is
   _____."

12. Look at the following statements and rate yourself by placing an x on the continuum.

I like to work a lot as it brings income and meaning.

Strongly Disagree   Strongly Agree

_____

I like free time as it makes life seem worth living.

Strongly Disagree   Strongly Agree

_____

I like an active social life. I like being out with people.

Strongly Disagree   Strongly Agree

_____

I like plenty of alone time, as it seems to be a balancer for me.

Strongly Disagree   Strongly Agree

_____

I like to spend my money to make our home a nice place (I like nice things and plenty of space and fun things to do at home).

Strongly Disagree   Strongly Agree

_____

I'd rather spend my money making interesting memories. Things aren't as important as memories.

Strongly Disagree   Strongly Agree

_____

13. Talk about your similarities and differences on the above continuum charts.

Chapter 4 Relationship Ready

1. From the list below, mark any areas of hurt you have experienced:

   • Past break-ups

   • Abuse

   • Abortion

- Rape/molestation
- Raised in a home that experienced any of the following: ·
  - Alcohol
  - Abandonment
  - Drugs
  - Other addictions (shopping, gambling, etc.)
  - Abuse (sexual, physical, mental, emotional, etc.)
  - Anger
  - Critical spirit
  - Lying
  - Stealing
  - Non-Christian belief patterns
  - Illegal activity
  - Divorce
  - An affair or sexual promiscuity
  - Poverty

2. Share how you think each area you marked might impact your relationship in the future.

3. What choices have you made that you believe created self-imposed hurt (examples: premarital sex, illegal drug use, dating people who showed you disrespect, etc.)?

4. How would you like the person you are dating to respond to these past choices? Ask for forgiveness and grace in areas you feel might have an impact on your relationship. (That is usually

pretty much all of the things on your list!) Note: We encourage you to speak in general terms. For example, say, "Please forgive me for not waiting until we married to have sex." This is better than listing off all your sexual partners and your detailed times with them. The Bible encourages us to walk in the light, so don't dwell in the darkness.

5. All these factors can undermine the trust you need to create a firm foundation for marriage. How can you learn to trust again? What can your girlfriend/boyfriend do to prove she/he is a trustworthy person?

6. Complete the following sentence: "If there is one thing I'd change about you it would be _____, and if there's one thing I'd change about our relationship, it would be _____."

7. When I fail you (and you *will* hurt each other), this is how I'd like you to tell me that I have failed you or hurt you:

8. Answer the following questions:

When I am angry I tend to

_____.

When I fear failure I tend to

_____.

When I am hurt I tend to

_____.

When we're in conflict, I want to (mark any that apply):

(a) Leave it alone and hope it just goes away with time

(b) Talk it out immediately

(c) Find out who is at fault

(d) Find a resolution

(e) Listen and see why the conflict happened in the first place

(f) Just do it my way

(g) Give in to you just to get peace

(h) Try to find a compromise

(i) Pray and seek God for a solution that will be good for both of us (a win-win)

(j) Decide whether talking it through or arguing is worth it or if I just want to forgive and let it go because it's not a big issue

(k) Hit you or punish you or get back at you somehow

(l) Run away

(m) Yell and let off steam

9. Create a conflict commitment. Here's an example:

When I disagree with you, I will not leave unless I feel it's necessary for your safety, and even then, I will always inform you and not just storm out. I will not tear you down with my words. I will seek to sit calmly and choose positive resolution procedures like praying, listening, and brainstorming options, and I won't let anger go unresolved. I will keep talking until I feel in love with you again.

Now work together to create your own conflict commitment.

Chapter 5: The Waffle Warrior

1. What did you learn about the way men operate, and how does this information impact your relationship?

2. Now consider your age. Men hit re-evaluation moments in their late twenties. (They ask questions such as, Is this the job I want to do for my lifetime? Do I want to marry? How many children do I want? What does success look like to me?) They hit a more difficult transition at 45-55, during midlife. (They ask questions such as, Am I fulfilled? Has my life become predictable or boring? Is this the career I want to stay in? Have I missed out on something in life? I'm getting older, what can I do to recapture my youth?) Will you be tackling either of these transitions early in your married life? If so, we recommend you learn more about midlife and men (midlife.com has some great resources).

3. Women, try talking out some of these issues ahead of time and make a game plan with your man that will allow him to keep a sense of adventure in his life even as he steps into the greater responsibility that comes with marriage. (Examples: an annual guys-only hunting trip, lessons to learn to fly, keeping involved in a sport he enjoys, or greater business or educational challenges such as a higher degree)

4. Guys answer this: Adventure to me is_____ _____. Gals answer this: I am comfortable with all kinds of adventure, except I probably won't join you if you _____. Even if you

decide to do _____
alone, I'd be very afraid for you and it may
impact our relationship. (For example, I, Pam,
would complete the above sentence like this: I
am comfortable with you and our sons doing all
kinds of adventures, except I might not join you
on some while I'm pregnant or nursing, and I'd
probably never be very good company on long
hikes or backpacking because I get heat exhaustion. But any water sport—I'm there! I may
bungee jump, *maybe*—but I will never go skydiving with you. In fact, I'd be very nervous if
you went skydiving, and that might impact our
relationship. I'd probably have issues with you if
you decided to sail around the world *alone*, but if
you had a trained crew, I'd be okay with that. On
the financial front, I'd be willing to risk going
into business with you or even having you run
your own business, but I'd freak out if you took
our family's savings to the racetrack to bet! However, I think I could live pretty much anywhere
in the world if you were there and if we had running water and a phone line.)

Chapter 6: The Pasta Princess

1. Men, what did you learn about the way women
   operate and how does this information impact
   your relationship?

2. Men: How do you see your girlfriend/fiancée fulfilling these areas of calling:

   • Her compassion: What are her strongest rela-
     tionship skills?

- Her contribution: Explain to her your level of commitment in regards to her calling. What sacrifices are you willing to make to see her become all God designed her to be?

- Her character: What are her strongest moral attributes?

3. Of all the information given about being a Pasta Princess, what got my attention was

_____.

4. Women: Give an honest evaluation of these following areas:

- My compassion: The relationship skills that are easiest for me are _____.
The ones that are more difficult for me are

_____.

- My contribution: I do want to follow God's call on my life. I want to become the woman He designed me to be. In doing so, I may need your help. A few ways I can see I might need your help are _____.

- My character: I think my strengths are

_____.

- I think my weaknesses are

_____.

5. Of all the issues that were mentioned in being a Pasta Princess, what impacted me most was

_____.

Note: If she has issues of abuse or abandonment, we recommend further counsel and, perhaps, more individual counseling.

Chapter 7: Waffles and Spaghetti in Love

1. Second Corinthians 6:14 explains that couples should be spiritually compatible. Are you *both* in a relationship with Christ and do you *both* want to grow in that relationship?

2. Research other key areas of compatibility:

   • How did you vote in the last election?

   • How do you decide what a person of integrity looks like?

   • List five key passionate beliefs you hold (examples: abortion/choice, education and home-schooling, censorship)

3. After reading the chapter together, what changes do you think need to happen in your relationship to:

   • Help build a deeper friendship

   • Help your romantic life

   • Help your future sex life

4. Having more information will help you romance one another. Please copy these questions with their answers on to a separate piece of paper that you will give to your dating partner/fiancé:

   • Here's a list of five *free* things you can do that express your love to me. (Examples: rub my shoulders, take out my trash, put gas in my car, open the doors)

   • Here's a list of five dates I'd love to someday go on with you.

   • If you gave me a gift under $5, I'd be so pleased to receive _____.

• I love being surprised by

_____.

• Things I collect are:

• My favorite stores or internet sites are:

• A perfect date, planned just to make me smile, would definitely have to include

_____.

Chapter 8: The Social Life of Waffles and Spaghetti

1. ***Look at the list of "A Life that God Blesses."*** Are there any changes you would need to make to have a life God can bless?

2. ***God knows us by name; we should know others by name.*** We'll be marrying into each other's families. Tell me what you are most proud of in your family circle or on your family tree.

3. ***God values a good reputation; we should know a person's reputation.*** Introduce the one you love to three people you think know you best and give the one you love permission to ask them anything. Then ask, "What new insights did you learn about me? What information that you already knew was reconfirmed that you think is vital to the future of our relationship?"

4. ***Inner character quality is valued higher than outward appearance.*** Ask, "What do I do that makes you feel valued as a person?"

5. ***Meet people in a way that keeps you in ministry.*** Ask, "How can we keep God and serving others as priorities in our dating relationship?" "How can we ensure God and serving others will stay priorities in our future?"

6. *Socialize to stay other-centered, not self-centered.* Each of you answer, "What can we do to make sure our life doesn't become all about us?"

7. *Each answer,* "When I hit a hard place in life, I react _____ and what I'd expect from you is _____."

Chapter 9: Waffles, Spaghetti, and Kids

Read Psalm 78:4; 127:1-5; Philippians 2:2-5

1. If you are marrying and you have children, it's imperative that you get good counseling for you as a couple, *and* some family counseling, especially if your children are old enough to have opinions on your relationship. You can discuss the questions below to give some basic information, but you'll need to discuss issues such as: discipline (Who will do it for which kids?), finances (Who pays for what in the child's life?), custody (When is couple time, when is family time?), and other issues (Who will talk to the ex and negotiate changes?). And there are many more issues, so it's well worth a few sessions of Christian counseling with someone specializing in family counseling.

If you don't have children yet, discuss these questions:

2. Describe a typical weekday in the home you grew up in. Describe how you spent the majority of weekends and free time/holidays.

3. How many children (if any) do you see yourself being able to parent well?

4. How will you as an individual know you are ready to have children? How will you know you are ready as a couple to have children?

5. Who handled the discipline of the children in the home you grew up in? Explain what would typically happen if you did something wrong (at each major stage of life. For example: How were you disciplined as a toddler? As an elementary student? As a teen?). What adjustments, if any, would you make in the family you will someday have?

6. How important is it to you to have a parent at home during childrearing years? How will you combine work and childcare at each stage? (For example: Who will care for a brand new baby? Who will care for a preschooler? Who will oversee the schedule and activity and off school hours of a child in school? A teen?)

7. What kind of child discipline are you comfortable with? How were you trained and disciplined growing up? What do you think your parents did well in this area? What would you change?

Chapter 10: God Loves Waffles and Spaghetti

1. Read the personalities and take a personality test (see options below). Discuss your results. What strength do you bring to the relationship? What weaknesses do you bring? How do your personalities mesh? What potential obstacles do you foresee?

Personality resources:
CLASS Personality Inventory (very inexpensive. Get one for each person in your family, or order a personality book by one of the Litteaurs.)
PO Box 66810
Albuquerque, NM 87193

DISC
Personality Insights
PO BOX 28591
Atlanta, GA 30358

2. The woman: What does your boyfriend do to make you feel more secure? Less secure?

3. The man: What does your girlfriend do to simplify your life? What does she do to complicate it?

4. How can we make God more of a priority in our relationship? (Read Deuteronomy 6:5; 30:16; Mark 12:30; Matthew 6:33.)

Successful couples have key choices they have made:

Studies say married couples who pray daily have the best sex lives. Also, married couples who have a group of friends who are positive and committed to marriage tend to have stronger marriages and more passion in their love lives. Also, couples who attend church regularly give their sex life the highest marks in passion. And the key trait in a lasting marriage is a deep friendship. Also, longevity studies say people live longer, healthier lives if they're "other" focused.

5. We can make prayer a daily priority by

_____.

(Example: Pray before or after dates, pray over meals, etc.)

6. We can find a group of friends who have a positive view of marriage by

_____. (Ideas:

Join a small group at church, look for a mentor couple, etc.)

7. We will make worship a priority by attending _____ church for the following events/activities: _____.

8. We will also grow in our relationship with God by _____.

9. We will nurture our friendship by _____ _____. (Ideas: take up a new activity you both enjoy, set aside weekly date times, read marriage/relationship books or watch relationship videos, etc.)

10. We will be other-focused by _____ _____. (Ideas: volunteering together, teaching or leading a group, serving at church or other organization.)

Notes

Chapter 1

1. Darleen Giannini, *Reader's Digest*, April 1995, p. 85.

2. Leah Ariniello, "Gender and the Brain." Available [Online]: <www.sfn.org/content/Publications/BrainBriefings/gender.brain.html>.

3. Malcolm Ritter, "Brains Differ in Navigation Skills," AP, Tuesday, March 21, 2000; 2:29 A.M. EST.

4. Ariniello, "Gender and the Brain."

5. Leon James, "Aggressive Driving Analyzed: The Effect of Age, Gender, and Type of Car Driven Across the States." Available [Online]: <www.DrDriving.com>.

6. Bernice Kanner, "Are you a normal guy?" *American Demographics*, March 1999, p. 19.

7. Nancy Ammon Jianakoplos and Alexandra Bernasek, "Are Women More Risk Averse?" *Economic Inquiry*, October 1998, pp. 620-630.

8. Sheila Brownlow, Rebecca Whitener, and Janet M. Rupert, "I'll Take Gender Differences for $1000!" *Sex Roles*, February 1998.

9. Ibid.

10. Ibid.

11. Jianakoplos and Bernasek, "Are Women More Risk Averse?"

12. Ibid.

13. Lillian Glass, *He Says, She Says* (New York: Perigee Books, 1993), p. 34.

14. Carol Watson, "Gender Differences, Do They Really Exist?" Available [Online]: <www.babyschool.com/bmcgende.html>.

15. Denise L Croker, "Putting It on the Table: A Mini-Course on Gender Differences," *English Journal*, January 1999, pp. 65-70.

16. Kanner, "Are you a normal guy?"

17. Ibid.

18. Ibid.

19. Sara E. Guiterres, Douglas T. Kenrick, and Jenifer J. Partch, "Beauty, Dominance, and the Mating Game: Contrast Effects in Self-Assessment Reflect Gender Differences in Mate Selection," *Personality and Social Psychology Bulletin,* September 1999, pp. 1126-1134.

20. Brownlow, Whitener, and Rupert, "I'll Take Gender Differences for $1000!"

21. Ibid. Halla Beloff, "Mother, Father, and Me: Our IQ" *The Psychologist,* 1992, pp. 309-311. D. S. Berry, "Vocal Attractiveness: Effects on Stranger, Self, and Friend Impressions," *Journal of Nonverbal Behavior,* 1990, pp. 141-153. A. Furnham and R. Rawles, "Sex Differences in the Estimation of Intelligence," *Journal of Social Behavior and Personality,* 1995, pp. 741-748. H. W. Hogan, "IQ: Self Estimates of Males and Females," *Journal of Social Psychology,* 1973, pp. 137-138.

22. Glass, *He Says, She Says,* p. 32.

23. Ibid.

24. Cheryl Lavin, "The Things Women Want," *Chicago Tribune,* May 7, 2000.

25. Cheryl Lavin, "Rules Guys Wish Girls Played By," *Chicago Tribune,* April 23, 2000.

Chapter 2

1. Paul Lee Tan, ed., *Tan's Encyclopedia of 7700 Illustrations* (Rockville, MD: Assurance Publishers, 1984), illustration #4995, "People Didn't Know Him."

2. Bonne Steffen, ed., "Getting Old—Having Fun," *The Christian Appeal.* Retrieved from PreachingToday.com.

Chapter 3

1. "Finally…Computer Games for Girls," *USA Today,* February 3, 1999.

2. Ibid.

3. Ibid.

4. Ibid.

5. Ibid.

6. L.C. Embrey and J.J. Fox, "Gender Differences in the Investment Decision-Making Process, *Financial Counseling and Planning,* vol. 8, no. 2, 1997, pp. 33-40.

7. Ibid.

8. Susan Roxburgh, "Exploring the Work and Family Relationship," *Journal of Family Issues,* vol. 20, no. 6, November 1999, pp. 771-788.

9. Maria Gardiner and Marika Tiggemann, "Gender Differences in Leadership Style, Job Stress and Mental Health in Male- and Female-Dominated Industries," *Journal of Occupational and Organizational Psychology,* vol. 72, pt. 3, September 1999, pp. 301-305.

10. Daniel J. Canary, et al., *Sex and Gender Differences in Personal Relationships* (New York: The Guilford Press, 1997), p. 156.

11. Sally Helgesen, *The Female Advantage: Women's Ways of Leadership* (New York: Doubleday, 1990), pp. 19-28.

12. Gary N. Powell, *Women and Men in Management* (Newbury Park, CA: Sage Publications, 1993), p. 167.

13. Ibid., p. 84.

14. Ibid., p. 162. Several studies showed males' aspirations and self-perception of leadership skills as higher than women's. See pp. 76-79, 105-106.

15. Ibid., p. 109.

16. Based on a survey by Kaia Rendahl, Jean Anderson, Kristin Hill, Anna Henning, Christopher Randall, Amy Davis at St. Olaf University.

17. Ahalya Krishnan and Christopher J. Sweeney, "Gender Differences in Fear of Success Imagery and Other Achievement-Related Background Variables Among Medical Students," *Sex Roles,* vol. 39, issue 3, August 1998, pp. 299-310.

18. Krishnan, et al., "Gender Differences."

19. Gardiner, et al. "Gender Differences."

20. Ibid.

21. Ibid.

22. Roxburgh, "Exploring the Work and Family Relationship."

23. Canary, et al., *Sex and Gender Differences in Personal Relationships,* p. 106.

24. For more on personalities: Florence Littauer, Marita Littauer, *Getting Along with Almost Anybody: The Complete Personality Book* (Ada, MI: Fleming H. Revell, 1998); Jim Brawner, Suzette Brawner, Gary Smalley, *Taming the Family Zoo: Maximizing Harmony and Minimizing Family*

Stress (Colorado Springs, CO: Navpress, 1998); and Bob Philips, *The Delicate Art of Dancing with Porcupines: Learning to Appreciate the Finer Points of Others* (Ventura, CA: Regal Books, 1989).

25. Patrick Morley, *The Man in the Mirror* (Brentwood, TN: Wolgemuth & Hyatt Publishers, Inc., 1989), p. 84.

Chapter 4

1. Bob Burns and Michael Brisset, *The Adult Child of Divorce: A Recovery Handbook* (Nashville, TN: Thomas Nelson, 1991).

Chapter 5

1. John Eldredge, *Wild at Heart* (Nashville, TN: Thomas Nelson, Inc., 2001), pp. 3-5.

2. John Nicholson, *Men and Women: How Different Are They?* (Oxford: Oxford University Press, 1984), p. 160.

3. Ibid.

4. Ibid.

5. *Harper's Magazine,* October 1998. Retrieved from PreachingToday.com.

6. Nicholson, *Men and Women: How Different Are They?* p. 170.

7. Ibid.

8. Ibid.

9. I (Bill) will always be indebted to John Eldredge for expressing this theme throughout *Wild at Heart.* Thanks John.

10. Nancy Ammon Jianakoplos and Alexandra Bernasek, "Are Women More Risk Averse?" *Economic Inquiry,* vol. 36, issue 4, October 1998, pp. 620-630.

11. Ibid.

12. Malcolm Ritter, "Brains Differ in Navigation Skills," AP, Tuesday, March 21, 2000; 2:29 A.M. EST.

13. Leah Ariniello, "Gender and the Brain." Available [Online]: <www.sfn.org/context/Publications/BrainBriefings/gender.brain.html>.

14. Ritter, "Brains Differ in Navigation Skills."

15. "Controlling Anger—Before It Controls You." Available [Online]: <www.apa.org/pubinfo/anger.html>.

16. Statistics are from the Office of National Drug Control Policy. See <www.whitehousedrugpolicy.gov/prevent.html>.

17. Statistics are from the National Council on Alcoholism and Drug Dependence. See <ww.ncadd.org>.

18. Neil S. Jacobson and John M. Gottman, "Anatomy of a Violent Relationship," *Psychology Today,* Mar/Apr 1998, p. 60.

19. Ibid.

20. Paul Lee Tan, ed., *Tan's Encyclopedia of 7700 Illustrations* (Rockville, MD: Assurance Publishers, 1984), illustration #3259, "Worth of a Man."

21. Ibid., #3259, "Worth of 'Energetic' Man."

Chapter 7

1. Ralph R. Behnke and Chris R. Sawyer, "Anticipatory Anxiety Patterns for Male and Female Public Speakers," *Communication Education,* vol. 49, issue 2, April 2000, pp. 187-195.

2. Ibid.

3. Ibid.

4. Ibid., p. 136.

5. Steven L. Nock, "A Comparison of Marriages and Cohabiting Relationships," *Journal of Family Issues,* vol. 16, January 1995, pp. 53-76. Susan L. Brown and Alan Booth, "Cohabitation Versus Marriage: A Comparison of Relationship Quality," *Journal of Marriage and Family,* vol. 58, August 1996, pp. 668-678. Many thanks to Focus on the Family. For more information, see Glenn T. Stanton, *Only a Piece of Paper: the Unquestionable Benefits of a Lifelong Marriage.*

6. John Roache, "Premarital Sexual Attitudes and Behaviors by Stages," *Adolescence,* vol. 21, no. 81, Spring 1986, p. 119.

7. Josh McDowell and Dick Day, *Why Wait?* (San Bernardino, CA: Here's Life Publishers, 1987), p. 207.

8. Statistics are from Free Teens Leadership Training. See <www.freeteens.org/stories/doubtcondom.htm>.

9. McDowell and Day, *Why Wait?* p. 50.

10. Ibid., p. 218.

11. Ibid., p. 41. Stephan, Berscheid, & Walster (1971) demonstrated that sexual arousal has been found to lead directly to greater general romantic attraction. Berscheid & Walster (1974) as well as Dutton & Aaron (1974) interpreted this to mean that "generalized physiological arousal, in the presence of an appropriate object of attraction is misattributed to feeling attraction to the object."

12. Roache, "Premarital Sexual Attitudes and Behaviors by Stages."

13. Ibid., p. 114.

14. Ibid., passim.

There were five categories of dating couples in this study: (1) dating with no particular affection, (2) dating with affection but not love, (3) dating and being in love, (4) dating one person only and being in love, (5) being engaged. The five groups were asked to give responses in eight behavioral categories: (1) no physical contact, (2) goodnight kiss, (3) several hugs and kisses, (4) prolonged kissing and hugging, (5) light petting above the waist, (6) heavy petting below the waist, (7) mutual masturbation, (8) sexual intercourse.

There are several interesting results of this study: (1) In every category the respondents were more active than they deemed proper. (2) In every category respondents thought others were more active than they were. (3) A majority of male respondents considered all eight behavioral categories as proper when at dating stage 3. (4) A majority of female respondents considered all eight behavioral categories as proper when at dating stage 4. (5) Men overall expected sexual activity sooner in the relationship than women. (6) By dating at stage 4, male and female responses to all eight behaviors were statistically the same. (7) Those respondents who considered religion to be important had more conservative attitudes and behaviors.

15. Harold Leitenberg, Evan Greenwald, and Mathew J. Terran, "Correlation Between Sexual Activity Among Children, Preadolescence and/or Early Adolescence and Behavior and Sexual Adjustment in Adulthood," *Archives of Sexual Behavior,* vol. 18, no. 4, 1989, p. 309.

16. Leitenburg, et al., "Correlation Between Sexual Activity Among Children Preadolescence and/or Early Adolescence and Sexual Adjustment in Adulthood," p. 311.

17. McDowell and Day, *Why Wait?* p. 257.

18. Tim and Beverly LaHaye, *The Act of Marriage* (Grand Rapids, MI: Zondervan, 1976), pp. 211, 223.

Chapter 9

1. John Nicholson, *Men and Women: How Different are They?* (Oxford: Oxford University Press, 1984), p. 131.

2. Ibid., p. 129.

3. Ibid., p. 131.

4. Ibid.

5. Ibid.

6. Ibid., p. 128.

7. Brenda Hunter, *Where Have All the Mothers Gone?* (Zondervan: Grand Rapids, 1982), p. 88.

8. Ibid.

9. Ibid, p. 89.

10. Nicholson, *Men and Women: How Different are They?* p. 124.

11. Barbara Kantravitz and Claudia Kalb, "Boys Will Be Boys," *Newsweek*, May 11, 1998.

12. Ibid.

For more resources to enhance your relationships and build marriages or to connect with Pam and Bill Farrel for a speaking engagement, contact:

Masterful Living
P.O. Box 1507
San Marcos, CA 92079-1507
(760) 727-9122
www.farrelcommunications.com
Email: info@farrelcommunications.com

OTHER BOOKS BY
BILL AND PAM FARREL

Men Are Like Waffles—
Women Are Like Spaghetti

Bill and Pam Farrel explain why a man is like a waffle (each element of his life is in a separate box), why a woman is like spaghetti (everything in her life touches everything else), and what these differences mean. Then they show readers how to achieve more satisfying relationships.

Biblical insights, sound research, humorous anecdotes, and real-life stories make this guide entertaining and practical. Readers will feast on enticing insights that include:

- letting gender differences work for them
- achieving fulfillment in romantic relationships
- coordinating parenting so kids receive good, consistent care

Much of the material in this rewarding book will also improve interactions with family, friends, and coworkers.

Every Marriage Is
a Fixer-Upper

Bestselling authors and popular speakers Bill and Pam Farrel provide readers with a tool chest of communication skills for do-it-yourselfers who want to get the most out of their marriage. HGTV watchers and *Better Homes and Gardens* readers will quickly connect with the home-improvement theme as the Farrels show couples how to...

- strengthen the foundation of their family
- inspect their marriage for hidden weak spots
- protect their relational investment with consistent maintenance and improvement

Filled with practical advice, biblical insights, and the Farrels' trademark warmth and wit, this manual is perfect for newlyweds as well as longtime marriage partners as they turn their fixer-upper marriage into the relationship of their dreams.